Vladim~

The Ri~

English transla ~ ~sworth

Published by **Ringing Cedars Press**
www.RingingCedars.com

Anastasia herself has stated that this book consists of words and phrases in combinations *which have a beneficial effect on the reader.* This has been attested by the letters received to date from thousands of readers all over the world.

If you wish to gain as full an appreciation as possible of the ideas, thoughts and images set forth here, as well as experience the benefits that come with this appreciation, we recommend you find a quiet place for your reading where there is the least possible interference from artificial noises (motor traffic, radio, TV, household appliances etc.). *Natural sounds,* on the other hand — the singing of birds, for example, or the patter of rain, or the rustle of leaves on nearby trees — may be a welcome accompaniment to the reading process.

Ringing Cedars Press is an independent publisher dedicated to making **Vladimir Megre**'s books available in the beautiful English translation by **John Woodsworth**. Word of mouth is our best advertisement and we appreciate your help in spreading the word about the Ringing Cedars Series.

Order on-line	**www.RingingCedars.com**	ordering
call / fax toll-free	**1-888-DOLMENS**	details
or call / fax	**1-646-429-1986**	see last page

Generous discounts are available on volume orders. To help spread the word as an independent distributor, or to place the books in your bookstore, or to be kept up to date about future book releases and events, please email us at:

info@ringingcedars.com

or write to the Publisher, Ringing Cedars Press, 120 Hana Hwy #9-230, Paia, HI 96779, USA. We also welcome reviews, poetry and artwork inspired by the Series.

Vladimir Megre

WHO ARE WE?

The Ringing Cedars Series
Book 5

Translated from the Russian by
John Woodsworth

Edited by
Leonid Sharashkin

Ringing Cedars Press
Paia, Hawaii, USA

Who Are We? by
Vladimir Megre

Translation and footnotes by
John Woodsworth

Editing, footnotes, design and layout by
Leonid Sharashkin

Cover art by
Alexander Razboinikov

Front cover font: *ShangriLaNF* by
Nick Curtis

Library of Congress Control Number: 2006920096

ISBN-10: 0-9763333-4-1
ISBN-13: 978-0-9763333-4-0

First edition, 2006

Published by
Ringing Cedars Press

www.RingingCedars.com

Contents

Chapter One

Two civilisations

We are always in a hurry to get somewhere or get something. There is hardly a single one of us who doesn't desire to lead a happy life, find love and establish a family. But how many of us will actually achieve our desire?

What determines our satisfaction or dissatisfaction with life? What determines our success or failure? What constitutes the meaning of life for each and every Man[1] and for all mankind on the whole? What kind of future awaits us?

These questions have been around a long time, but nobody has managed to come up with an intelligible answer. But I wonder: what kind of country will we be living in five or ten years from now? What kind of world are we leaving to our children? We really don't know. And, let's face it, none of us can ever picture our own future, because we are always hurrying off somewhere... but to where?

Strange, but true: the first clear glimpse I ever had about the future of our country came not from statisticians or politicians but from Anastasia, a recluse living in the wilds of the taiga. And not only did she present a picture of a marvellous future, but showed step-by-step its feasibility even for our generation — a design, in fact, for the development of the whole country.

---

[1]The word *Man* (with a capital *M*) is used throughout the Ringing Cedars Series to refer to a human being of either gender. For details on the word's use and the important distinction between *Man* and *human being* please see the Translator's Preface to Book 1.

It was while I was on my way from Anastasia's glade to the river[2] that this firm conviction, for some reason, came to my thought: *her plan is capable of changing so much in this world of ours.* When we consider that everything her thought conceptualises inevitably turns into a real-life embodiment, we see we are already living in a country with only a splendid future ahead of it. As I walked along, I thought about what Anastasia had said about our country's splendid future, which might even come about in our generation's lifetime. It will be a country without regional conflicts, criminal gangs and diseases, a country without poverty. And while I didn't understand all the thoughts she came out with, there wasn't a single thing she said this time that I felt like doubting. On the contrary, I felt as though I wanted to show everyone how *right* she was.

I firmly resolved to do everything within my power to bring her plan to fruition. On the surface it seems simple enough: each family should be allotted a hectare[3] of land for lifetime use, whereon to set up its own 'kin's domain',[4] its own 'piece of the Motherland'.[5] But my thought was immersed in the details of this plan. They were utterly simple in themselves, and yet at the same time utterly incredible.

Amazing! It isn't an agricultural scientist but a reclusive woman from the taiga that has shown that, with the right planting arrangement on a plot of land, it can take just a few short years to dispense with the need for fertilisation. Not only that, but even soil that isn't terribly fertile will be significantly improved.

---

[2]*from Anastasia's glade to the river* — see the last part of Book 4, Chapter 33: "School, or the lessons of the gods".

[3]*hectare* — 1 hectare is equivalent to approx. 2.5 acres in the Imperial system.

[4]*kin's domain* — see footnote 7 in Book 4, Chapter 33.

[5]*Motherland* — see footnote 1 in Book 4, Chapter 24: "Take back your Motherland, people!"; also the Translator's and Editor's Afterword to Book 4.

As a basic example Anastasia referred to the situation in the taiga.[6] The taiga has been around for thousands of years, and everything grows in it, even though it has never been fertilised. Anastasia says that all the things growing in the earth constitute the materialised thoughts of God, and that He has arranged everything so that Man has no need to worry about difficulties in finding food. One needs only to try to understand the Creator's thought and create splendid things together with Him.

I can cite an example of my own. The island of Cyprus, which I have visited, has a very rocky soil. But the ground wasn't always this way. Centuries ago the island was home to some splendid cedar forests and orchards, and its many rivers were filled with the purest spring water. The whole island was like an earthly Paradise. Then the Roman legions invaded the island and began to cut down the cedars to build their ships. Whole groves were felled. Today the larger part of the island is covered with stunted growth, the grass looks burnt even in the springtime, summer rains are a rarity and there is not enough fresh water. The residents have had to import fertile soil by the bargeload to be able to grow anything at all. So the upshot is: not only has Man failed to improve what has been created on the island, but his barbarous interference has actually made things worse.

In outlining her plan, Anastasia said that it was essential to plant a family tree, and that people should not be buried in a cemetery but right there on the beautiful terrain they themselves have nurtured. No headstone of any kind need be placed on the grave. It is a Man's living creations, not something dead, that will serve as a memorial for his relations. And not only that, but his soul will be able to take on a material embodiment again, in his earthly garden of Paradise.

---

[6]*taiga* — the Russian name given to the boreal forest that stretches across much of Siberia and northern Canada.

People buried in a cemetery cannot end up in Paradise. Their souls cannot be embodied in matter as long as there are relatives and friends around thinking about their death. Headstones are monuments to death. Funeral rites were thought up by the dark forces for the purpose of confining, at least temporarily, the human soul. Our Father has never produced any kind of suffering or even grieving for His beloved children. All God's creations are eternal, self-sufficient, self-reproducing. Everything living on the Earth, from the outwardly simple blade of grass to Man, is a self-constituted harmonious and eternal whole.

Here too, I think, she is right. Just look at how things have turned out. Today scientists tell us that human thought is material — but if that's the case, it means that the deceased person's relatives, in thinking of him as dead, thereby keep on holding him in a deadened state, which torments his soul. Anastasia maintains that Man, or, more precisely, Man's soul, can live forever. It has the capacity to constantly re-embody itself anew, but only under certain conditions. These conditions are brought about by a *kin's domain* established according to Anastasia's design. I am simply a believer in this design. As to proving or disproving her claims about life and death, I'll leave that to esoteric scholars who are no doubt more qualified for the task.

"I say, you're going to get a lot of opposition on that one," I observed to Anastasia. To which she only laughed and replied:

"It will all happen very simply now, Vladimir. Man's thought is capable of materialising and changing the shape of objects, predetermining events, creating the future. So it works out that any opponents who try to argue for the frailty of Man's existence only end up destroying themselves, for they will bring about their own decease by their very thoughts.

"Those who are able to comprehend their purpose and the meaning of infinity will start to live a happy life, eternally re-embodying themselves, for they themselves will produce with their thoughts their own infinity of happiness."

I liked her plan even better when I began to calculate its economic potential. I have become convinced that any Man, with the help of a family domain he establishes according to Anastasia's design, can ensure a poverty-free existence for himself as well as for his children and grandchildren. It is not merely a question of providing one's children with good food to eat or a roof over their heads. Anastasia said that the fence around the domain must be made of living trees, and that at least a quarter of the hectare should be given over to forest.

That means about 300 trees. They'll quite likely be cut down in, say, eighty to a hundred years, yielding about 400 cubic metres of lumber.[7] Even today, lumber well-dried and processed for finishing fetches at least one hundred dollars[8] per cubic metre, meaning a total income of $40,000. Of course, one shouldn't cut down the whole forest at once, just the number of mature trees that are needed at the time, and then immediately plant new ones in their place. The overall value of a kin's domain set up according to Anastasia's design may be estimated at a million dollars or more, and any family can build one, even those with an average income.

The house can be quite modest to start with. The main treasure will be the plot of ground, accurately and æsthetically laid out. Even today, wealthier citizens are paying big money to firms specialising in landscape design. There are about forty such firms in Moscow right now, and they are always busy. For upwards of $1,500 they will take just the hundred square metres of ground around your house and turn it into a landscape designed with detailed accuracy and æsthetic beauty.

---

[7] *400 cubic metres of lumber* — equivalent to 170,000 board feet.

[8] *dollars* — in this case, American dollars, the currency most familiar to Russians after their own rouble.

It costs around $500 to plant a single conifer about 6 metres high, but people who want to live in beautifully appointed surroundings are willing to pay big money for that. They end up paying it because it never entered their parents' heads to establish a family domain for their children. You don't need to be rich to do something like that, you need only to get your priorities straight. How can we raise our children properly if we ourselves don't grasp such simple things? Anastasia's right when she says that education begins with ourselves.

I myself have had a strong desire to establish my own family domain — to take a hectare of land, build a house and — most importantly — to put in all sorts of plantings around it. I want to set up my piece of the Motherland just as Anastasia described, and have it surrounded by other people's beautifully appointed plots. Anastasia and our son could establish themselves there too, or at least come visiting, and eventually our grandchildren and great-grandchildren. Maybe our great-grandchildren will want to work in the city, but they will still be able to come to their family domain to relax.

And once a year, on the 23rd of July, the All-Earth holiday,[9] the whole extended family will gather at home. I shan't be around then myself, but the domain I set up will remain, and the trees and garden it contains. I'll hollow out a little pond and put in some hatchlings so there'll be fish. The trees will be planted in the special arrangement outlined by Anastasia. Some things my descendants will like, others they may want to change, but either way I shall be remembered.

And I shall be buried in my own domain, with the request that my grave not be marked in any way. I don't want anyone putting on a show of grief or making a sad face over it. In fact, I don't want there to be any grieving at all. I don't want a headstone with an inscription, just fresh grass and bushes

[9]See Book 2, Chapter 9: "Dachnik Day and an All-Earth holiday!".

growing over the body — maybe some sort of berries too, which will be useful to my descendants. What's the point in a grave-marker? There isn't any — only grief. I don't want people coming to my domain to remember me with sadness, but with joy. Yeah, they'll see how I've set things up, and arranged all the plantings!...

My thoughts kept intertwining in a kind of joyful anticipation of something grand: *I'd better begin as quickly as possible, somehow start the ball rolling. I've got to get back to the city quicker, but it'll still be another ten kilometres just to get through this forest. If only I could get through it sooner!*

And all at once, out of the blue, statistics on Russia's forest lands floated to the surface of my memory. I didn't remember all the figures, but here's what I saw one time in a statistical report:[10]

"Forests constitute the basic type of vegetation in Russia, covering 45% of its land mass. Russia has the most extensive forest reserves in the world, amounting to 886.5 million hectares in 1993, with a timber volume of 80.7 billion. This means Russia holds 21.7% and 25.9% (respectively) of the world's forest and timber resources. The higher figure for timber reflects the fact that in terms of its wealth of mature and productive forests, Russia is way above the world's average.

"Forests play a huge role both in the gas balance in the atmosphere and in regulating climate on our planet. According to B.N. Moiseev's calculations, the gas balance of Russia's forests is 1,789 million tonnes[11] for carbon dioxide and 1,299 million tonnes for oxygen. Annual carbon deposits in Russia's forests amount to 600 million tonnes. These huge volumes

---

[10]This description appears, among other places, in an environmental atlas of Russia which may be found on the Russian "Practical Science" website at: www.sci.aha.ru

[11]*tonne* (metric ton) — 1 tonne = 0.98 UK (long) tons or 1.1 US (short) tons.

of gas exchanges significantly contribute to the stabilisation of the gas composition and climate of the whole planet."

Just look at what's happening! I've heard it said some kind of special mission lies ahead for Russia — but that's not in the *future,* it's already unfolding.

Just think: people all over the planet — to a greater or lesser extent, it isn't important — are breathing Russia's air. They're breathing the oxygen produced by this very forest I'm walking through right now. I wonder whether it's simply oxygen that this forest is supplying all life on the planet with, or maybe something even more important besides.

My solitary walk through the taiga this time provoked no feeling of trepidation within me as it did before. It felt pretty much the same as walking through a safe park. In contrast to a park, of course, there are no laid out pathways, and my journey was sometimes blocked by fallen trees or thick underbrush, but this time there was nothing that irritated me.

Along the way I would pick berries — raspberries and currants, for example — and for the first time my attention was drawn to the tremendous variety in appearance even among the same kind of trees. And the vegetation, too, was arranged in so many different patterns — no two scenes were alike.

For the first time I really examined the taiga, and it seemed a kinder place than before. No doubt this impression was due in part to the awareness that it was right here in the taiga that my very own son was born and was now living. And then, of course, there's *Anastasia*... My encounter with this woman has changed my whole life.

In the middle of this endless taiga is Anastasia's little glade, which she has no desire to leave for any length of time. She would never exchange it for any — even the fanciest — apartment in town. At first glance the glade appears to be just another empty space — no house, no tent, no household facilities — and yet look at how she brightens with joy every time she approaches it! And now on my third visit I've caught a similar feeling, something like the sense of comfort one feels upon returning home after a difficult journey.

Funny things have been taking place lately all over our world. It seems that, for millennia now, human society has been struggling for the happiness and welfare of the individual, but when you come right down to it, it turns out that this same individual, even though he lives at the very centre of society, at the centre of the most modern and civilised city, finds himself more and more often in a state of helplessness. He gets into a traffic accident, or gets robbed, or constantly falls into the grip of all sorts of aches and pains — he can't live without a drugstore nearby — or some dissatisfaction he can't even explain to himself provokes him into suicide. The suicide rate is increasing particularly in civilised countries with a high standard of living. Mothers from various regions of the country are seen on TV pleading for help for their families threatened with starvation because they can't afford to feed their children.

Yet here is Anastasia, living with a little boy all alone in the taiga, in what can only be called *another civilisation*. Not a single thing does she ask from our society. She needs no police or home security forces to protect her. She gives the impression that nothing bad can possibly happen in this glade to either her or her child.

It's true: we live in different civilisations, and she proposes to take the best of both these worlds. In which case the lifestyle of many people on the Earth will change, and a new and joyous commonwealth of humanity will be born. This commonwealth will not only be interesting — it will be new and unusual. For example...

CHAPTER TWO

Take a taste of the Universe

For a long time it bothered me that Anastasia appeared so content to leave her nursing child all by himself. She would simply put him down on the grass under some bushes or next to the dozing she-bear or she-wolf. I was already convinced that not a single creature would touch him. On the contrary, they would defend him to the death. But from whom? If all the animals around were acting like nannies, then who would they need to protect him from? Still, it was unusual to leave a nursing baby all alone, and I tried to dissuade Anastasia, saying:

"Just because the animals won't touch him, that doesn't mean that there are no other misfortunes out there that could befall him."

To which she responded:

"I cannot imagine, Vladimir, what misfortunes you have in mind."

"There are a lot of things that could happen to helpless children. Let's say he crawls up a hillock, for example, and then tumbles down it, twisting his ankle or his wrist."

"Any height of ground the baby could crawl up on his own would not cause him any harm."

"But say he eats something harmful. He's still too young, everything goes into his mouth, so it won't be long before he poisons himself, and then who's going to be around to flush out his insides? There aren't any doctors in the neighbourhood, and you don't even have an enema to flush out his intestines in case of emergency."

Anastasia just laughed.

"What need is there for an enema, Vladimir? The intestines can be flushed out another way, and much more effectively than with an enema."

"How so?"

"Would you like to try it? It will do you a world of good! I shall simply bring you a few little herbs..."

"Hold on, don't bother. I understand. You want to give me something to make my stomach upset."

"Your stomach has been upset for a long time, Vladimir. The herb I have in mind will expel anything causing your stomach harm."

"I get it — in case anything happens you can give a herb to a young child and it will make him go to the bathroom. But why take things to such lengths when it comes to a baby?"

"It will not go that far. Our son will eat nothing that is going to harm him. Children — especially those who are nursing and accustomed to the taste of their mother's milk — will never eat anything else in any significant quantity. And our son will only take a little taste of any berry or herb. If he finds it noxious or bitter — a substance that could harm him, he will spit it out himself. If he eats a little of it and it begins to affect his stomach, he will vomit it, and that will help him remember and he will not try it again. But he will come to know the whole Earth — not from someone else's reports, but by tasting it on his own. Let us allow our son to taste the Universe for himself."

No doubt Anastasia is right. It is true nothing bad has happened to the little one so far, not even once. Besides, I noticed a particularly interesting phenomenon: the creatures around her glade themselves train or teach their young how to interact with Man. I used to think Anastasia was the one that did this, but later I became convinced that that is not something she wastes her time on.

This is what I saw on one occasion: we were sitting in the sun at the edge of the glade. Anastasia had just finished nursing our son, and he was blissfully lying in her arms. Initially he seemed to be having a nap or just dozing, but then all at once his little hand began touching Anastasia's hair, and he broke into a smile. Anastasia looked at her son and smiled back, whispering something in his ear with her tender voice.

I saw the she-wolf come out into the glade with her brood — four cubs, still quite young. The wolf came over to us, and stopped about ten metres away and lay down on the ground. The cubs trailing along behind her quickly began nuzzling up to her belly. Upon seeing the wolf and her cubs lying there, Anastasia rose from the ground, babe in arms, and went over to her. She squatted down about two metres away and began inspecting the wolf's brood, her face all smiles, and saying:

"Oh, what beauties our clever wolf has borne! One of them will most certainly be a leader, while *this* little one is the spitting image of her Mama. She will be a joy to her Mama, and a worthy inheritor to carry on the family line."

The mother wolf seemed to be dozing, her languishing eyes closed tight either from drowsiness or from the soft caressing of Anastasia's voice. The cubs turned away from their mother's belly and began looking at Anastasia. One of them, still unsure of his step, began making his way over to her.

The mother, who just a second before had looked so drowsy, suddenly sprang up, seized the cub with her teeth and dropped him back among the others. Then the same thing occurred with a second cub, then the third and the fourth, all trying to get closer to Anastasia. The inexperienced cubs continued their attempts, but the mother would not let them go until they had finished their little adventures. Two of the cubs began tussling with each other, the other two sat meekly and kept a watchful eye on us.

The baby in Anastasia's arms also noticed the wolf family. He began watching them, and then his legs began kicking impatiently, and he uttered some kind of beckoning sound.

Anastasia reached out her hand toward the wolves. Two of the cubs began heading, with unsure step, in the direction of the outstretched human hand. This time, however, the mother didn't try to stop them. On the contrary, she began nudging the other two cubs, who were still at play, in the same direction. And before long all four were right at Anastasia's feet.

One of them began nibbling on one of her fingers, a second got up on its hind legs and rested its forepaws on her arm, while the other two crawled over to her leg. The boy started to squirm in Anastasia's arms, evidently wanting to get closer to the cubs. Whereupon Anastasia let him down on the ground and he started playing with them, oblivious to anything else! Anastasia went over to the mother wolf, and after giving her neck a gentle stroking, came back to me.

I realised that the wolf had been trained never to disturb Anastasia without being invited, and would approach her only upon a predetermined gesture. Now she was teaching this same rule to her offspring. The wolf, no doubt, had been taught this by her own mother, who in turn had learnt it from *her* mother, and so on from generation to generation — all the creatures transmitted to their young the rules of interaction with Man. A reverent and tactful interaction, it must be said. But who taught them that other kind of interaction and how — to attack Man?

My exposure to the life of the Siberian taiga recluses[1] raised a whole lot of different questions — questions I could not have even imagined asking earlier. Anastasia has no intention of changing her reclusive lifestyle.

---

[1] *recluses* — referring to Anastasia, her grandfather and great-grandfather, introduced in Book 1, Chapter 2: "Encounter".

But... stop right there! When I think of Anastasia as a 'recluse', each time I associate the word *recluse* with someone who has isolated himself from society, from our contemporary information systems. But what is really going on? After each visit to her glade I end up putting out a new book. A book that is discussed by all sorts of people, young and old, scientists and religious leaders. The way it turns out, it is not *I* who bring *her* information from our over-informed society, but it is *she* who offers *me* information that proves to be of great interest to our society.

So then, who is the real recluse? Haven't we got caught up so much in the abundance (or, more correctly, the seeming abundance) of information at our fingertips that we have set ourselves apart, distanced ourselves from the true source of information? It's simply amazing when you think about what's really going on — Anastasia's remote taiga glade serves as a real information centre, like a launch pad propelling us into the other dimensions of our existence. Then, *who am I, who are we? And who is Anastasia?*

In any case, perhaps it isn't all that important. Something else is much more important, namely, her latest sayings concerning the possibility of transforming the life of any individual Man for the better. Or, for that matter, any country, or even human society as a whole. And this is effected through changing the living conditions of an individual.

It's all incredibly simple: just give a Man at least one hectare of land, and she goes on to explain what to do with this land, and then... Incredible, how simple it is! And Man will always be surrounded by the energy of Love. Those in marital relationships will love their spouses. Their children will be happy, many diseases will be eradicated, wars and catastrophes will cease. Man will draw closer to God.

She has, in fact, proposed the construction of a whole lot of glades similar to her own in the proximity of major cities. But this doesn't mean she rejects making use of our civilisation's achievements — "Let what is negative be pressed into service on behalf of good," she says. And I have come to believe in her plan. I believe in that splendid turn of events that is to come about as a result of implementing her ideas in our lives. And a lot of them seem so logical to me. All we have to do is go over everything, think everything through, in the right order. We have to adapt her proposal to each location.

I was especially struck by Anastasia's idea regarding land and its development. I could hardly wait to get home and see what scientists have to say about similar communities — does anything along this line exist anywhere in the world? I wanted to see if I could start by designing a new community in all its detail, and then start building it through the concerted efforts of those desiring to participate in its construction. Naturally, neither I nor anyone else can undertake the responsibility for getting this marvellous community of the future going all on our own. It is something we need to do together! We shall have to examine all the information collectively and design our community, taking into account mistakes other people have made.

Chapter Three

Dreams of Auroville

During the first months after returning from my visit with Anastasia I set about making an intensive search and study of any information about eco-communities I could lay my hands on. Most of my sources told about experiments abroad. Altogether I collected information on 86 communities in 19 countries (Belgium, Canada, Denmark, England, France, Germany, India and others). But I wasn't particularly struck by any of the reports I had collected. No country could boast any kind of large-scale eco-movement, nor did I come across any communities capable of exercising a significant influence on the social situation in their respective countries.

One of the largest and best-known communities that came to my notice is located in India. It goes by the name of *Auroville*. I'd like to elaborate a little on this one.

Auroville was initiated in 1968 by the wife of the founder of the Integral Yoga movement Sri Aurobindo, Mirra Richard.[1] It was thought that the community, once begun, would eventually grow into a thriving city of 50,000 on lands allocated

[1] *Sri Aurobindo* (1872–1950) — Hindu mystic, scholar, poet and evolutionary philosopher, considered by his followers to be an 'avatar', or incarnation, of the Supreme Being. His *Integral Yoga* is actually a synthesis of the three yogas: *bhakli, karma* and *jnana,* embodying and integrating all aspects of life. His 'spiritual partner', *Mirra Richard* (1878–1973), born in Paris to Egyptian parents, first came to Aurobindo's *Ashram* (Hermitage) in 1914 and eventually settled in Pondicherry in 1920. Commonly known as 'The Mother', she supervised the operations of his *Ashram* and related organisations. Upon Aurobindo's death in 1950, she succeeded him as spiritual leader, and went on to found the Auroville community in 1968.

by the Indian government near Pondicherry, where Sri Aurobindo's *Ashram* — a centre for Integral Yoga adherents —
had been operating since the 1940s. Auroville, or the 'City
of Dawn', was supposed to embody the idea of unity of people — people united by a common goal of building a harmonious material world which in no way would find itself at odds
with the world of the spirit.

The community's charter, written by Mirra Richard,
states:

"Auroville will be a site of material and spiritual researches
for a living embodiment of an actual human unity."

The idea of building a city wherein people will live in harmony with the world of Nature, in the harmony of the spirit
and love, was approved by the Indian government (and personally by Indira Gandhi) as well as by UNESCO. It received
financial support from the Indian government along with
a large number of sponsors. Representatives of 121 nations
and 23 Indian states attended the opening ceremonies, after
which this splendid city — no doubt the dream of a lot of
people the world over who call themselves 'spiritual' — began
to take shape.

However, following the death of Mirra Richard in 1973,
one of Aurobindo's disciples by the name of Satprem[2] spoke
out strongly against the Auroville community, calling it nothing but a 'commercial enterprise'. Sri Aurobindo's Ashram,
which controlled most of the 'enterprise's' finances, claimed

[2] *Satprem* (birth name: Bernard Enginger, 1923–) — French author, who discovered the teachings of Sri Aurobindo while serving in the French colonial
administration of Pondicherry in the 1940s, and later worked closely with
Mirra Richard. It was she who gave him the name *Satprem* ('the one who
loves truly') in 1957. Later he published *The Agenda* — a mutli-volume account of his collaboration with Richard, disseminated through his Institute for Evolutionary Research in Paris. This was followed by a number of
other books he wrote on his experiences in India.

authority over everything going on in the city, but the residents considered that their community belonged to the whole world and was not under the Ashram's jurisdiction. A serious confrontation ensued between the spiritual leaders on both sides — a confrontation which was not confined to the ideological level but became more and more physical. In 1980 the Indian government was obliged to pass a decree removing Auroville from the control of Sri Aurobindo's society, and a permanent police detachment was assigned to the community. The Auroville situation led to a general crisis in Sri Aurobindo's movement and teachings.

Today Auroville has about 1,200 residents, instead of the 50,000 or more envisaged by its initiators. The whole region, including the local population, comprises 13 villages and 30,000 people.

Quite possibly the downfall of the Auroville dream was precipitated by the following situation: while any resident may obtain permission to buy land and build himself a house (at his own expense), legal title to the land on which the house stands belongs to the city. Thus it turns out that full confidence is placed in Auroville as a city, but is not accorded any of its individual residents. Every resident lives in a state of dependency on the community as a whole. And yet the whole project was worked out by people who considered themselves highly spiritual. It seems that in the case of spirituality there is another side of the coin to be considered.

I am extremely disturbed and upset by the situation of Auroville today. While it has not provoked any doubts about Anastasia's project, I cannot say my mind is entirely free from negative thoughts. If things did not work out with a model community in India — a country considered practically the leader in the spiritual understanding of human existence, especially with the financial backing of the Indian government, UNESCO and sponsors from a variety of countries, then how can Anastasia possibly foresee on her own all the pitfalls that lie ahead? Even if it isn't all on her own, and the masses of readers sharing her views try to make calculations, think everything through and foresee the future — even then there is no guarantee such concerted efforts will succeed, as nobody has any experience along this line.

If anyone knew where to find the foundation on which to build a happy life for both the individual and society as a whole, a happy society would have probably been built somewhere. But it doesn't exist — anywhere in the world! The only experience we have is negative. Where can one find anything positive?

"In Russia!" replied Anastasia.

CHAPTER FOUR

Harbingers of a new civilisation

"The first shoots of a new and splendid future are to be found in the Russian *dachniks!*"[1] These words sounded within me, all by themselves. Anastasia was not around at the time. It took but a moment to recall the enthusiasm and joy with which she talked to me about the Russian dachniks four years ago. She believes that it was thanks to the dachniks that a global catastrophe on the Earth was avoided in 1992. So it turns out that it was in Russia that this amazing movement began, a movement which has had a kindly influence on a part of the Earth. I remember her telling me:

"Millions of pairs of human hands began touching the Earth with love. With their *hands*, you understand, not a bunch of mechanical contraptions. Russians touched the ground caressingly on these little dacha plots. And the Earth felt the touch of each individual hand. The Earth may be big, but it is very, very sensitive. And the Earth found the strength within itself to carry on."[2]

Back then, four years ago, I didn't take this saying seriously, but now, after learning of all the various attempts by people of different countries of the world to create spiritual-ecological communities, I suddenly realised something: with no noisy fanfare, appeals, advertising or pompous ceremonies, the

---

[1] *dachniks* — people who spend time at their *dacha,* or cottage in the country, surrounded by a garden where fruits and/or vegetables are grown to feed the family all year long (for further details see Book 1).

[2] See Book 2, Chapter 9: "Dachnik Day and an All-Earth holiday!".

most massive-scale project has come to fruition right here in Russia — a project having significance for all humanity. When seen against the backdrop of all the various Russian dacha communities, all the reports from various countries on the creation of eco-communities there sound quite ludicrous.

Judge for yourselves: here spread out in front of me is a pile of articles and collections of reports seriously discussing the question of how many people should live in an eco-community — a population of no more than 150 is advised. Considerable attention is paid to the governing bodies of such communities and their spiritual leadership.

But Russia's dacha co-operatives have existed for years, sometimes comprising 300 families or more. Each co-operative is managed by one or two people, usually somebody retired from their regular job — if in fact you can call the chairman of a Russian dacha co-operative a manager. He's actually more like a registrar, or a manager who simply carries out the will of the majority.

Russia does not have any centralised management system for its dacha movement. However, according to data published by *Goskomstat* (the State Statistics Committee), in 1997 14.7 million families had fruit-growing plots, while 7.6 million had vegetable plots. The overall land area cultivated by these families amounted to 1,821,000 hectares. These households independently grew 90% of Russia's potatoes, 77% of its berries and fruit, and 73% of its vegetables.[3]

[3]These figures have further increased since the book was written, making Russian gardeners the backbone not only of the country's agriculture, but the economy as a whole. Thus, according to the official statistics published by *Goskomstat*, in 2004 Russian gardening families — without any heavy machinery, hired labour or government subsidies — have grown on their free time and using predominantly organic methods 33 million tonnes of potatoes, 11.5 million tonnes of vegetables and 3.2 million tonnes of fruit and berries, which represent 93%, 80% and 81% respectively of the country's total output of these crops. Russian gardeners now produce more products than the whole commercial agricultural apparatus all told. In 2004 the

No doubt the theoreticians who have been designing eco-communities and eco-villages for years will protest that a dacha co-operative is not the same as an eco-community. To which I wish to immediately respond: it is not the name but the content that is important.

The overwhelming majority of Russia's dacha co-operatives conform to eco-community guidelines. Not only that, with no thunderous declarations on spiritual self-improvement and the necessity of a careful approach to Nature, the dachniks have proved their spiritual growth not by words but by their way of life. They have planted millions of trees. It is thanks to their labours on hundreds of thousands of hectares thought to be infertile and good for nothing — so-called marginal lands, that orchards are now flourishing.

We keep hearing how in Russia part of the population is on the verge of starvation. We see strikes by teachers, then by miners, and our politicians are scratching their heads in their attempts to bring the country out of crisis after crisis. More than once during the *perestroika*[4] period Russia was but a hair's breadth away from a massive social upheaval. But it didn't happen.

And now let's try mentally deducting from just the past few years of our lives the 90% of potatoes, 77% of berries and 73% of vegetable production, and substitute a heightened anxiety level on the part of millions of people. This you would have

value of the Russian gardeners' production represented 51% of the country's total agricultural output — approx. US$14 billion, or 2.3% of Russia's gross domestic product (GDP). The contribution of dachniks and rural family growers to the Russian economy exceeds that of any of the following industries: steel; electric power generation; chemical and pharmaceutical; forestry, timber, pulp and paper; building materials; or oil refining, natural gas and coal industries taken together.

[4]*perestroika* — the policy of restructuring the economic and political system of the Soviet Union, which led to the collapse of the Communist Party's hold on power and the break-up of the USSR in the late 1980s and early 1990s.

to do if you were going to exclude from the past few years the calming effect of the dachas. You don't have to be a psychologist to see how dachniks are calmed by their contact with the vegetable plots they have planted. So, if we take away that factor, what would we have been left with in 1992, 1994 or 1997? In any of those years a colossal social upheaval could have come about. What kind of result might such an upheaval have led to on a planet chock full of deadly weapons?

But no catastrophe occurred. Anastasia maintains that in 1992 a catastrophe on a global scale was avoided thanks only to Russia's dachniks, and now, having read all the reports explaining the situation, I tend to agree with her.[5]

It's not so important any more to know just which 'smart head' in our nation's government came up with the idea of giving the green light to the dacha movement in Russia (still the Soviet Union back then). Or maybe it was Providence itself that saw fit to accord this privilege specifically to Russia? What's important now is that the movement exists! And it is proof positive that there is indeed a possibility of achieving stability in human society — maybe even that stability so many peoples on various continents having been trying without success to achieve for thousands of years!

Anastasia says that the dacha movement in Russia represents a momentous turning-point in the development of the human commonwealth. Dachniks are the harbingers of a splendid future which will come after them, she has said, thinking of the future communities she has sketched out. And I myself would very much like to live in one of these splendid communities — a community located in a flourishing country, whose name just happens to be... Russia.

---

[5]See Book 2, end of Chapter 8: "The answer". Some of the factors portending a social upheaval in 1992 are detailed in footnote 1 of Book 1, Chapter 17: "The brain — a supercomputer".

CHAPTER FIVE

A search for evidence

Russia of the future... A splendid land, in which many of to-day's generation will be able to live a happier life.

Russia of the future — a land which will lead the human commonwealth of the whole planet to a happier life. I have seen this splendid country coming into bloom. She, Anastasia, showed me the future of our country. And it is absolutely unimportant and insignificant just *how* this fiery, untiring recluse living alone in the Siberian taiga is able to travel to other planets, or into the future or into the past, or by what means or unseen threads she brings together the hearts of people living in different countries into a single, exciting creative impulse. What is important is that *this impulse exists.* Does it really matter where she obtained such a colossal amount of all kinds of information and knowledge of our life? What matters immeasurably more is the *result* of this knowledge — the fact that people living in different cities, once put in touch with the information she possesses, are now planting cedar allées, that people have started producing cedar nut oil, and that more and more songs and poems about what is beautiful in life are coming to light.

This is simply amazing! She dreams about something, I write about it, and... *presto,* it turns into reality! Like a kind of fantasy! Yet this fantasy, after all, is embodied in real life for everyone to see. Now she has dreamt about a splendid country. Shall not that too come to pass? Of course it must! And we must help in any way we can!

Going over in my mind and analysing everything Anastasia has said or showed has only made me more and more convinced of the reality of a splendid future. I believe in it.

Even though I'd begun to believe all Anastasia's words, there was still no way I could put together and publish a chapter on the future of Russia. It wasn't included in the previous book, *Co-creation*. And the release of this present volume has been delayed more than once for the same reason. I wanted everything I wrote to look sufficiently real and convincing. So that not just I but a whole lot of people could believe and set things in motion to create a splendid future. But there are certain sayings of Anastasia's that have prevented me from being less than fully convincing.

In *Co-creation* I published Anastasia's statement that what our whole natural environment comprises is precisely the materialised thoughts of God. If Man is able to comprehend these, even in part, he will not need to spend so much effort in his search for food, fertilising the ground (since the ground itself is capable of re-establishing its own fertility) or to waste energy on trying to fight noxious pests and weeds. His thought will be liberated from the problems of everyday living, and Man will be able to get involved in tasks more suited to his existence — the co-creation, with God, of splendid worlds. I wanted her words to be believed by a majority of people. But how can people trust her if even the whole agriculture industry, both in Russia and abroad, cannot dispense with the fertilising process?

So many factories in various countries of the world are involved in the production of all sorts of chemicals for 'enriching' the soil. On a number of occasions I have put this question to various agricultural scientists, but each time I've got pretty much the same condescending reply, namely that of course one could set up a Paradise garden on a single hectare of land, but you would need to tend this garden from morning 'til night. And you could not possibly expect a good harvest unless you added fertiliser to the soil, and made use of toxic chemicals, otherwise your harvest would be ruined by a whole bunch of pests. When I brought up Anastasia's argument that everything grows in the taiga without human assistance, the scientists countered:

"Let's assume it grows. But if your recluse is to be believed, the taiga has been programmed directly by God. Man needs a lot more than what can grow in the taiga. For example, the taiga doesn't have any fruit orchards. That's because orchards need to be cared for by Man. They can't grow all by themselves."

I've made several visits to such stores as "Everything for your garden", "The Gardener", "The Dachnik", and seen so many people buying different bags of chemicals. I watched these people and thought that they'll never believe what Anastasia says, and so there's no point in writing about the future of Russia — they simply won't believe in it. They won't believe in it because this future is first and foremost linked to a new conscious awareness, a different attitude to the Earth and our environment.

But there is not a single person today who could confirm what she said, not a single real-life example bearing out her words. On the contrary, everything *contradicts* her position. And the factories producing toxic pesticides continue to operate. There is a whole chain of stores selling fertilisers and chemicals. And a great many people are involved in agricultural research.

The absence of significant evidence to back up Anastasia's statements had such a strong effect on me that I came to the point where I was no longer able to write anything at all. It was for that reason that I accepted an invitation to go to Innsbruck in Austria. A German publisher rang me and said that the director of a bio-energy institute by the name of

Leonard Hoscheneng had invited me to speak on Anastasia at a gathering of the most prominent healers of Europe. The institute would pay my travel and lodging expenses, and was prepared to pay me 1,000 marks for every hour I spoke. I didn't go on account of the money, but in search of convincing arguments that a lot of people could understand either for or against Anastasia's plan — her affirmations about the future of Russia.

Dr Hoscheneng, who invited me to speak to the healers, was himself a professional doctor and a prominent healer, as his father and grandfather had been before him. His grand-father had treated the Japanese Imperial family and many other highly placed dignitaries. His personal domains, apart from the institute building, included several small, cozy ho-tels (where a great number of patients coming from Euro-pean countries stayed), along with a restaurant, a park, and some other buildings in the city centre. He was a millionaire, though, in contrast to the image many Russians have about the lifestyle of a Western millionaire, Leonard, as I found out, handles all the serious work involved in people's treatment himself. He personally treats every one coming to see him — which can mean as many as fifty patients a day. Indeed, his working day can sometimes stretch to 16 hours. Only occa-sionally he has entrusted his consultation task to... a healer from Russia.

I spoke to the gathering of healers at Innsbruck, aware that they were interested first and foremost in Anastasia. I devoted the larger part of my presentation to her, and ended up talking a little about her project, with the secret hope that the audience would either confirm or discredit her ideas on the future of Russia. But they neither confirmed nor discred-ited them; they just kept constantly asking for more details.

That evening Hoscheneng threw a 'banquet' in his restau-rant. I would simply have called it a supper. Even though everyone could order what they liked, they were all modest, giving preference to the salads. Nobody drank alcohol or smoked. I too refrained from ordering any alcoholic beverages. Not because I was afraid of looking like the proverbial black sheep in their eyes — it was just that for some reason I didn't *feel* like having meat or alcoholic drinks.

At the supper-table the talk again turned to Anastasia. A saying was born (though I don't remember who said it first): *The splendid future of Russia is linked with the Siberian Anastasia.* The phrase caught on, and was in time repeated with various interpretations by healers from Italy, Germany, France and other countries.

I was waiting for specifics as to why and by what means the splendid scenario of the future would unfold, but nobody could offer any specific evidence. The healers were relying on some kind of intuition, whereas I needed proof: can the Earth feed Man without a special effort on his part, simply by virtue of Man correctly understanding the thought of a God whom nobody could see?

After returning to Russia, I recalled the words of the European healers, and continued my search for concrete evidence, for which I was prepared to travel anywhere. But I didn't have to travel very far. An extraordinary coincidence, as though deliberately set up by someone, not only offered theoretical evidence, but proved to be a real and living confirmation of Anastasia's words.

It happened this way...

CHAPTER SIX

A garden for eternity

I set off on a day-trip to the country along with employees of the Anastasia Cultural Foundation of Vladimir.[1] We stopped by the picturesque shore of a small pond. The women went about preparing a variety of salads for lunch, while the men attended to building a fire. I stood at the edge of the pond, gazing at the water and lost myself in thought. I was in a pretty gloomy mood. All at once Veronika, a resident of a nearby village, came up to me and said:

"Vladimir Nikolaevich, just about seven kilometres from here, in the middle of these fields, there are two former manorial estates. There's nothing left of the buildings, but the fruit orchards have been preserved. Nobody looks after them, but they still bring forth fruit year after year. They give a lot more fruit than the village orchards which are tended to and fertilised.

"In 1976 there was an extremely cold winter in these parts, and a lot of people lost their orchards and were forced to

---

[1]*Vladimir* — in this case the name of one of Russia's oldest cities (founded in 1108 by Prince Vladimir Monomakh on the site of a much earlier settlement), which once served as the Russian capital. Situated on the Klyazma River about 180 km east of Moscow, it has a current population of about 340,000. Like neighbouring Suzdal (former patriarchate of the Russian Orthodox Church) and a chain of other historic towns, Vladimir forms part of Russia's circular tourist route known as the *Golden Ring* (*Zolotoe kol'tso*). It is here that the author of the Ringing Cedars Series, Vladimir Nikolaevich Megre, resided at the time this book was written. The name *Vladimir* — though now commonly interpreted as meaning "ruler of the world" — is an ancient Slavic name originally meaning "in harmony and peace".

plant new ones, but these two, out among the fields, weren't touched by the cold at all, and not a single tree was lost."

"Why didn't the cold touch them?" I asked. "Maybe they were a special variety, cold-resistant?"

"Just the usual variety. But the way everything was set up on these former estates — the way they did it on just a single hectare of land — *wow!* It's pretty much the way Anastasia describes it in your books. Two hundred years ago people planted Siberian cedars all around it along with local oak trees... Another thing: the hay from the grass that grows there is a lot richer. It keeps for a long time.

"If you like we could go see the place right now. It's just a dirt trail through the fields, but your jeep can make it."

I couldn't believe my ears. Who? How? A gift like this — and just at the right place and at the right time. Are such 'coincidences' really coincidental after all?

"Let's go!" I said.

The trail ran across fields belonging to a former state farm.[2] I said 'fields', though they were really more like hayfields or meadows, all overgrown with tall grasses.

"They've really cut back their growing areas here," observed Evgeny, Veronika's husband. "The farm company doesn't have enough money for fertiliser... Anyway, the ground's getting a rest. And not just the ground. The birds have started singing again this year. You didn't hear such happy twittering before. What are they so happy about? Maybe 'cause there are no chemicals on the fields now. Before the revolution there were villages here in these meadows — my grandmother told me about them. But there's no trace left of them now.

"Look — there it is, to the right of the trail — a former estate."

---

[2] *state farm* (Russian: *sovkhoz*) — in the Soviet period, a farm where workers were paid a monthly wage, as in a factory.

In the distance I could see tall trees growing densely together. They appeared to cover about a hectare of ground. This place seemed simply like a green isle of forest, all surrounded by fields and meadows. As we drew closer, I could see in amongst the dense grove of two-hundred-year-old oak trees and bushes an entrance leading to a woodland oasis inside. We went in through the entrance and...

There we were inside... Just imagine: there inside were ancient apple trees with gnarled trunks, spreading their branches out into space. Branches literally dripping with fruit. They hadn't been dug around — they were just growing there amidst the grasses, they hadn't been sprayed for insects, but these old apple trees were bearing fruit, and their fruit showed no sign of worm infestation. Some of the trees were real oldies, their branches were breaking under the weight of the fruit. Real oldies — quite possibly this was their last year for bearing fruit.

They will soon die off, but alongside each ancient tree you could already see shoots of a new tree breaking through the soil. The thought actually came to me that these trees probably wouldn't die — at least not until they saw the fresh and healthy shoots coming from their seed.

I walked through the orchard, took a taste of the fruit, wandered among the oak trees growing all around, and it seemed as though I could discern the actual thoughts of the Man who had created this splendid oasis. It was as though I could hear him thinking:

"Right here, around the orchard, I should put in an oak grove. It will protect the orchard from the winter cold, as well as from summer heat in dry years. Birds will make their nests in the tall trees and stop the caterpillars from taking over. I'll plant a shady oak allée by the shore of the pond. When the trees grow up, their tops will come together, giving shade to the spacious allée below."

And all at once a kind of vague thought made my blood course faster through my veins. What was it demanding of me, this thought? And then... it came in a flash: of course, Anastasia! Naturally you were right when you said that we could feel God in coming into contact with His creations and in continuing His creations. Not by wild antics, jumping up and down and new-fangled rituals, but by directly turning to Him, to His thoughts, it is surely possible to understand His wishes and our own purpose in life. Here I am standing beneath the oak trees on the shore of a man-made pond and I can literally read the thoughts of the Man behind this living creation. And he — this Man, this Russian, who lived here two hundred years ago — no doubt felt more than others the thoughts of the Creator, which enabled him to bring about this Paradise creation. His own garden, his own family nest.

He may have died, this Russian, but his orchard has remained, and is still bringing forth fruit, and feeding the children of the neighbouring villages, who come here every autumn to delight in the fruits. Some people gather them up and sell them. And you, my fine Russian fellow, no doubt wanted your grandchildren and great-grandchildren to live here. Of course you did! I can tell that because you didn't put up just a mansion with a limited life-span, but something that will last for eternity.

But where are your grandchildren and great-grandchildren today? Your family domain has been abandoned, it's all grown over with grasses, and your pond is drying up. But your allée, for some reason, didn't get overgrown with wild grass. In fact the grass beneath it is like a carpet. Your corner of Paradise which you created — your family domain — is no doubt still awaiting the return of your descendants. Decades go by, even centuries, but it is still waiting. So where are they? Who are they now? Whom do they serve? Whom do they worship? Who chased them away from here?

We did have a revolution — maybe that's to blame for everything? Of course it is. Only a revolution is made by people when some sort of qualitative change takes place in the consciousness of the majority. What happened in the minds of your contemporaries, my fine Russian fellow, that your family domain has gone to waste?

The local old-timers told me how the ageing Russian landowner headed off a blood-bath on his domain.

When a group of revolutionary-inclined residents from two nearby villages, pumped up on local beer, marched en masse to pillage his family domain, the old landowner came out to meet them with a basket of apples, only to be slain by a bullet from a double-barrelled gun. He had known already the night before that they were planning to pillage his house, and he had persuaded his grandson, a Russian officer, to leave the domain. The grandson, a front-line veteran, decorated with St George's Cross, fled together with his comrades-in-arms with front-line Mosin rifles[3] slung over their shoulders; their open wagon also carried a trusty, battle-worn machine gun. He probably went into emigration and now has grandchildren of his own growing up.

Your descendants, my fine Russian fellow, are growing up in another land, while in Russia, in your kin's domain, the leaves of the trees in your orchard are rustling in the breeze, and every year your old apple trees are bringing forth fruit, astounding all the residents around with a luxuriant harvest. There isn't even a trace of your house left, all the outbuildings have been torn down, but the orchard lives on in spite of everything — no doubt in the hope that your descendants will return to taste the best apples in the whole wide world. Yet your descendants are still not coming.

---

[3] *Mosin rifle* (Russian: *vintovka Mosina*) — the standard army-issue three-line (*triokhlineika*) rifle in both the Imperial and Soviet Russian armies, developed in 1891 by Sergei Ivanovich Mosin (1849–1902).

Why have things turned out like this and who is making us seek our own happiness at the expense of others just like us? Who is making us breathe air filled with noxious gases and dust instead of floral pollen and beneficial ethers? Who is making us drink water deadened by gases? Who? Who are we today? Why do not your descendants come back, my fine Russian fellow, back to their family nest?

In the second domain the apples were even tastier than in the first. Around this orchard had been planted beautiful Siberian cedars. Local residents informed me that there had even been more cedars earlier — now only twenty-three of them were left. During the days following the revolution when they still had a day-labour system, they said people were paid for their work with cedar nuts. Now the nuts were there to be collected by anyone who wanted to. The only thing was, sometimes they would beat the trees very hard with logs[4] to make the cones fall to the ground.

Twenty-three Siberian cedars, planted by the hand of Man two hundred years ago, still stood there all in a row, like soldiers protecting this splendid orchard from freezing winds and harmful pests. There had been more of them, but one by

---

[4]The customary process of harvesting cedar nuts involves 5 to 10 strong men putting a log on their shoulders and, with a running approach, hitting the trunk of the cedar with one end of the log. This is the most 'efficient' method of knocking the cones off the tree to the ground, yet the most damaging to the tree. A milder alternative is to hit the trunk with a special bat, while the best option — recommended by Anastasia (see Book 2, Chapter 31: "How to produce healing cedar oil") — is to gather the ripe cones that fall naturally to the ground (or to climb the tree and pick them by hand).

one they perished, since in Siberia the cedars were always sur-rounded by tall pines. A single cedar by itself could not with-stand the blasts of wind, as its root system is not all that exten-sive. Cedars are nourished not only through their roots, but also absorb the surrounding space through their tops. That is why the pines or young cedars protect them. Whereas here the cedars were all standing in a row. They lasted the first hundred and fifty years, but then, after their tops expanded, they began falling, one after the other.

For the past fifty years nobody thought of planting pines or birches beside them, and so the cedars were left to defend the orchard, standing up against the angry winds all on their own. It was probably just last year that one of them began falling, but came to rest against the top of the one next to it in the row. I looked at the sharply leaning tree trunk, whose top was intertwined with that of its neighbour. Their branches had grown together, and the falling tree was still living. Both trees were green and bearing seed. There were only twenty-three left. They are still standing there, supporting each other, bearing seed and protecting the orchard.

Oh you Sibiriaks![5] Hang in there, just a little longer, please! I'm going to write about you...

Oh, Anastasia, Anastasia! You taught me how to write books, but why didn't you teach me to write words that would be understandable to a lot of people right off the bat? To a whole lot of people?! Why can't I manage to write in an understandable way for a great many people? Why does my thought get confused? Why do the cedars fall, and people only *look* at them and not *do* anything?

Not far from these former domains, which have preserved right up to our day their splendid orchards and shady allées,

---

[5] *Sibiriak* (pronounced: *sibir-YAK*) — a native of Siberia, in this case referring to the trees.

are located several villages. The sight of these villages spoils the whole surrounding landscape. If you look at them from afar, you get the impression that some sort of worm ran amuck, laid everything waste and dug up the flower-covered meadows. Slums full of grey village houses, farm buildings thrown together out of various rotting materials, dirt from roads broken down under the wheels of lorries and tractors, all contribute to this impression.

I asked the local residents whether they had been to the orchards laid out among the cedar and oak trees. Many had been there, tasted the apples. Young people were accustomed to going to the place for picnics.

"It's lovely there!" was chorused by young and old alike.

But when I asked why nobody had tried to set up their own homestead in the same 'image and likeness', I got pretty much the same answer each time:

"We don't have the kind of money the landowners who created this beauty had."

Older residents said that the cedar saplings had been brought here by the landowner directly from Siberia.

When I asked how much it cost just to take a cedar nut from one of these trees and plant it in the ground, I got a strained silence in reply.

Which brings me to the thought that it is not the lack of opportunity or financial means, but our own inner coding that is somehow to blame for all our woes.

Nowadays people with money are putting up a lot of fancy houses in the country. The land around these houses has been either dug up or buried in asphalt. In twenty or thirty years these houses are going to be in need of repair; they won't look like new any more. And their children won't need this old derelict. They won't be needing a family domain — a Motherland — like that, and so they'll go off to find themselves a new one.

But they'll be taking with them this same mysterious coding they got from their parents and repeating their life as temporary caretakers on the land, instead of creating something for eternity. Who will be able to remove it and how — this mysterious coding for hopelessness?

Perhaps what Anastasia has said and shown about the future of Russia will somehow help in this regard. And just to allay the doubts of the sceptics, I have put on the inside covers of this book photographs of these amazing Russian orchards, spreading out their fruit-laden branches to the Russia of the future.

CHAPTER SEVEN

Anastasia's Russia

As Anastasia was telling me about the communities of the future which would be comprised of family domains, I asked her:

"Anastasia, please *show* me the Russia of the future. I know you can."

"Yes, I can. What place in the future Russia would you like to see, Vladimir?"

"Well, how about Moscow?"

"Would you like to go to the future alone, Vladimir, or together with me?"

"It'd be a lot better with you. You can explain anything I see and don't understand."

The touch of Anastasia's warm hand at once induced a sleepy state, and I started to see...

Anastasia showed me the future of Russia the same way she showed me life on another planet. At some point scientists will probably understand just how she does this, but the means she used are quite irrelevant in this case. In my view, the most important thing is information about what specific actions will enable us to bring about this splendid future.

The Moscow yet to come was nothing like I had imagined. The city had not expanded its geographical boundaries. There were no skyscrapers, as I might have expected. The walls of the old houses were decorated in cheerful colours, and many were painted with pictures — landscapes and flowers. I later found out that this was the work of foreigners. First they covered the walls with some kind of plaster, and then artists —

also from abroad — added the ornamentation. Intertwining vines hung down the roofs of many of the houses, their leaves rustling in the wind, as though greeting the passers-by.

Almost all the streets and avenues of the capital were planted with trees and flowers. Right down the middle of Kalinin Avenue (or the New Arbat,[1] as it is called) stretched a green boulevard about four metres wide. Concrete kerbs rose about a half-metre above the pavement, enclosing earthen beds from which sprouted grass and wild flowers, interspersed at brief intervals with various kinds of trees: rowans with their clusters of red berries, birches, poplars, currant and raspberry bushes and a host of other plants such as one might find in a natural forest.

There were similar boulevard strips down the centre of many of Moscow's avenues and broad streets. And on the reduced traffic portion of these streets there didn't seem to be very many motorcars — mainly buses carrying passengers who did not look at all Russian in their appearance. The same could be said of many of the pedestrians on the sidewalks. I wondered for a moment whether Moscow had been occupied by a technically more developed country. But Anastasia reassured me, saying that the people I was seeing here were not occupiers, but simply foreign tourists.

"And what draws them to Moscow?" I asked.

---

[1] *New Arbat* (in Russian: *Novy Arbat*) — a broad thoroughfare leading west from the Kremlin and city centre to the Novy Arbat Bridge across the Moskva River (*Moskva* is also the Russian name of the city itself). Officially known as Kalinin Prospekt (Avenue) in Soviet times (after Mikhail Kalinin — see footnote 1 in Book 1, Chapter 1: "The ringing cedar"), Novy Arbat was constructed in 1963 parallel to the old Arbat Street, which still runs a short distance to the south and from 1974 to 1986 was turned into a pedestrian mall. Novy Arbat's imposing row of modern high-rise apartment blocks gave 1960s Moscow a new Western appearance, complete with contemporary-looking shops and restaurants.

"The atmosphere of a grand creation, refreshing air and water," came the reply. "Look and see how many people are standing along the banks of the Moskva River and collecting water in containers on strings they let down from the high embankments, and drinking the river water with great delight!"

"But how can they drink water straight from the river without boiling it first?"

"Look and see, Vladimir, how pure and transparent the water is in the Moskva River. It contains living water, not water deadened by gases like the kind sold in bottles throughout the world."

"It must be a fantasy — something impossible to believe!"

"A fantasy? But when you were little, would you and your friends have believed it if someone told you that before long people would be selling water in bottles?"

"You're right: when I was young nobody would have believed that. But how was it possible to make the water so pure in such a big city as Moscow?"

"Stop polluting it, stop throwing harmful waste into it, stop littering the river banks."

"It was that simple?"

"Exactly. Nothing fantasy-like — it is actually all quite simple. Today the Moskva River is protected even from the runoff water flowing over the pavement, and it is closed to dirty ships. They used to consider the Ganges in India sacred, but now the whole world adores the Moskva River and its water, they adore the people who restored the water to its pristine vitality. And people come here from many countries to see this wondrous marvel, taste the water and find healing."

"And where are all the local residents? Why are there so few passenger cars in the streets?"

"There are only about a million-and-a-half Muscovites actually living in the capital now, though the number of tourists from various countries can be more than six times that figure," replied Anastasia, and added: "There are fewer cars because the remaining residents have managed to arrange their day on a more rational basis, reducing their need to move around. Their work is usually close by, close enough to walk. And the tourists get around using just the metro[2] and the buses."

"And what's happened to all the other Muscovites?"

"They live and work in their splendid family domains."[3]

"Then who works in the plants and factories? Who looks after the tourists?"

And Anastasia told me the following:

"As the year 2000 (according to the accepted Earth calendar of the time) was drawing to a close, the Russian leadership was still in the process of determining the country's path of future development. The majority of Russian citizens were not particularly inspired by the path the so-called prosperous countries of the West were taking.

"Russians had already tried the food products from these countries, but did not have much of a taste for them. It turned out that the development of what was termed technical

[2]*metro* — Moscow's "metropolitan", or subway system, which has been operating since May 1935. Over the years it has expanded to twelve lines and some 200 stations.

[3]The whole description of the Russia of the future in this chapter and elsewhere in the Series bears striking similarities to the ideas of one of Russia's greatest economists, Alexander Chayanov (1888–1937). Back in the 1920s he already foresaw the eventual return of the country to predominantly rural living after the fall of communism, and even described the Moscow of the future as a garden-city populated mostly by tourists. He also accurately predicted the rise of the dacha movement that would eventually dominate the country's agriculture. Some of these views are expressed in his insightful *A journey of my brother Alexey to the land of peasant Utopia* (dubbed a 'utopia' only to allow the publication of the work under the Soviet censorship in 1920). After Stalin publicly attacked Chayanov's views in 1929, he was incarcerated and, after years in prison, executed on Stalin's personal order. Today Chayanov's works are better known abroad than in his native Russia.

progress in these countries came hand-in-glove with various diseases of both the body and the soul. Crime and drugs became increasingly rampant, and women were less and less inclined toward child-bearing.

"Russians were not attracted to the conditions in which the peoples of the 'developed' nations lived. Neither did they wish to revert to the old social order, but they had not yet seen any new path. An increasing mood of depression took hold of the country, affecting the whole society in ever greater numbers. Russia's population was ageing and dying.

"At the beginning of the new millennium, at the initiative of the Russian President, a decree was signed granting free and unconditionally to each willing family one hectare of land whereon to establish a family domain. The decree allotted this land to the family for lifetime use, with the right to pass it on to their heirs. Any produce grown in this domain would not be subject to taxation of any kind.[4]

"Russian parliamentarians supported the President's initiative and the Russian Constitution was amended accordingly. The primary aims of the decree, in the eyes of the President and the parliamentarians, were: reducing unemployment in the country, guaranteeing a minimum income level to needy families, and solving the refugee problem. But what subsequently happened was something none of them could have fully imagined.

[4]On 7 July 2003, less than three years after this book was released in Russian, Russian President Vladimir Putin signed into federal law the "Private Garden-plot Act" (*Zakon o lichnom podsobnom khoziaistve*). According to this law, Russian citizens can receive free of charge from the state plots of land in private inheritable ownership. The maximum size of plots differs from one region to another, but in most cases is between 1 and 3 hectares. The produce grown on the plots is not subject to taxation. Subsequently, on President Putin's instructions the Russian government developed and introduced into the Russian parliament another law to further facilitate the acquisition of land for gardening. This second law was passed in June 2006.

"When the first allocation of land was made for organising a community numbering more than two hundred families, the plots of land in question were taken up not just by the needy, the unemployed or poverty-stricken refugees, but primarily by middle-income families and wealthy entrepreneurs who had read your books, Vladimir. They had been anticipating this turn of events. And they were not just idly waiting for it — many of them had already been growing their own family trees in their apartments from seeds planted in clay pots, and the mighty cedars and oaks of the future were already sprouting their first little shoots.

"It was these entrepreneurs who initiated and financed plans for a community with an infrastructure facilitating a convenient lifestyle, as you wrote in your book *Co-creation*. These plans provided for a store, a medical clinic, a school, a club, roads and a lot else besides. In fact, entrepreneurs made up about half the number of people who expressed their desire to rearrange their life and daily routine to live in the first of the new communities.

"They all had their own businesses, their own source of income. For the actual construction work and setting up their plots of land they required a labour force. The ideal solution, they discovered, was to hire their neighbours from among the needy families as construction and landscape workers. That way some of these families got jobs right away, which gave them the wherewithal to finance their own construction projects. The entrepreneurs realised that nobody would prove to be more meticulous and efficient workers than those who were planning to live in the community themselves, and so external specialists would be hired only where such could not be found among the future community residents.

"Only the establishing of the future orchard and forest and the planting of the family trees and living fences was something each family endeavoured to do on their own.

"Most of them did not yet have enough experience or knowledge as to how best to establish their plot, and as a result among the future residents the elderly people who did have this knowledge commanded considerable respect. The principal focus was not on temporary structures or even houses *per se,* but on the development of the landscaping. In each case the actual buildings people were going to live in were considered just one small part of the larger living house of God.

"Within five years houses for permanent residence had been built on all the lots. They were quite varied in size and architectural style, but it was soon evident that the greatest treasure of each domain was by no means the size of a house. The greatest treasure lay elsewhere, and it was not long before it took form and outline in the splendid landscaping elements of each plot in particular as well as of the community as a whole.

"The oaks and cedars planted in each plot were still very young, and each plot was surrounded by a living fence, which was only starting to grow. But with each new spring, apple and cherry trees, even though still quite small, came stridently into bloom in the young orchards, along with grass and flower beds that were doing their very best to resemble a splendid living carpet. The spring air was filled with delightful aromas and floral pollen. The air became truly invigorating.

"And every woman living in this new community had a desire to bear children. This happened not only in young families but even people considered elderly suddenly began to bear children. People felt that even if they themselves did not live to see the splendid piece of their Motherland their hands had created, they wanted their children to — they wanted their children to delight in the sight and continue the co-creation begun by their parents.

"At the beginning of the new millennium, in each plot, all living shoots represented the first shoots of a splendid, happy future for the whole Earth. The people that established for centuries to come the first family domains had still not completely felt the significance of what they had done — they simply began looking more joyfully at the world around them. They were still not consciously aware of the great joy their actions were bringing to their Heavenly Father. The Father was sending tears of joy and tenderness upon the Earth amidst the drops of the falling rain. And He smiled with the sunshine, and was endeavouring to use the little branches of young trees to give a secret caress to His children who had suddenly become aware of eternity and had come back to Him.

"The Russian press began writing about the new community, and many people wanted to see this splendid phenomenon for themselves so that they could create one of their own like it.[5] Perhaps even create a better one.

"Millions of Russian families were seized with the inspired desire for a splendid co-creation. Communities similar to the first one sprang up simultaneously in various regions of the country. An entire movement began, not unlike our contemporary dacha movement.

"Within nine years after the first decree was signed allowing people to establish their lives independently and make their lives happy, more than thirty million families had become involved in creating their own kin's domains, their own piece of the Motherland. They have been cultivating their

[5]This too came to pass. On 12 November 2002, less than two years after this book was published in Russian, *The Moscow Times*, Russia's largest English-language daily newspaper, featured an article (entitled "Urban group dreams of eco-friendly settlement") on *Rodnoe*, one of Russia's first eco-villages created by inspired readers of the Ringing Cedars Series. This article, describing the emerging Russia-wide eco-village movement which sprang from the ideas expressed in Vladimir Megre's books, was followed by hundreds of other reports in newspapers and in other mass media. Both *Rodnoe* and other eco-communities now receive a steady flow of visitors from all over Russia and abroad.

splendid plots of ground, using, in the process, living, ever-lasting materials created by God. And, by so doing, they were creating together with Him.

"Each of these families turned their hectare of land provided for their lifetime use into a little corner of Paradise. Against the backdrop of the vast spaces of the Russian Motherland, a single hectare seemed like a very small piece indeed. But there were many such pieces. And all of them together made up a vast Motherland. Through these pieces, all created by loving hands, the whole Motherland flourished like a garden in Paradise! This was their Russia!

"On each of the hectares were planted both evergreens and deciduous trees. People were already aware how the trees themselves would fertilise the ground and the balance in soil composition would be maintained by the grasses growing all around. And nobody had it even cross their mind to use chemical fertilisers or toxic chemicals.

"The quality of Russia's air and water improved and became health-giving. The food shortage problem was completely resolved. Each family was able — easily and without undue effort — not only to provide for themselves from what grew in their domain, but also to sell their surplus.

"Every Russian family with its own domain started to become rich and free, and Russia as a whole began to grow into the most rich and powerful state in comparison with other countries in the world."

CHAPTER EIGHT

The richest state

"Hold on, Anastasia, I don't understand how the state as a whole suddenly got rich. You yourself said that the produce from family domains wasn't subject to any kind of tax, so what has made the state so rich?"

"How can you possibly ask *what?* Think about it more carefully, Vladimir. You are an entrepreneur, after all."

"Well, since I am an entrepreneur, I happen to know that the state has always tried its hardest to squeeze just a little more tax out of every citizen. And here you tell me it's gone and axed thirty million families from the tax roll. The families, of course, could have got very rich, but at the same time it should mean bankruptcy for the state."

"The state did not go bankrupt. First, unemployment was completely eliminated, since any Man who found himself without a job in the industrial, commercial or public sectors (as we know them today) was able to devote himself either fully or partially to work — or putting it more specifically, to *co-creation* in his own domain. The total elimination of unemployment freed up significant financial resources.

"The abundant supply of food provided by the families with their own domains spared the state from any kind of expenditure on agricultural production. But, more importantly, thanks to the vast number of families who established their domains in accordance with the Divine plan, the Russian state received an income significantly higher than it realises today from the sale of oil, gas and other resources traditionally regarded as its basic sources of income."

"What could possibly bring it more income than oil, gas and arms sales?"

"A great deal, Vladimir — for example, air, water, ethers, loveliness, contact with the energy of co-creation, the contemplation of pleasant things."

"It's still not completely clear, Anastasia. Couldn't you put it in more specific terms? Where did the money come from?"

"I shall try my best. The extraordinary changes taking place in Russia attracted the attention of many people all over the globe. The world press began writing about the major change in lifestyle most Russians were experiencing. This became a burning issue for a good deal of the world's population. A huge flood of tourists began pouring into Russia. There were so many that wanted to come, it was impossible to accept them all, and many had to wait their turn, even as long as several years. The Russian government was forced to limit the length of stays by foreign tourists, since many of them, especially the elderly, were attempting to stay months and even years here.

"The Russian government collected huge levies from each foreigner entering the country, but this by no means reduced the number of those applying to come."

"But why did they want to visit here in person, if they could see it all on TV? You did say the world press was enlightening people about life in the new Russia."

"People all over the world wanted more — they wanted to breathe Russia's air which had become so health-giving. They wanted to drink its living water. To take a taste of fruits unlike any other in the world. To talk with the people who were stepping forward into God's millennium and thereby both slake their souls' thirst and heal their suffering bodies."

"And what unusual kinds of fruit appeared? What were they called?"

"The same as they were called before, only the quality was completely different. You already know, Vladimir, how much better tomatoes and cucumbers taste when they are grown in the open air under the direct rays of the Sun, in comparison to hothouse varieties. Well, fruits and vegetables grown in soil free from harmful chemicals are even tastier and more healthful. And they have even greater healing properties when grown in the company of different kinds of herbs and trees. The mood and attitude of the grower also plays a role. And the ethers contained in the fruit also have a tremendous benefit for Man."

"What do you mean by *ethers?*"

"Ethers are fragrances. A fragrance you detect signifies the presence of an ether which feeds not only the body but also the invisible essence of a Man."

"Still not clear. Are we talking about the brain, perhaps?"

"One could say that ethers strengthen mental energy and feed the soul. Such fruits were grown only in Russia, and the greatest benefit is realised when used by Man on the day they are picked, and that is why so many people have come to Russia from all over the world — to taste these fruits, among other things.

"Produce from the family domains very quickly took over the market, squeezing out not only imported fruits and vegetables but those that were still growing in the ordinary large-acreage fields. People began to appreciate and feel the difference in the quality of the produce. Pepsi-Cola and the other soft drinks so popular today were replaced by fruit beverages made from natural berries. And even the most sophisticated and expensive liqueurs in today's society could not compete with the sweet wines prepared from natural berries right in the domains.

"These drinks also contained beneficial ethers, since the people preparing them in their domains knew that once the berries were picked, they had only a few minutes to begin making them into fruit liqueurs and wines.

"An even greater source of income for families living in their domains was the sale of medicinal plants which they gathered from their groves, gardens and surrounding meadows.

"In time the harvests of medicinal herbs from Russia became a far more sought-after commodity than drugs manufactured abroad — but only the herbs collected in the family domains and not those grown in specialised operations on huge tracts of land. A herb grown in a huge field among others of its own kind cannot take from the soil and surrounding space all the ingredients that are needful and useful to Man. Even though the produce from the domains cost a great deal more than what was produced by the so-called industrial method, people all over the world still preferred it."

"And why did the owners of the domains jack up the price?"

"The minimum price was set by the Russian government."

"The government? Why would it care? It doesn't get anything from family domain production. Why would it take pains to enrich individual families?"

"You must remember, Vladimir, that the state itself consists of individual families, who, as the need arose, took to financing the infrastructure network in their communities — schools and roads, for example. Sometimes they would put money into projects on a national scale. Politicians and economists would publish their projects, but only those which people put their money into passed."

"Tell me, what kinds of projects were the most popular among the majority?"

"The buying up of chemical conglomerates abroad, arms factories and scientific institutes."

"Now there's a switch! You told me that these families had a conscious awareness of the Divine, a sense of goodness.

That it was thanks to them that the whole world was being transformed into a garden of Paradise, and now you're talking about buying up chemical plants and arms manufacturing companies."

"But these ventures were not aimed at *producing* weapons or harmful chemicals, but at destroying the factories making them. The Russian government was involved in the redirection of the international monetary flow. The energy of money, which had been feeding what was fatally harmful for mankind, was now aimed at the liquidation of the same."

"And what happened — did the Russian government have enough money for such extravagant projects?"

"It did. Russia not only became the richest country in the world but it became immeasurably richer than all the other countries. The whole world's capital started flowing into Russia. Not only the wealthy, but even people of modest means flocked to deposit their savings exclusively in Russian banks. Many wealthy people simply willed their savings to the development of Russian projects — these were people who realised that the future of all mankind depended upon these projects being carried out. Foreign tourists who had visited Russia and seen the new Russians could no longer live by their former set of values. They excitedly told their friends and acquaintances about what they had seen, and the flood of tourists kept getting bigger, and bringing ever increasing profit to the Russian state."

"Tell me, Anastasia, those people, you know, who live in Siberia, what projects could they undertake to become as wealthy as the people in central Russia? After all, in Siberia the summer is shorter and you won't get very rich on growing garden produce."

"People in Siberia, Vladimir, also began setting up their domains. Siberians used their plots of ground to grow things suitable to their climate, and they had one big advantage over

residents of more southern climes. Siberian families received
state allotments in the taiga, and each family took care of its
own lands and harvested their gifts. And out of Siberia came
health-giving berries and herbs. And... cedar nut oil."

"And how much did cedar oil fetch on the international
market, in terms of dollars?"

"One tonne of cedar oil cost four million dollars."

"Wow! Finally it was priced at its true worth, which is eight
times higher than what it was fetching before. I wonder how
much of this cedar oil the Siberians would have prepared in a
season?"

"In the year you are looking at now: three thousand tonnes
were produced."

"Three thousand?! Wow! That means they would have got
twelve billion dollars just for harvesting cedar nuts."

"More, in fact. You forgot that pressed cedar nuts can be
made into excellent flour."

"So how much would an average Siberian family make in a
year from their labours — in terms of dollars?"

"On average, three to four million dollars."

"Wowee! And you mean to tell me they still don't pay any
tax?"

"No tax at all."

"In that case, where on earth could they spend money like
that? Back when I worked in Siberia, I saw that anyone in
a Siberian village who wasn't lazy could provide enough for
himself by hunting and fishing. But here you're talking huge
sums!"

"Like other Russians, they invested their money in national
government projects. For example, initially, when the Russian
people still had not discovered how to control the movement
of the clouds, a great deal of the Siberians' money went to the
purchase of aeroplanes."

"Aeroplanes? What would they need planes for?"

"To ward off clouds containing harmful deposits. These clouds would form over countries where deadly industrial pollution was still permitted. They were fought off by Siberian aviators."

"And what about hunting — has it been confined to reserved family allotments in the taiga?"

"Siberians have totally stopped all hunting and the killing of animals. Many of them built summer residences on their allotments and spent their summers collecting herbs, berries, mushrooms and nuts. Young creatures of the forest right from birth saw human beings as not a threat to them, and got accustomed to Man as an integral part of their territory. They began communicating with people, making friends with them.

"The Siberians taught many creatures to help them. For example, squirrels would throw down cedar cones with ripe nuts onto the ground, which gave the squirrels no end of pleasure. Some people trained bears to pull heavy baskets and sacks with nuts, and clear away trees felled by the wind."

"Really! They even got bears helping!"

"There is nothing surprising in that, Vladimir. In times which people today call 'ancient', a bear was one of the most irreplaceable helpers in the household. He would use his paws to dig edible tubers out of the ground and put them in a large basket, and then take it upon himself to drag the basket on a rope to a pit cellar hollowed out of the ground not far from Man's dwelling. He would climb trees in the forest to fetch log-hives filled with honey and bring them back to Man's dwelling. He would take Man's children into the forest to gather raspberry treats, as well as do a lot of other things for the household."

"Wow! The bear replaced both the tractor and the plough, and brought home things to eat, and minded the children!"

"And all winter long he slept, needing no maintenance or repairs. And when spring came he would return to Man's dwelling once more, and Man would treat him to the fruits of the previous autumn."

"I see what's going on: a reflex was trained in those bears to make it seem as though Man had stored up those supplies just for them."

"You could call it a reflex, if that helps you gain a clearer understanding, but you could also say that is the way it was designed by the Father. I will only tell you that tubers were not the most important thing for the bear in the springtime."

"What was, then?"

"After sleeping all alone in his lair the whole winter long, when he awoke in the spring the first thing the bear did was hurry over to see Man, to feel Man's caresses and hear his praise. All the creatures need Man's caresses."

"If dogs and cats are any example, you're right. But what about the other creatures in the taiga — what did they do?"

"Gradually all the other taiga dwellers found themselves a niche too. And the highest reward for these tamed residents of the territory was a tender word or gesture, or petting or scratching for those who had done an exceptionally good job. But they could get jealous of each other some times, if one of them seemed to win special favour from Man. They could even have a quarrel over this."

"And what have Siberians been doing during the winter?"

"Processing the nuts. Instead of husking the cones right after gathering them, the way it is done in our time for ease of transport, they keep the nuts stored in their resinous cones. The nuts keep that way for several years. Also during the winter women do handicrafts. For example, a hand-made shirt woven out of nettle fibres and embroidered by hand fetches quite a handsome price today. And in wintertime Siberians receive people from all over the world and treat their ills."

"But, Anastasia, if Russia has indeed become such a rich land for Man to live in, surely that means that many other states have a desire to conquer Russia? Especially since, as you said, the arms factories have been shut down. Are you telling me Russia has become in fact an agrarian country, unprotected against an external aggressor?"

"Russia has not been transformed into an agrarian country. It has become a centre for world science.

"And the factories manufacturing destructive weapons in Russia were eliminated only after people discovered an energy, before which the most up-to-date kinds of armaments not only proved useless, but even represented a threat to those countries which maintained them."

"What kind of energy is that? Where does it come from and who discovered it?"

"This energy was possessed by the Atlanteans. But they got hold of it too early, and so Atlantis disappeared from the face of the Earth. And it was rediscovered by the children of the new Russia."

"Children?! You'd better run all this by me in the proper order, Anastasia."

"Very well."

Chapter Nine

Good shall prevail on the Earth[1]

In one of the Russian domains lived a happy family — a husband, wife and two children: a boy, Konstantin, who was eight, and a little five-year-old girl named Dasha.[2] Their father was considered one of the most talented computer-programmers in Russia. His study at home contained several state-of-the-art computers on which he compiled programmes for a government military agency. Sometimes he would linger at his computers well into the evening hours, completely absorbed in his work.

The other members of the family, accustomed to gathering in the evenings, headed for his study, where each busied themselves with their own activities. The wife sat in a comfortable armchair and sewed. Their son read or drew sketches of the landscapes of the new settlements. Only five-year-old Dasha would not always find herself an activity to her liking, in which case she would curl up in a chair with a good view of everyone else, and spend a long time carefully observing each member of the family. Occasionally she would close her eyes, and her face would show a whole range of emotions.

On what seemed to be a fairly routine evening the family had gathered in the father's study as usual, each one busy in their own way. The study door was open, which meant that

[1]The whole of Chapter 9 and the first few paragraphs of Chapter 10 are told directly in Anastasia's words.

[2]*Dasha* — the diminutive form of the name *Daria*; family and friends might also call her *Dashenka*, or (indicating a momentary negative emotion) *Dashka*. *Konstantin* may also be known informally as *Kostia* or *Kostienka*. They in turn could address their parents as *Mamochka* and *Papochka*.

they could hear the cuckooing of an old-fashioned mechanical cuckoo clock on the wall of the children's room next door. Usually it would sound off only during the daytime hours, but now it was already evening. So the father glanced up from his work and stared at the door, while the other family members gave an astonished look in the same direction. All except for little Dasha, who simply sat in her chair, her eyes closed, apparently oblivious to everything. A smile — first barely noticeable, then quite evident — crept across her lips. All at once the clock cuckooed a second time, as though someone standing in the children's room had moved the hands forward to announce the next hour. Ivan Nikiforovich,[3] as the father of the household was called, turned his swivel chair in his son's direction and said:

"Kostia, please go see if you can fix the clock or at least stop it. We've had it a long time, that gift of Grandfather's. Strange how it got broken like that... Strange... See if you can do something about it, Kostia."

The children were always obedient. Not out of fear of punishment — in fact, they were never punished. Kostia and Dasha loved and respected their parents. They got the highest pleasure out of doing something together or carrying out their parent's wishes. Upon hearing his father's request, Kostia at once rose from his seat, but, to his mother's and father's surprise, did not head for the children's room. Instead, he just stood and stared at his younger sister sitting in the armchair with her eyes closed. Then once again they heard a cuckooing from the next room. But Kostia still stood there and stared, his eyes fixed on his sister.

Galina, their mother, looked concernedly at her son, who remained rooted to the spot. All at once, she got up and cried out in fright:

[3]*Nikiforovich* — a patronymic, derived from Ivan's father's first name *Nikifor.*

"Kostia... Kostia, what's the matter with you?"

The eight-year-old boy turned to his mother, wondering what she was frightened about, and replied:

"Everything's fine with me, Mama. I wanted to do as Papa asked, but I can't."

"Why not? Are you unable to move? You're unable to go to your room?"

"I can move," replied Kostia, waving his arms about and stamping his feet on the spot to prove it, "but there's no point in my going to our room — she's here and she's stronger."

"*Who's* here? *Who's* stronger?" Mother started getting more and more upset.

"Dasha," Kostia replied, pointing to his younger sister sitting in the armchair, her eyes closed and with a smile on her face. "She's the one who's been moving the hands forward. I tried to put them back in place, but I can't do it when she —"

"What are you talking about, Kostienka?" Mother interrupted. "You and Dashenka are both here with us — I can see you. How can you two be here and at the same time move the clock hands in the other room?"

"Well yes, we're here," answered Kostia, "but our thoughts are in the other room, where the clock is. Only *her* thought is stronger. That's why the clock keeps cuckooing — her thought is speeding up the hands. She's been playing a lot of tricks like that lately. I told her not to. I knew it might upset you, but Dasha doesn't care. All she has to do is fall into a state of contemplation, and she starts thinking up something."

"What is Dasha contemplating on?" Ivan Nikiforovich broke into the conversation. "And Kostia, why didn't you say anything about this earlier?"

"You yourself can see how she's contemplating. The clock hands aren't important — she's just amusing herself. I can move the hands too when nobody's interfering. Only I can't contemplate like Dasha. When she's in a state of contemplation like that there's no way anyone can counteract her thought."

"What is she contemplating on? Do you know, Kostia?"

"Sorry. Why don't you ask her yourself? I'll stop her contemplation before she thinks up anything else."

Kostia went over to the chair his sister was sitting in and said distinctly in a louder than normal voice:

"Dasha, stop thinking! If you don't stop, I shan't speak to you for a whole day. And besides, you've frightened Mama."

With a flutter of her eyelashes the little girl surveyed everyone present in the room with an observing glance and, as though literally waking up, jumped up from her chair and hung her head apologetically. The cuckooing stopped, and for a while the study was enveloped in complete silence — a silence eventually broken by little Dasha's apologising voice. She raised her head, looked at her Mama and Papa with her sparkling, tender eyes and said:

"Mamochka, Papochka, forgive me for frightening you. But I had to... I just had to finish thinking it through — this thought I had. Now I can't help but think it through. I'll be thinking it through tomorrow too, when I've had a rest." The girl's lips trembled, it seemed just as though she were about to break into tears, but she continued:

"You, Kostia, can refuse to talk with me if you like, but I'll go on contemplating it all the same, until I think it through."

"Come to me, daughter dear," said Ivan Nikiforovich, trying to act restrained. He held out his arms to his daughter, ready to embrace her.

Dasha rushed toward her father, jumped up on his knees and put her little arms around his neck, pressed her cheek briefly against his, then jumped down and stood beside him, bending her head down to him.

Ivan Nikiforovich for some reason had a hard time hiding his emotion. He began telling his daughter:

"Don't worry, Dashenka! Mama will no longer get frightened when you contemplate. Just tell us what you're thinking about. What is so important to think through and why do the clock hands move forward so fast when you're thinking?"

"You see, Papochka, I want to make everything that's nice even bigger in time, and everything that's bad tiny and unnoticeable. Or even... I want to think it through so that the hands skip over the bad things and they aren't there any more."

"But what is nice and what is bad doesn't depend on the clock hands, Dashenka."

"It doesn't depend on the hands, Papochka. I realise that. But I move them along so's I can feel the time. The cuckoo counts off the speed of my thinking, 'cause I have to get it done in time... That's why I move the hands."

"How do you do that, Dashenka?"

"It's simple. I picture the hands of the clock out of the corner of my thought, then I think they should go faster — and they go faster when I start thinking fast."

"What do you want to achieve, daughter dear, by speeding up time? What don't you like about the present time?"

"I like it. I realise now that time isn't to blame. It's people themselves who spoil their time. You, Papochka, are so often at your computer, and then you go away for a long time. You, Papochka, spoil the time when you go away."

"Me? Spoil it? How so?"

"We have a good time when we're all together. When we're together we have very good minutes and hours, even days. Everything around is joyful. Do you remember, Papochka, when the apple tree began to bloom just a little? You and Mama saw the first buds, and you took Mama in your arms and twirled around. And Mamochka laughed so brightly that everything around was joyful with us — the leaves on the trees, and the little birds too. And I didn't feel sore at all about your twirling Mama around in your arms instead of me, 'cause I love our Mamochka very much. I was so happy with that time, just like everyone else.

"But then a different time came. I realise now that it was you, Papochka, who made it different. You went away from us for a very long time. Baby apples had even begun to appear on the apple tree. But still you didn't come home. And Mamochka went up to the apple tree and stood there all by herself. But there was nobody there to twirl her around, and she didn't laugh brightly, and nothing around had anything to be joyful about. And Mamochka has quite a different smile on her face when you're not around. It's a sad smile. And that is a bad time."

Dasha spoke quickly and excitedly. All at once she seemed to choke on something inside her, and then burst out:

"You shouldn't make it bad when it is good... Time... Papochka!"

"Dasha... You're right about one thing... Of course... But you don't know everything about the times we're all in. The times we live in..." Ivan Nikiforovich spoke disconnectedly.

He was feeling tense. Somehow he needed to explain how necessary it was for him to go away. To explain it in such a way that his little daughter could understand. Finding no better alternative, he began telling her about his work, showing her rocket models and schematics on the computer.

"You see, Dashenka. Of course it's good for us here. And it's good for those who live in our neighbourhood too. But there are other places, other countries in the world. And they've got a lot of weapons, all sorts of them... To protect our splendid garden, and the gardens and the houses of your friends, sometimes Papa has to go away. Our country must also have a lot of up-to-date weapons to defend itself.

"But recently... Dashenka... You see, recently in another country, not ours, they came up with a new kind of weapon.

For the time being it is stronger than ours. Look here, on the screen, Dashenka!"

And Ivan Nikiforovich gave a tap on the keyboard, and the image of a strange kind of missile appeared on the screen.

"Look, Dashenka. This is a large missile, and it holds fifty-six smaller missiles. The large rocket takes off at Man's command and heads for its assigned target, to destroy everything living there. This missile is very hard to shoot down. When any object approaches it, an on-board computer kicks in and sends out one of the smaller missiles to destroy the object.

"The smaller missiles can travel faster than the big one, since when they're launched they can use the inertia speed of the larger missile. To shoot down just one such monster, we need to send fifty-seven missiles out against it.

"The country producing this so-called 'cassette' missile has only three working models at the moment. They have been carefully concealed in various places, in shafts deep underground, but it only takes a single radio-transmitted command to launch them. A small group of terrorists are already blackmailing a number of countries, threatening to wreak havoc on them. So you see, Dashenka, I have to decode the programme of the cassette missile's on-board computer."

Ivan Nikiforovich got up and walked around the room. He continued talking rapidly, getting more and more absorbed in his thoughts about the programme, seemingly oblivious to his little girl standing beside the computer. Ivan Nikiforovich quickly went over to the monitor showing the external image of the missile, gave a tap on the keyboard, and the screen showed a schematic of the missile's fuel supply system, then one of the targeting radar devices, and then, once more, an overall image. Even as he was switching the screen images, Ivan Nikiforovich was no longer paying any attention to his dear little daughter. He kept reasoning aloud:

"They have obviously equipped each of the smaller missiles with a targeting radar device. Of course, that would apply to every single one. But there can't be any difference in the programmes. The programmes have to be identical..."

All at once one of the other computers emitted an alarm sound, demanding immediate attention. Ivan Nikiforovich quickly turned to the respective monitor and froze in his seat. The screen showed a blinking text message: "EMERGENCY ALERT... EMERGENCY ALERT..." Ivan Nikiforovich gave a quick tap on the keyboard, and an image of a man in a military uniform appeared on the screen.

"What's happened?" Ivan Nikiforovich asked him.

"Three unusual explosions have been recorded," responded the man. "The whole defence complex has been put on Emergency Alert. Explosions of lesser magnitude are continuing. There's been an earthquake in Africa. Nobody's offered any explanations. According to international information exchange networks all military blocs on the planet have been ordered to high alert. Still no determination where the attack originated from. The explosions are continuing and we're trying to shed light on the situation. All personnel have been ordered to set about analysing the situation."

The officer on the screen spoke in a clipped, military fashion. At the end, his voice was already betraying signs of concern:

"Explosions continuing, Ivan Nikiforovich, explosions continuing. I'm signing off..."

The officer's image disappeared from the screen. Ivan Nikiforovich, however, continued to stare at the darkened monitor, intensely absorbed in thought. Slowly and pensively he turned in the direction of his chair, where Dasha was still standing as before.

All at once an incredible conjecture made him shudder. He saw how his little daughter, her eyes screwed up and unblinking, was staring at the screen showing the image of the modern missile. Suddenly her little body gave a start. Then, letting out a sigh of relief, she hit the 'ENTER' button on the keyboard. When the image of the new missile appeared, she screwed up her eyes again and began staring intently at the monitor.

Ivan Nikiforovich stood as though paralysed, incapable of budging from the spot, feverishly asking himself — though only in his thoughts — the same question over and over again: *Could* she *have set off the explosions? Set them off by her thought, because she doesn't like the bombs? Did she blow them up? Could that be true? How?*

He wanted to stop his daughter and called out to her. But he did not have the strength to speak very loudly, and could only whisper:

"Dasha, Dashenka, my dear daughter, stop it!"

Kostia, who had observed the whole scene, quickly got up from his seat, ran over to his sister, gave her a little pat on her bottom and began talking at a rapid pace:

"Now, Dashka, you've gone and upset Papa this time. Now I shan't speak to you for two whole days — one day for Mama, the other for Papa. D'you hear? Do you hear what I'm saying? You've frightened them!"

Gradually emerging from her state of concentration, Dasha turned to her brother and let her face resume its normal appearance as she looked him pleadingly and apologetically in the eye. Kostia noticed Dasha's eyes were filling with tears. Putting his hand on her shoulder, he spoke to her with a less severe tone than before.

"Okay, I got carried away about not talking to you, but you'll have to tie your own hair ribbon in the mornings. You're not so little any more, you know."

And telling her not to think about crying, he embraced her tenderly. The little girl nuzzled her face up against her brother's chest, her shoulders trembling, as she sorrowfully repeated:

"I've gone and frightened them again. I'm a very naughty girl. I wanted to do the best I possibly could, but I've gone and frightened them."

Galina came over to the children, squatted down beside them and began stroking Dasha's head. The girl threw her arms around her mother's neck and sobbed quietly.

"How does she do it, Kostia? How?" Ivan Nikiforovich asked his son as he slowly came to himself.

"The same way that she moves the hands of the clock, Papa," replied Kostia.

"But the clock is right here, while the missiles are a long ways away, and their location is classified as 'top secret'."

"Papa, it doesn't matter to Dasha where they're located. All she needs to see is the outward appearance of the object."

"But the explosions... In order to set them off, the circuits have to be connected. Quite a few circuits at that. There are safety mechanisms, codes..."

"But Papa, Dasha's able to go through all the circuits until a connection is made. Before, it took her a long time to do that, maybe fifteen minutes, but lately she's got it down to a minute and a half."

"*Before?!*"

"Yes, Papa, only not with missiles. That was the way we played. After she started moving the clock hands forward, I showed her my old electric car I used to love riding in when I was little. You see, Papa, I opened the bonnet and asked her to connect the headlamp wires together, since it was hard for me to get at them myself. She did it. And when she asked to take it for a drive, I told her she was still too young and wouldn't be able to brake properly, or even switch on the motor. But then when she kept insisting, I gave in. I explained how to switch the motor on, but Dasha did it all her own way.

"I tell you, Papa, Dasha simply sat down behind the wheel and took off without switching on anything. She thought she was switching it on, but I could see that she wasn't doing anything with her hands. Or rather, she was switching it on, but she did it mentally. Besides, Papa, she's made friends with microbes. They obey her."

"With *microbes*?! What microbes?"

"With the ones that are very prolific, that live everywhere, all around us and inside us. We can't see them, but they're there. D'you remember, Papa, over on the edge of our domain, in the forest, there used to be the remains of two metallic posts sticking out of the ground? They belonged to an old high-voltage electricity line."

"I remember them. What of them?"

"They were rusty, resting on concrete foundations. One day when Dasha and I went mushroom-picking, she noticed these remains, said what a bad thing they were, that they weren't allowing the berries and mushrooms to grow on that spot. Then she said: "You should eat them up very, very fast!""

"And...?"

"And a couple of days later those rusty remains and the concrete foundations were gone. There was only bare earth there, without grass, at least for now. The microbes had eaten the metal and the concrete."

"But why — oh why, Kostia, didn't you tell me earlier about everything that was going on with Dasha?"

"I was afraid, Papa."

"Afraid of what?"

"I was reading up on history... In the recent past people with unusual abilities have been subject to forced isolation. I wanted to tell you and Mama all about it, but I couldn't find the right words so that you'd understand and believe..."

"Kostia, you know we always believe you. Besides, you could show us. Or rather, ask Dasha to demonstrate her ability, only with something harmless."

"That's not what I was afraid of, Papa. Of course she could show you." Kostia fell silent, and when he spoke again, his voice was emotional. "Papa, I love you and Mama... And even though I'm strict with Dashenka sometimes, I love her very much, too. She is kind. Dasha is good to everything around her. She wouldn't even hurt a little bug. Nor would they hurt her. She went up to a bee-hive one day, sat right down by the hive entrance and watched. She watched how they flew. The bees... A lot of bees crawled over her arms and legs and even over her cheeks, but they didn't sting her. She held out her hand to the bees buzzing around her — they landed on it and left something there. Afterward she licked the palm of her hand and laughed. She's kind, Papa."

"Calm yourself, Kostia. Don't worry. Let's calmly examine what's going on here. Yes, we have to think about it calmly... Dasha is still a child. She's blown up several state-of-the-art missile complexes. She could start a world war. A terrible war. But even without a war... Say she looked through some pictures showing not only enemy missiles, but our own... Say she started detonating all the missiles in all the countries that have them, the world would be on the verge of a global catastrophe! Hundreds of millions of human lives could be lost!

"I too love our little Dasha. But millions!... I need some advice. We must find a way out. But for now — I simply don't know... Dashenka needs to be isolated somehow. Somehow... Yeah... Maybe she needs to be put to sleep for a while. Maybe... But what's the solution? How can we possibly find a way out?"

"Papa, Papa... Hold on. Maybe... maybe it's possible to eliminate all the deadly missiles she doesn't like from the whole face of the Earth?"

"Eliminate? But... We'd need a multilateral agreement. From all the military blocs. Yeah... But there's no way we can get one quickly. If we can get one at all. In the meantime..."

Ivan Nikiforovich gave a sudden start and rushed over to his computer, where the monitor still showed the image of a missile, which Dasha was prevented from destroying. He switched off the monitor, then sat down at his communications computer and began to transmit the following text:

To: Headquarters.
The following memo should be transmitted at once to all military blocs and international news media. The series of missile complex explosions was caused by bacteria capable of connecting circuits. These bacteria are controllable. It will be necessary to destroy all images of any live ammunition. All images!!! From the most minute bullet to the most modern missile complex. The location of the explodable object is immaterial to the controller of the bacteria, who only needs to see its shape in an image.

Ivan Nikiforovich looked at Dasha, who by this time was smiling and having a lively conversation with her Mama. He then added the following text:

The locttation of the installation controlling the explosions is unknown.

Finally, Ivan Nikiforovich encoded the transmission and despatched it to headquarters.

The next morning there was an emergency meeting of Russia's Security Council. A security detachment was posted to stand guard around the community where Ivan Nikiforovich's domain was situated. The security personnel dressed as road-repair workers, so as not to draw attention to themselves. They pretended to be 'building' a five-kilometre-long road around the perimeter of the community (working on all five kilometres at once), maintaining round-the-clock shifts.

Video cameras were set up in Ivan Nikiforovich's domain which followed every move of little Dasha's life. The video images were transmitted to a central monitoring station resembling a launch-site mission control. The video monitors were manned in shifts by dozens of specialists — including psychologists and military personnel — ready to issue the required orders in case of an emergency situation. The psychologists used special communications devices to give a constant stream of recommendations to Dasha's parents on how to distract her, whatever way they could, and keep her from falling into a state of contemplation again.

The Russian government put out an international statement — which many people thought strange — to the effect that in Russia there were forces capable of blowing up any type of live ammunition, no matter where it was located in the world. These forces, it said, were not entirely under the control of the Russian government, although negotiations were underway.

The extraordinary nature of this statement called for some kind of confirmation to back it up. At an international council meeting it was decided to prepare a series of unusual-looking projectiles, mounted in square casings. Each country participating in the experiment took twenty such projectiles and hid them in various places on their respective territories.

"Why did they make the projectiles with square casings? Why couldn't they have just used ordinary ones?" I asked Anastasia.

"They were afraid, Vladimir, that not only all the existing projectiles in the world might explode, but that all the bullets in police and army pistols might get blown up as well, wherever there were guns with live ammunition."

"Yes, of course... And how did the square-projectile experiment go?"

Calling his daughter into his study, Ivan Nikiforovich showed her a photo of a square projectile and asked her to blow them up.

Dasha took a look at the photo and said:

"I love you very much, Papochka, but there is no way I can do what you ask."

"Why?" asked Ivan Nikiforovich in amazement.

"Because it won't work with me."

"What d'you mean, Dashenka? It worked before — you blew up a whole series of modern missiles, and now it won't work?"

"You know, back then I was really upset, Papochka. I didn't want you to go away, or to spend so many hours in front of your computer. When you're at your computer, you don't talk with anyone and you're not doing anything that's interesting. But *now*... well, you're with us all the time. You've become very good, Papochka, and I can't make any more explosions."

At this point Ivan Nikiforovich realised that Dasha was unable to blow up the square projectiles because she didn't understand the purpose of the explosion — what it was for. Ivan Nikiforovich started nervously pacing back and forth, feverishly searching for possible solutions and trying to convince Dasha to do something. But even as he was talking to his daughter, it seemed as though he were mainly reasoning it out for himself.

"It won't work... No, it won't... Pity. Wars have been around for thousands of years. While wars have ended between some countries, others have begun fighting. Millions of people have perished, and they are still perishing today. Tremendous resources are being wasted on armaments... And here finally is an opportunity to stop this endless disaster scenario, but alas..." Ivan Nikiforovich looked at Dasha sitting in the chair.

His daughter's face was composed. She watched with interest as he walked about the room, constantly talking. But she was not fascinated by what he was actually saying. She did not have a full comprehension of what wars meant, what resources her father was talking about and who was wasting them.

She was immersed in her own thoughts: *Why is Papa so agitated, walking back and forth amidst these computers which don't show any affection and don't give us any energy? Why doesn't he want to go out into the garden, where the trees are in bloom and the birds are singing, where every blade of grass and every branch of a tree caresses the whole body with something invisible? That's where Mama and Kostia are right now. I only wish Papa would finish his boring conversation and the two of us could go together to the garden. Mama and Kostia will be so happy to see us. Mama will smile, and Kostia promised yesterday he would tell me about how to touch a faraway star by putting your hand on a stone or a flower. Kostia always keeps his promises...*

"Dashenka, are you bored listening to me? You don't understand what I've been saying? You're thinking about something else?"

"I've been thinking, Papochka: why are we here, and not in the garden, where they're waiting for us?"

Ivan Nikiforovich realised that he had to speak to his daughter sincerely and in specific terms. So he took a different tack.

"Dashenka, when you blew up the missiles by looking at their image, they wanted you to test that ability once more. Or rather, to show the whole world Russia's ability to destroy all the ammunition on the planet. Then there won't be any point in making it any more. It would be senseless and dangerous. As for the ammunition already existing, the people themselves will destroy it. A global disarmament will begin. The square projectiles were made especially so that you could show your ability without killing anyone. Blow them up, Dashenka!"

"I can't do that any more, Papochka."

"Why? Earlier you could, now you can't?"

"I promised myself I would never blow up anything again. And now that I've made that promise, I don't have the ability to do it any more."

"You can't? But why did you make such a promise to yourself?"

"Kostia showed me some pictures from a book of his — pictures of parts of bodies strewn all over after an explosion. He showed me how people are frightened by explosions, how trees fall and die from explosions — and so I promised myself —"

"Dashenka, does that mean you'll never be able to now? Just once more... Just once. You see these square projectiles..."

Ivan Nikiforovich again held out the photo of a square projectile for his daughter to see.

"They were specially made for this experiment and are hidden away in secluded places in various countries. There are no people around, or anywhere near them. Everyone's waiting to see whether they'll explode or not. Blow them up, daughter dear! That won't be breaking your promise. Nobody will perish. On the contrary..."

Dasha again looked at the photo indifferently and calmly replied:

"Even if I go back on my promise, these projectiles still won't explode, Papochka."

"But why not?"

"Because you've been talking for so very long, Papochka. When I first looked at the photo, I couldn't stand these horrid things right off. They're ugly, and now —"

"Now what? Dashenka — what?"

"Please forgive me, Papochka, but you went on talking for so long after you showed me the picture, that by now they've been almost all eaten up."

"Eaten up? What's been eaten up?"

"Those square projectiles. They're almost all eaten up. As soon as they realised I couldn't stand the projectiles, they got into action and began to eat them up very fast."

"Who are *they*?"

"You know, the 'little ones'. They are everywhere around us and inside us. They are good. Kostia calls them bacteria, or micro-organisms, but I've got my own name for them, a better name — I call them my 'little ones', my 'goodies'. They like that name better. I play with them sometimes. People pay hardly any attention to them, but they always try to do good for everyone. When Man is joyful — they feel good too from the joyful energy; when Man is angry or hurts something living — a lot of them perish. Others rush in to replace them. But sometimes the others don't manage to replace the ones that have died — and Man's body becomes ill."

"But you are here, Dashenka. And the projectiles are far away in various countries, hidden underground. How is it possible for — well, for those 'little ones' of yours in other lands — to find out so quickly about what you desire?"

"You see, they tell everything to each other very fast along a chain, a lot faster than the electrons run in your computer."

"Computer... Communications... That's it... I'll check it all now — video cameras have been set up around all the projectiles on our territory. It'll just take a moment."

Ivan Nikiforovich turned to his communications monitor, which was showing a picture of a square projectile. Or rather, what remained of a projectile. The casing was rusty and full of holes, while the warhead was lying to one side, significantly reduced in size. Ivan Nikiforovich switched to another camera, and then another, but the same thing was happening to all the projectiles. Now the screen showed an image of a man in military uniform.

"Hello, Ivan Nikiforovich. You've seen it all yourself by now."

"What conclusions has the Council come to?" asked Ivan Nikiforovich.

"The Council members have divided into groups and are currently in consultation. Our security forces are trying to work out supplementary measures to ensure the object's safety."

"I'll thank you not to call my daughter an object."

"You're nervous, Ivan Nikiforovich. That is not permissible under the circumstances. In ten minutes you'll be getting a visit from a panel of experts, comprising prominent specialists — psychologists, biologists, radio-electronic engineers. They're already on their way. I want you to set up an interview for them with your daughter. Prepare her ahead of time."

"What opinion is the majority of the Council inclined to favour?"

"At the moment they are leaning toward totally isolating your family within the confines of your domain. You need to immediately remove all technical pictures from your daughter's sight. Stay close to her and try to follow her every move."

Upon arriving at Ivan Nikiforovich's domain, the panel of experts sent by the Russian Security Council engaged little Dasha in a lengthy conversation. After the child had been patiently answering all the adults' questions for about an hour and a half, everyone, including the observers following the interview on the huge video monitors at the Security Council's communications centre, were suddenly thrown into a state of utter bewilderment when the door of Ivan Nikiforovich's study opened and in walked Dasha's brother Kostia, carrying the cuckoo clock which was now cuckooing incessantly. Kostia put the clock down on the table. The hands showed eleven o'clock, but no sooner had the mechanical bird given the requisite number of cuckoos than the big hand on the clock quickly traced a full circle around the clock face and the cuckooing began all over again. Those present were amazed at this strange operation of the clock, alternating their silent gaze between the clock and Dasha.

"Oh!" all at once Dasha exclaimed. "I quite forgot. I have to go on a very important errand. That's my friend Verunka[4] turning the clock hands. That was our arrangement, just in case I forgot. I have to go."

Two guards blocked the door of the study.

"What might you have forgotten, Dashenka?" Ivan Nikiforovich asked his daughter.

"I might have forgotten to go to the domain where my friend Verunka lives and stroke her little flower and water it. And it really misses being caressed. It loves people to look at it tenderly."

"But it's not *your* flower," observed Ivan Nikiforovich. "Why can't your friend stroke it herself? Her own flower?"

"Papochka, you see, Verunka's gone visiting with her parents?"

"Where's she gone visiting to?"

"Somewhere in Siberia."

From all around the room whispered exclamations could be heard:

"She's not alone!"

"What kind of abilities does her friend have?!"

"She's not alone!"

"How many of them are there?!"

"How can we tell who they are?!"

"We need to take measures immediately regarding every child like that!"

But all the exclaiming ceased directly an elderly grey-haired gentleman rose from his seat at the side of the room.

[4]*Verunka* (pronounced: *ve-ROON-ka*) — diminutive of the name *Vera*.

This man had the most senior title and position of all, and not just in relation to those present in Ivan Nikiforovich's study. He was the chairman of Russia's Security Council. Everyone turned to him in reverent silence.

The elderly fellow looked at Dasha sitting in her little wooden chair, and a tear rolled down his cheek. Then he slowly went over to Dasha and knelt down on one knee in front of her, holding out his hand to her. Dasha rose and took a step to one side. Holding the frilled hem of her dress, she made a curtsy, and put her little hand in his huge palm.

The elderly man looked at her for some time. Then, bowing his head, he kissed Dasha's hand in respect, saying:

"Please forgive us, little goddess!"

"My name is Dasha," the girl answered.

"Yes, of course, your name is Dasha. Tell us, Dasha, what will prevail on our Earth?"

The little girl looked into the elderly man's face in surprise, bent closer to him and with the palm of her hand carefully wiped away the tear from his cheek, then touched his moustache with her finger. Then she turned to her brother and said:

"Kostienka, you also promised to help me talk with the lilies on Verunka's pond. Remember you promised?"

"I do remember," Kostia replied.

"Then let's go."

"Let's go."

In the doorway, having already passed by the guards which had stepped aside as she approached, Dasha turned in the direction of the elderly fellow still standing on one knee, smiled at him and stated confidently:

"On the Earth shall prevail... *Good shall prevail!*"

Six hours later, speaking before an expanded session of Russia's Security Council, the elderly chairman said:

"Everything in the world is relative. Relative to our generation, those in the new generation may seem to us to be like gods. It is not up to them to align themselves with us, but for us to align ourselves with them. The entire military might of the planet with its unique technological achievements has proved itself powerless before a single little girl of the new generation. And our job, our duty, our obligation to the new generation is simply to clear away the garbage. We must make every effort to rid the Earth of any kind of armaments. Our technological achievements and discoveries, embodied in the most modern and, it seemed to us, unique military complexes, proved nothing more than useless scrap in the face of the new generation. And we must clear it away."

Chapter Ten

The disarmament race

An international congress was held, with delegates from the security councils of the military blocs of various countries and continents, to work out a plan for the emergency conversion of military hardware and ammunition. Scientists from different parts of the world exchanged their expertise. Psychologists kept appearing in the media in an effort to head off panic among a population possessing a considerable variety of firearms. Panic had broken out after news of the Russian phenomenon had been leaked to the media, and the facts had become somewhat distorted.

A number of Western news sources were reporting that Russia had launched an emergency programme to convert all the ammunition on its territory, and at a designated hour would be blowing up the ammunition reserves held by other nations, destroying a large part of their population in the process. People began disposing of their firearms and ammunition in rivers, or burying them in wasteland sites, since the official conversion centres could not keep up with the demand.

Heavy fines were levied for unauthorised conversion. And even the fact that independent 'brokerage firms' started charging huge sums for each bullet or shell they accepted did not deter the flood of people wishing to escape from something that threatened the lives of whole families. People living in cities situated in the proximity of military bases demanded the authorities immediately get rid of all military facilities. But the arms industry, which had now been reoriented toward the conversion of the very products it had previously manufactured, was working to the limits of its capacity.

In many Western countries the press began circulating a flurry of rumours to the effect that Russia was threatening the world with disaster. The world was not in a position to free itself from its accumulation of armaments so quickly, and even though conversion plants were operating at full tilt, it was impossible for them to destroy in a few months a stock of arms that had been accumulating over decades.

Accusations were made that the Russian government had known for some time about the existence of children with unusual abilities, and that it had long been preparing for the conversion of deadly weapons. To back up this claim, it was noted that the Russian government had been buying up and dismantling ecologically unsound enterprises — not just on its own soil but in neighbouring countries as well. And that if Russia could become the first to rid its territory of explosive armaments, it would also be able to destroy nations that were lagging behind in the disarmament race.

All sorts of destructive scenarios of an impending world disaster and its consequences were deliberately exaggerated in the media. This was quite advantageous for companies involved in conversion, escalating the price of their services. Anyone handing in bullets from a handgun, for example, was obliged to pay twenty dollars for each bullet. Unauthorised burial or disposal of a weapon was treated as a criminal act. Another source of panic was the lack of proposals for any real defence against the abilities which had come to light in certain Russian children.

The Russian President then took what seemed to all to be a desperate and ill-conceived action: he decided to go live before the world's TV cameras in the company of children with extraordinary abilities. And on the appointed day and hour practically the whole planet gathered in front of their TV sets to hear what the Russian President had to say.

In advance of the broadcast many factories stopped, stores closed, streets emptied — all eyes were focused on Russia. The President wanted to calm people's fears and show the whole world that the newly-emerging generation of young Russians were not bloodthirsty monsters, but kind, ordinary children, whom there was no reason to fear.

To appear even more convincing, the President asked his advisers to invite thirty children with extraordinary abilities to the Kremlin, proposing to remain alone with these children in his office during the broadcast. All this was carried out as he requested.

"And what did the Russian President have to say to the world?" I asked Anastasia.

"If you like, you can watch this scene for yourself and listen to what he said, Vladimir."

"I'd like that very much."

"So take a look and see."

The Russian President stood on a small podium next to his desk. On either side of the podium sat children of varying ages, from about three to ten years old. On the opposite side of the room were arrayed a group of correspondents and a flock of TV cameras. The President began speaking.

"Ladies and gentlemen! My fellow-citizens! I have specially invited these children to meet you. As you can see, I am with them here alone, with no bodyguards or psychologists or parents. These children are not monsters, as some Western media are attempting to portray them. You can see for yourselves that these are just ordinary children. There are no signs of aggressiveness in their faces or actions. Some of their abilities we regard as unusual. But are they really? It is quite possible that the abilities which have begun to reveal themselves in the rising generation are entirely normal for the human individual. Our own creations, on the other hand, may turn out to be inimical to human existence. The human commonwealth has created a communications system and military potential capable of fomenting global disaster.

"Peaceful negotiations between states possessing the greatest military potential have gone on for centuries, yet the arms race has still not ceased. Today we have a real opportunity to do away with this endless destructive process. Today the countries in the most advantageous position are those that do not have a concentration of deadly weapons on their territories.

"We tend to think of such a situation as unnatural. But let us ponder the question of why, on the other hand, the production of life-destroying weapons which now threaten whole nations, has ever seemed natural to the human commonwealth, and why such a conviction is so deeply rooted in our consciousness.

"The children of the new generation have changed our priorities, causing us to take steps in the opposite direction — namely, *disarmament*. The fear and panic and feverish activity surrounding this process are largely due to a misrepresentation of the facts. The Russian government has been accused of knowing for a long time about the extraordinary abilities of children in our country. Such accusations are unfounded. Up until now a huge military potential has been present on Russian soil, and we, like many other countries, are doing the best we can to effect its conversion.

"The Russian government has been accused of not taking sufficient measures to identify all children with extraordinary abilities and to isolate them — in other words, to force them into a state of narcosis until the disarmament process is complete. But that is a step the Russian government is not about to undertake. The children of Russia are equal citizens of our country.

"And let us not overlook the question of why people might desire to isolate those who reject murderous weapons instead of those who manufacture them! The Russian government *is* taking measures to prevent spontaneous emotional outbursts in the children that might possibly transmit a signal and blow up any kind of armaments they didn't like.

"All Russian television channels have completely banned films showing murderous weapons. All toy guns have been destroyed. Parents are constantly minding their children in a bid to head off any negative reactions. Russia —"

The President broke off his speech abruptly. A tow-headed boy of about five rose from his seat and approached one of the videocamera tripods. At first he just examined the screws on the tripod, but when he touched them with his hand, the camera-operator stepped back in fright and hid behind the row of correspondents. The President rushed over to the boy, took him by the hand and led him to the chair where he had been meekly sitting before, admonishing him along the way:

"Would you please sit there quietly until I finish."

But he could not continue with his speech. Two boys, about three or four years of age, were now standing at the communications console, fiddling with the equipment. The children who had been sitting quietly right from the start of the President's speech were now wandering all over the office, each one looking into whatever they liked. Only the older children — and they were few in number — still sat quietly in their seats, their eyes focused on the correspondents and the TV cameras.

One of them was a little girl with ribbons in her braids. I realised right off who it was. It was Dasha, the one who had blown up the missile complexes. She was not behaving childishly, but attentively and intelligently sizing up the situation, observing the reaction of the correspondents.

People all over the world with their eyes glued to their TV sets caught a glimpse of the rather distraught face of the Russian President. He surveyed the children now dispersed around the room. Seeing two boys fiddling with the government communications console, he glanced over at the door, on the other side of which his assistants, along with the parents of the invited children, were waiting, but he did not call on anyone for help. Excusing himself for the interruption, he rushed over to the boys who were already in the process of pulling one of the telephones off the desk, seized them one under each arm and told them:

"Look, these are not toys!"

One of the boys looked over and saw his chum hanging from the President's other arm and burst out laughing. The second boy managed to reach out and give a tug on the President's necktie, uttering the word *Toys!*

"That's what you think, but they are not toys," the President responded.

"Toys!" the smiling lad cheerfully repeated.

The President noticed several other youngsters, evidently attracted by the sounds and the flashing coloured lights, approach the console and start fingering the telephone receivers. After setting the two fidgeters down on the floor, he rushed over to the console, pressed one of the buttons and said:

"Cut all communications to my office immediately."

Next he quickly laid out on his desk a number of blank sheets of paper. On each one he put a pencil or pen, turned to the children clustering around the desk and said:

"Here you are. You can draw whatever you like. Start drawing, and later we'll decide all together who's come up with the best picture."

All the children gathered around the desk and began taking paper and pen or pencil in hand. To those who were not tall enough to reach the desk, the President offered chairs, either seating or standing the littlest ones on the chairs.

Satisfied that he had succeeded in occupying the children's attention with drawing, the President once more went over to the podium, smiled to the television viewers, took a deep breath, and was about to go on with his speech. But to no avail. A little boy came up to him and began tugging on his trousers.

"What is it? What do you want?"

"Pee..." said the boy.

"What?"

"Pee..."

"Pee, pee? You mean you want to go to the bathroom?" And once more the President's gaze turned toward the door leading out of his office.

The door opened, and immediately two of his assistants or bodyguards rushed toward him. One of the men, who had a sombre and rather tense expression on his face, bent down and took the little boy's hand. But the boy, still clinging to the President's trouser leg, wriggled free, shaking his hand loose from the grip of the sombre-looking man attempting to take him out of the office. He held up his hand to the other men approaching — a gesture of protest which caught them completely off guard. Once more the boy raised his head, looking up to the President from below. Tugging on his trouser-leg, he repeated the word *pee* and began to crouch down just a little.

"This isn't the right time for your 'pee'," said the President. "Not only that, but you're being pernickety too."

At that point the President picked up the boy in his arms, excused himself to the media representatives and headed out of the office, saying in passing: "We'll be right back."

In hundreds of millions of homes people watched as the TV cameras switched back and forth between the children playing, drawing and chatting with each other — and, more often than not, the now-deserted presidential podium.

And then little Dasha rose from her seat. Dragging a chair over to the podium, she climbed up on it, looked at the correspondents and then directly into the lenses of the TV cameras focused on her. She straightened the ribbons in her braids and began to speak.

"My name is Dasha. And our Uncle President — he's a good chap. He'll be back in a moment. He'll come back and tell you everything. He's just a little anxious right now. But he'll be able to tell everyone how life is going to be good everywhere you look on the Earth. And that nobody need be afraid of us. My brother Kostia told me how people are afraid of us children because I blew up some big new missiles. But it wasn't that I wanted to blow them up. I just wanted my Papa not to go away for such a long time and for him not to think so much about these missiles. Or look at them so much. He should look at Mama instead. She's much better than any missile. And she likes it when Papa looks at her and talks with her. But when he goes away for a long time or looks at the missiles, Mama's sad. And I don't want Mama to be sad.

"Kostia, my brother, is very clever and intelligent, and Kostienka told me that I've frightened a lot of people. I shan't blow up anything else. It's quite boring, really. There are other things to do that are much more important and interesting. They bring joy to everyone.

"You take care of dismantling the missiles yourselves. See to it that nobody ever blows them up. And please don't be afraid of us.

"Do come visit us. All of you. We'll give you living water to drink. My Mama told me how people here used to live. They kept so very busy building all kinds of plants and factories and got so carried away that before they knew it there was no more living water. The water had become dirty. And water was something you could only buy in bottles in stores. But the water in the bottles was dead, suffocated, and people began to get sick. That was how it used to be, but there's no way I can imagine how people could possibly dirty the water that they themselves drank. But Papa said that even now on the Earth there are whole countries where there is no clean living water, and that people in these countries are dying from painful diseases. And there are no tasty apples or berries in these countries — everything living is sick, and the people eat sick things and feel wretched.

"Do come visit us, all of you come. And we'll treat you to healthy apples and tomatoes and pears and berries. When you've tried them and go back home, you'll say to yourselves: 'Don't do dirty things, it's better to live clean!' Then later when everything's clean in your country, we'll come visit you and bring you presents."

The President, who by this time had come back, still holding the little boy in his arms, stood in the doorway and listened to Dasha's speech. When she finished, he walked over to the podium. With the little one still comfortably nestled in his arms, he echoed Dasha's words:

"Yes, of course... Do come, really, we have treatments for the body here. But that's not the main thing. We all need to gain a better understanding of ourselves and our purpose. We really have to understand that. Otherwise we'll be swept off the face of the Earth like garbage. We've got to get together and clear away all this dirt we ourselves have brought forth.

"Thank you all for your attention."

The scene in the President's office faded. And Anastasia's voice continued:

"It is difficult to say whether it was the President's or Dasha's speech that had the greater effect on the viewers watching this live broadcast from Russia. But people were no longer inclined to believe the rumours that had been spread about Russia's aggressiveness. People wanted to live, and live a happy life — they believed that a happy life was possible. After the live broadcast from the Kremlin the numbers of people wanting to visit Russia or even live there increased dramatically. And upon coming back home from Russia these visitors could no longer live the way they did before. A new conscious awareness was sparked in each individual, like the first ray of the Sun at the dawn of a new day."

Chapter Eleven

Science and pseudo-science

"Anastasia, how have Russians managed to cope with such a huge influx of visitors? It must have been quite a challenge for them. I can just imagine living with your family in your kin's domain with a whole bunch of gawkers staring at you from the other side of the fence."

"The tourists and foreigners coming to Russia for treatment, Vladimir, have been housed in the cities, in the flats vacated by Russians. They get produce from the domains delivered to them, but tourists are not allowed to go to the domains themselves. Only a few have managed to visit the places where the New Russians reside. Psychologists are constantly reminding the owners of the domains that whatever hospitality they show to visitors — especially visitors from what used to be considered highly developed countries — can lead to a nervous breakdown. The psychologists are correct. About forty percent of foreigners who did visit the domains returned home only to fall into a state of depression bordering on suicide."

"How so? Why? You yourself said, Anastasia, that everything in the domains is perfect — the surrounding countryside, the food, the way family members help each other."

"That is true, but for many foreign visitors what they saw turned out to be *too* perfect. Imagine if you can, Vladimir, an elderly person who has lived most of their life in a large city. Someone who has tried as hard as they could to earn as much as they could — just to be, so they thought, no worse off than others. In return for this money they received a roof over their heads, clothing to wear, a car to drive and food to eat. And here is this person sitting in their furnished flat with a car in the garage and food in the fridge."

"Well, I am imagining it, and so far everything seems normal. What next?"

"'What next?', Vladimir, is a question you should be able to answer yourself."

"Next... Well, maybe this person will take a trip somewhere, maybe they'll buy some new furniture or a new car."

"And then?"

"And then? I haven't the foggiest!"

"And then this person dies. He dies forever, or at least for millions of Earth years. His second self, his Soul, cannot regain the earthly plane of being. It cannot because over the course of his earthly existence he created nothing good for the Earth. Each of us realises this intuitively, and that is why people are so terrified of death. When a majority of people have the same aspirations and a similar way of life, they have the impression that they can and should live only the way everybody else does.

"But here Man has seen a totally different way of life on the Earth. He has seen in fact an earthly Paradise — the Space of Love — which can be created by Man's own hand in the Divine image, and this makes him look upon his own life as already gone by and spent in hell, and this Man dies in torment, and his sufferings last millions of years."

"But why doesn't everybody fall into this state of depression after seeing the Russians' new way of life?"

"There are some who realise intuitively that even in their advanced years, if they put their weakening hand to creating a Space of Love on the Earth, the Creator will prolong their life. And after straightening up and with a smile brightening their face, they go and give a hand to younger people."

"Still, Anastasia, it doesn't seem right that people who come to Russia from so far away aren't able to at least spend a little time walking down the streets of the new Russian communities and breathing the clean air."

"Even the tourists who stay in the cities have the opportunity to feel the fresh breath of the Earth and drink health-giving water. The cities are caressed by breezes which infuse them with cleanliness, ethers and pollen from the luxuriant greenery of the domains. And when they go on out-of-town excursions, tourists can observe these oases of Paradise — only from a respectful distance so as not to disturb the families living there. Take a look and see how it all happens."

And once again I glimpsed another scene from the future. I saw the highway which runs between the city of Vladimir and another town named Suzdal[1] thirty kilometres away — a highway I had travelled a number of times before. Earlier I had only caught the rare glimpse of tourist motorcoaches taking visitors to see Suzdal's ancient cathedrals and monasteries. Most of the cars on the road had borne local licence plates. But now the highway was quite different. Beautiful motorcoaches rolled along a roadway that was twice the width of the old one. Electric vehicles, no doubt — I couldn't detect any exhaust gases or motor noise, only the quiet hum of the tyres. The coaches were filled with tourists of various nationalities. Many were observing their surroundings through field glasses.

About a kilometre from the main road, beyond a motley host of treetops, I could make out the roofs of detached houses. That was where the Russians' family domains were situated, each surrounded by an evenly planted hedge, or 'living fence'. On either side of the road, approximately two kilometres apart, were located nice-looking two-storey buildings

[1]*Vladimir, Suzdal* — see footnote 1 in Chapter 6: "A garden for eternity".

housing shops and dining salons.[2] Each of these was fronted
by a small asphalt lot where an electric vehicle could park if
there was a space free. The electric motorcoaches spewed
forth a stream of tourists, who were impatient to taste the local delicacies on the spot or to buy some to take home.

All the shops and cafés sold food products grown in the
domains. They also had hand-made Russian shirts, towels,
woodcarvings and many other things made by skilled craft-
speople. Anastasia explained that visitors were eager to buy
these handicrafts because they knew that a shirt embroidered
by the kind hands of a happy woman is immensely more valuable than something off a mechanised conveyor belt.

If you looked down from above at what was behind the
strip of forest visible from the highway, you would be able to
glimpse shady allées and domains outlined by living fences.
The strip of forest surrounded a community containing about
ninety family estates. About a kilometre distant, across open
fields, was another community surrounded by a strip of forest, and so on for the next thirty kilometres or so.

Even though they were the same size, the domain plots
were far from uniform in appearance. Some were dominated
by orchard trees, others featured wild-growing trees — slender pines, loosely spreading cedars, oaks and birches.

Each domain invariably had a pond or a swimming pool.
The houses, surrounded by flower beds, were also quite different from one another — some were large two-storey detached houses, others were smaller bungalows. They had
been built in various styles — both flat and sloping roofs were
to be seen. Some of the little houses were all white, resembling the huts found in Ukrainian villages.

---

[2]*dining salons* — the Russian word here is *trapeznye* (pronounced: *TRAH-pez-
nih-yeh*), originally designating refectories in monasteries, but more recently
used in reference to ornately decorated halls (often with arched ceilings)
where large groups of people can gather to enjoy traditional Russian meals.

Science

I saw no motorcars on the lanes running between the domains. Nor, for that matter, could I detect any special activity or work being done in the domains themselves. I had the impression that all this extraordinary beauty was the creation of Someone on high, and that all people needed to do was to delight in His creation.

In the middle of each community there were beautiful large two-storey structures. Around them scurried a host of active children at play. That meant that schools or clubs had been built in the centre of the settlements.

"You see there, Anastasia, in the centre of the community, where there's a school or a club, there's some kind of visible life, but in the domains themselves it looks pretty much like Dullsville. If their owners have managed to arrange the plantings so that there is no need to fertilise or to battle with pests and weeds, what is there left for them to do? In any case, I think that Man actually finds greater joy in intensive labour, creativity and inventiveness, but there's none of that here."

"Vladimir, right here in these splendid domains people are involved with the very things you mention, and their deeds are meaningful. It demands a significantly higher level of intelligence, mindfulness and inspiration than the work of artists and inventors in the world you are accustomed to."

"But if they are all artists and inventors, then where are the results of their work?"

"Vladimir, do you consider an artist someone who takes brush in hand and paints a beautiful landscape on a sheet of canvas?"

"Of course I do. People will look at his picture and, if they like it, they will either buy it or put it on display in an art gallery."

"Then why would you not consider as an artist someone who has taken, instead of a canvas, a hectare of land, and used it to create an equally beautiful or even a more beautiful landscape? After all, in order to create a beautiful landscape out of living materials, the creator needs more than artistic imagination and taste — he also needs a knowledge of the properties of a great many living materials. In both instances it is the task of what has been created to call forth positive emotions in the viewer, and to delight the eye.

"But in contrast to a picture painted on canvas, a living picture has a variety of functions besides. It cleanses the air, it produces beneficial ethers for Man and feeds his body. A living picture changes the nuances of its colours, and it can be constantly perfected. It is connected to the Universe by invisible threads. It is incomparably more meaningful than something painted on canvas, and so the artist who creates it will be that much the greater."

"Yes, of course, I really can't disagree with that. But tell me, why do you consider the owners of these domains to be inventors and scientists to boot? Do they have any relation to science at all?"

"They have a relation to science too."

"What kind of relation, for example?"

"For example, do you, Vladimir, not consider as a scientist someone who is involved in plant selection and genetic engineering?"

"Of course. Everybody thinks of them as scientists, they work in scientific research institutes. They come up with new varieties of fruits and vegetables, and other plants as well."

"Yes, of course, they come up with these, but what is important is the *result* of their work, its significance for humanity."

"Well, the result is that varieties of vegetables and potatoes are brought forth that are frost-resistant and that will not be eaten by the Colorado beetle. In highly developed countries they have managed to grow a living being from a simple cell. Now they are working on cultivating various organs for transplanting into patients — kidneys, for example."

"Yes, that is true. But have you not wondered, Vladimir, why in these highly developed countries there are also appearing more and more types of diseases? Why is it that these same countries have the highest cancer rates of all? Why do they need an increasing number of drugs for treatment? Why do an ever-increasing number of people suffer from infertility?"

"Well, why?"

"Because many of those you call scientists are not rational beings at all. Their human essence is paralysed, and the forces of destruction work through their merely external human form.

"Think about it, Vladimir: these so-called scientists have begun to fundamentally change the plants existing in Nature, thereby also changing the fruits they bring forth. They have begun changing them without first determining what purpose these fruits have. After all, in Nature, as in the Universe, everything is so closely interconnected.

"Let us take your car, for example. Suppose a mechanic were to remove or alter some part — a filter, let us say — the car might go for a while, but what would soon happen?"

"The fuel-feed system would go out of whack, and the motor would choke."

"In other words, every part of a motorcar has its function, and before touching a part, it is necessary to determine its function."

"Of course! You don't have to be a mechanic to see that."

"But Nature, after all, is also a perfect mechanism, and nobody has yet fully fathomed it. Every part of this great living mechanism has its purpose and is closely interconnected with the whole structure of the Universe. A change in properties or the removal of a single part inevitably affects the work of the whole mechanism of Nature.

"Nature has many protective devices. First, it will signal an impermissible action. If that does not work, Nature will be obliged to destroy the 'mechanic' who fails in his calling. Man uses the fruits of Nature for food, and if he begins to feed himself with mutant fruits, he will be gradually transformed into a mutant himself. Such an adulteration is inevitable, given the consumption of adulterated produce.

"This is already coming about. Man is already experiencing a weakening of his immune system, his mind and feelings. He is beginning to lose the abilities unique to him alone, and is being transformed into an easily manipulable bio-robot. He is losing his independence. The appearance of new diseases only confirms this — it is a sign that Man has tried undertaking an impermissible action."

"Well, let's say you're right, Anastasia. I myself don't think much of these hybrid plants. There was a lot of hoopla about them at first, but now quite a few national governments, including our own, have started mandating special labelling of genetically modified produce sold in stores. And many people try to avoid buying these mutant products. But they say there's no way to avoid them altogether, at least for the time being — there's too many of them. There's not enough real produce, and it's so much more expensive."

"There, you see, that is because the forces of destruction have managed to lure humanity into a state of economic dependency. They have managed to convince Man that if he does not consume their products, he will die of starvation. But that is not true, Vladimir. Just the opposite: Man will die if he does eat them."

"Maybe, Anastasia, but not everyone will die. Many already know about this and won't eat mutant products."

"How do you, for example, Vladimir, manage to tell the difference?"

"I don't eat imported vegetables, for one thing. What local residents sell at the markets from their own household plots is a lot tastier."

"And where do they get their seeds?"

"What d'you mean, where do they get them? They buy them. There's a lot of firms dealing in seeds now. They sell them in pretty coloured packaging."

"So, does that mean that people buy seeds according to the information on the package, without knowing for absolute certain how accurate that information is?"

"You mean to say that even the seeds they buy may be mutant?"

"Yes. For example, on the Earth today there are only nine apple trees left bringing forth original fruit. The apple is one of the most healthful and delicious of all God's creations for Man. But it was one of the first to be subjected to genetic manipulation. Even the Old Testament warns us against grafting. But people went ahead stubbornly and did it, and as a result the apples disappeared. What you now find in orchards or grocery stores does not correspond to the Divine fruit. Those that violate and destroy the original purity of God's creation you call scientists. But what can we call those who are *restoring* the functioning of all the parts of Nature's mechanism?"

"They're scientists too, but more literate, no doubt, more knowledgeable."

"The Russian families living in the domains which you see here are the same ones who are restoring that which was ruined before."

"And where did they acquire greater knowledge than the geneticists and the biologists involved in genetic selection?"

"This knowledge has existed in every Man right from the beginning. The goal, thought and conscious awareness of their purpose afford each of these the opportunity to reveal itself."

"Wow! So it turns out that the people living in the domains are both artists and scientists. Who then are *we* — I mean, the people living on the planet today?"

"Everyone can supply their own definition if they manage to free their thought for at least nine days."

CHAPTER TWELVE

Do we have freedom of thought?

"What do you mean — *to free their thought?* Everybody has freedom of thought."

"In the context of your technocratic society, Vladimir, Man's thought is enslaved by the limits and conventions of this world. In fact, the technocratic world can only exist when the freedom of Man's thought is nullified and the energy of his thought is absorbed by it."

"Something's not clear to me here. Every Man over his lifetime can do a lot of thinking about a lot of different things. There are limits on freedom of speech, for example. There are countries in which there is greater freedom of expression, in other countries less, but everyone is free to *think* whatever they wish."

"That is an illusion, Vladimir. The majority of people are compelled to think about one and the same thing their whole lives. This is easier to see if you take the topics a typical Man of your world thinks about and analyse them in terms of distinct time segments, adding up the time he spends thinking about each particular subject. By this simple method you can determine the prevailing thought in contemporary human society."

"Interesting. Let's try determining this prevailing thought together, you and I."

"Very well. Then tell me, what would you consider Man's average life expectancy today?"

"Is that important?"

"Not all that important, given the uniformity of Man's

thinking, but we need some sort of figure for our subsequent calculations."

"Okay. In our time let's say a Man lives eighty years."

"So, a Man is born. Or, to put it more accurately, he has attained the material plane of his being."

"Let's just say he is born — it's easier to understand."

"All right. Even as an infant he is looking at the world, which is waiting for him to get to know it. Clothing, housing and food are provided for him by his parents. But the parents also attempt, either consciously or subconsciously, through their behaviour, to impart to him their thoughts and the way they see the world around them. The visible process of getting to know what life is all about lasts approximately eighteen years, and over the whole course of these years the technocratic world attempts to impress the young Man's thought with its own importance. Then, over the remaining sixty-two years of his life, let us assume that Man himself can control the tendencies of his own thought."

"Indeed he can. But you were saying there's something trying to enslave his thought."

"Yes, I did say that. So let us try and calculate how much time he is free to think for himself."

"Okay, let's."

"For a certain number of hours each day Man sleeps or rests. How many hours a day does he spend on sleep?"

"Eight, as a rule."

"We took 62 years of Man's life as a basis. If you multiply that by eight hours per day, taking leap years into account, you find that Man sleeps for 587,928 hours of his life. Thus, sleeping 8 hours a day equates to 22 years of constant sleep. Now we subtract these 22 years from the 62 years of his life and we have 40 years when he is awake.

"Now, at some point during their waking hours most people are involved with the preparation of food. How much time do you think Man spends on cooking and eating food?"

"It happens that women generally do the cooking, while men are obliged to spend more time earning the money to pay for groceries."

"And how many hours would you say, Vladimir, go into the preparation and consumption of food every day?"

"Well, if you take into account the time spent on buying groceries, preparing breakfast, lunch and dinner, that's probably about three hours — on a weekday, that is. Only not everyone in the family is involved in the cooking. The rest of us... well, we eat, and maybe help do the grocery shopping, or wash the dishes, so that I'd say about two and a half hours, on average."

"In fact it is more, but let us take your figure, two-and-a-half hours per day. Multiply that by the number of days a Man lives and it comes to 61,242.5 hours, or 25,517 days, or 7 years. Subtract this number from the 40 and there are 33 left.

"Now, in order to be able to obtain food, clothing and housing, a Man dwelling in the technocratic world is obliged to perform one of the functions essential to this world — namely, *work*. And I should like to draw your attention, Vladimir, to this fact: Man is obliged to work or engage in some business not because he really likes it but for the sake of the technocratic world itself, otherwise Man will be deprived of what is vitally important to him. How much time do most people spend each day on work?"

"In our country it's eight hours, with another two hours or so spent getting to and from work, but every week they get a couple of days off."

"So now try to calculate how many equivalent years of his life does a Man spend on work which is rarely satisfying?"

"It would take me quite a while to figure out without a calculator — you tell me."

"All told, for the thirty years of so-called work activity he spends ten years constantly working for someone — or, rather, for the technocratic world. And now from those 33 years of life we have to subtract another 10, leaving us 23.

"Now, what else does a Man do every day over the course of his life?"

"He watches TV."

"For how many hours a day?"

"No less than three."

"These three hours amount to 8 years of constant sitting in front of a television screen. If we take them away from the 23 remaining, we are left with 15. But even this time is not free for activities native to Man alone. Man's thought is subject to inertia. It cannot make a sudden switch from one thing to another. Some time is spent processing and making sense of information received. All told, the average Man spends only 15 to 20 minutes of his life reflecting on the mystery of creation. Some do not think about it at all, while others spend years contemplating it. Anyone can figure it out if he looks back over the years of his life. Each individual is unique — he is more important than all the galaxies taken together, for he is capable of creating them. But each Man is a particle of the human commonwealth, which may be regarded in its entirety as a single organism, a single essence. And once humanity has fallen into the trap of technocratic dependence, this great essence of the Universe becomes closed within itself, it loses genuine freedom and becomes dependent, at the same time activating the mechanism of self-destruction.

"Another way of life, quite distinct from your world's everyday norm, is lived by people in the communities of the future. Their thought is both free and humane — it has merged into a single aspiration, and is leading humanity out of its dead end. The galaxies quiver in joyful anticipation when they see the human dream merging into a single whole. Creation will soon witness a new birth and a new co-creation. Their human thought will materialise a beautiful new planet."

"Wow! How grandiloquently you describe these community dwellers! But outwardly they're just ordinary people."

"Even their outward appearance is distinctive. It is imbued with the radiance of great energy. Look more closely — here come a grandmother and her grandson riding along..."

CHAPTER THIRTEEN

Equestrienne from the future

I saw a wagon emerging from the settlement, or rather a carriage with a folding top, drawn by a sorrel mare. On the carriage's plush seat sat an elderly woman, with baskets of apples and vegetables at her feet. Up in front a shirtless boy about seven years old held the reins, but did not appear to be controlling the horse. No doubt they had been along this route many times before and the horse was simply trotting leisurely along a familiar route.

The boy turned to the elderly woman and said something to her. His grandmother smiled and began to sing. The boy started singing along with her, picking up on the refrain. As for the tourists in their electric motorcoach passing by on the parallel highway about a kilometre distant, there was no way they could catch the sound of their song.

Practically the whole coach had their field glasses trained on the carriage and its passengers. They watched the spectacle unfold with bated breath, as though they had seen a miracle or an interplanetary alien, and again the thought came to me that there was something not quite right here: people had come from such a long ways away and couldn't even carry on a normal conversation with the local residents, but were limited to observing them from a distance. And the two occupants of the carriage weren't even looking their way.

One of the tourist coaches slowed down to keep pace with the horse's trot. The coach was filled with children visiting from abroad, excitedly waving their hands at the little boy and his grandmother riding in the handsome carriage, but not once was there even a glance in return.

All at once a young equestrienne emerged from one of the gates of the settlement, which were beautifully enwreathed with living vegetation. Her chestnut-coloured racehorse maintained a heated gallop in a bid to catch up to the carriage, and was soon prancing daintily alongside. The elderly woman smiled, listening as the young equestrienne spoke to her.

Even though the boy may not have been too happy at having their duet interrupted, his voice could not help but betray an inner joy as he said:

"Oh, Mamochka, you're a regular jumping jack! You can't stay still for a moment!"

The young woman laughed, reached into her canvas saddle bag and took out a *pirozhok,*[1] handing it to the little boy. He took a bite of it and then offered it to the elderly woman, saying:

"Here you are, Granny, try it — it's still warm!"

The boy gave a tug on the reins and stopped the carriage. He leant down and with both hands picked up a basket of yummy-looking apples. He held it out to the woman rider with the words: "Please, Mama, take these to *them,*" nodding in the direction of the touring coach with the visiting children on board.

Grasping the heavy basket of apples easily with one hand, with the other hand she gave her prancing steed a pat on its neck, and galloped off toward the children's motorcoach. Several other tourist coaches in the meantime had pulled up beside it, all eyes fixed on the young woman rider galloping toward them over the fields clutching the basket of apples with one hand.

---

[1] *pirozhok* (plural: *pirozhki*) — a small Russian pastry with a filling, akin to a Ukrainian pierogie. See footnote 2 in Book 2, Chapter 11: "A sharp about-turn".

Dashing up to the children who had now spewed forth out of the coach, she reined in her steed, and without leaving the saddle, deftly bent down and placed the apple basket on the ground in front of the excited children.

After managing to give a dark-haired little boy a pat on the head, she waved a greeting to all and headed off on her steed right down the middle of the dual motorway. The driver of the children's coach was talking on his two-way radio:

"She's galloping right down the median strip! She's marvellous!"

Many of the touring coaches along the motorway pulled over to the side and stopped. People quickly got out and spread themselves along the roadside, watching the beautiful young equestrienne galloping along at full speed. No shouts, but rather whispers of excitement emanated from many people's lips. And here was really something to be excited about. Sparks flying from his hooves, the steed flew along unhindered in his heated gallop. His rider carried no whip in her hand, or even a switch, yet the steed kept quickening his step, his hooves barely touching the asphalt, his mane streaming from the brisk headwind. No doubt he was extremely proud of his rider and wanted to prove worthy of this beautiful woman on his back.

Indeed, she was exceptionally beautiful in appearance. Of course one could get excited about her perfect facial contours, her light-brown braid and thick eyelashes. Of course, beneath her white hand-embroidered blouse and flowered skirt with white camomiles one could easily picture a shapely supple waist on this girl with such a magnificent figure, whose smooth, feminine lines seemed to frame some sort of irrepressible energy. The blush playing on her cheeks gave but a glimpse of the majesty and boundless possibilities of this unfathomable energy. The young equestrienne's unusually healthy-looking appearance (she looked like a girl in her late teens!) quite distinguished her from that of the people standing by the side of the road. She sat upright on her frisky steed with not a trace of tension in her body. She wasn't holding on to the pommel of her saddle, or even the reins. And her legs were thrown over one side of the horse's rump without a stirrup on either foot.

As she rode along with her eyelids lowered, she gracefully wove her wind-tossed hair into a tight braid. And she had only to raise her eyelids to inflame one of the crowd of people with some kind of invisible but captivating fire. Whoever caught her gaze felt himself straighten up inside and stand tall.

It seemed that these people could feel the light and energy emanating from the equestrienne and were trying to let it at least partially fill their being. She understood their desire, and generously shared what she had, galloping on and just being beautiful.

All of a sudden an excited Italian man ran out across the motorway right in front of the oncoming steed. He waved his arms wildly to each side, crying out in excitement: *Rossiya! I love you, Rossiya!*[2] The young rider was completely unmoved by her steed rearing up on its hind legs and prancing on the spot. With one hand simply holding on to the pommel of her saddle, she used the other to pluck a flower of the garland adorning her hair and toss it down to the Italian. Catching his gift, he pressed it tenderly to his chest like a valuable treasure, constantly repeating: *Mamma mia! Mamma mia!*

But the beautiful equestrienne was no longer paying attention to the impetuous Italian. She had only to touch the reins and the horse broke into a lightly prancing walk, and headed over to the people standing on the roadside. As the crowd parted, the young equestrienne gave a sprightly leap down from her steed, coming face to face with a woman of European appearance who was holding a baby girl fast asleep in her arms.

[2] *Rossiya* (pronounced: *ros-SEE-ya*) — the Russian name for *Russia,* which is similar in a number of European languages.

The mother was slouching a little, her face was pale and eyes fatigued, and she seemed to have a hard time holding her baby still without waking her. The equestrienne gave the woman a big smile, and the two mothers' glances met.

It was not difficult to notice the difference in the two women's mental states. The mother with the baby had a depressed look, which gave her the appearance of a fading flower in comparison with the young woman who had just approached her — a woman whose countenance suggested an irrepressible explosion of blossoms from thousands of gardens.

The two women looked each other in the eye without a word between them. And then all at once, as though startled by a new conscious awareness of something, the woman holding the sleeping baby straightened up, and her face broke into a broad smile. With a graceful, very feminine movement of her hands, the Russian woman took the beautiful garland from her own head and placed it on the head of the mother holding the baby, though they still didn't say a single word to each other.

Once more the beautiful equestrienne deftly mounted her steed which had been standing meekly at her side, and headed off. For some reason the people all gave her a round of applause. The now-smiling slender woman, whose baby daughter had by this time awakened with a smile of her own on her little face, kept watching as the figure of her new-found friend receded into the distance. As for the impetuous Italian, he was running after her holding an expensive watch he had taken off his wrist, calling out to her: *A souvenir, mamma mia!* But by this time the beautiful rider was already far away.

The adventuresome racehorse turned off the highway in front of a patio decked out with long tables, where another group of tourists was sitting, drinking *kvass*[3] and berry drinks. They were

---

[3]*kvass* — a fermented beverage made from rye, barley or other natural products.

also sampling other delicacies waiters kept bringing to them out of a building replete with beautiful Russian carvings.[4]

Another building was in the finishing stages of construction next door. Two people were attaching to one of the windows of the new building — probably a shop or dining salon — a beautiful carved wooden *nalichnik*. Upon hearing the hoofbeats, one of the men turned in the direction of the approaching rider, said something to his fellow-worker and jumped down from the scaffolding. Reining in her horse, the impetuous equestrienne sprang down to the ground and, quickly unfastening her canvas bag from the saddle, ran over to the man and gently handed it to him.

"*Pirozhki...* With apple filling, just the way you like them. They're still warm."

"You're my little jumping jack, Ekaterinka,"[5] the man said tenderly. Whereupon he reached into the bag, took out a *pirozhok* and bit into it. His face writhed with pleasure.

The tourists sitting at the tables stopped their eating and drinking, admiring the young lovers. There stood the pair face to face — the man working on the building and the beautiful young equestrienne just dismounted from her fiery steed — as though they were not already married with children, but a courting couple fervently in love. And here was this beautiful woman, who had just ridden fifteen kilometres, who seemed so invincible and as free as the wind under the excited gaze of the tourists, calmly standing in front of her beloved, first

---

[4]*Russian carvings* — these might include sacred solar symbols, such as a horse at the front of the roof finial, believed to protect the house and its occupants from evil. Such carvings are found on many a Russian *terem* (mansion) or *izba* (hut). Some of these carvings are featured on a decorated board known as a *nalichnik* (see footnote 3 in Book 3, Chapter 10: "Work out your own happiness").

[5]*Ekaterinka* — like *Ekaterinushka,* a diminutive of the Russian name *Ekaterina* (pron. *ye-ka-te-REE-na*) equivalent to *Catherine* in English.

looking him in the eye, then lowering her eyelids in embarrassment. All at once the man stopped eating and said:
    "Ekaterinushka, look, a wet spot has broken out on your
blouse — that means it's time to feed Vanechka."[6]
    She covered the little wet spot on her milk-filled breast with
the palm of her hand and answered, somewhat embarrassed:
"I'll manage it. He's still sleeping. I'll take care of everything."
    "Better hurry. I'll be home soon, too. We're just finishing
up here. D'you like what we've done?"
    She took a look at the windows framed by the decorative
carved *nalichniks*.
    "Yes. Very much. But there's something else I wanted to tell you."
    "Go on."
    She came up close to her husband and stood on tiptoe
as if to whisper something in his ear. He leaned over to listen, but she just gave him a quick kiss on his cheek. Then,
without even turning around, she sprang into the saddle of
her steed standing alongside her, her happy trilling laughter
mingling with the hoofbeats. Then it was off to home she galloped — this time not along the asphalt motorway, but across
the grasses of the open fields. As before, the tourists could
not take their eyes off her so long as she remained in sight.
    What was so special about this young woman — a mother
with two young children — riding across the open fields on
her adventuresome steed? Yes, she was beautiful. Yes, one
could feel her overflowing energy. Yes, she was kind. But why
couldn't anyone take their eyes off her as she rode away?
    Perhaps it was more than just a woman riding a horse across a
field. Perhaps it was Happiness incarnate hurrying home to feed
an infant and later welcome her beloved husband? And people
couldn't help but admire Happiness hurrying back to her home.

---

[6] *Vanechka* — a diminutive of the Russian name *Ivan* (corresponding to the English name *John*).

CHAPTER FOURTEEN

City on the Neva

"And have such changes been taking place in St. Petersburg too, as well as in Moscow?" I asked Anastasia.

"Events happened somewhat differently in the city on the Neva,"[1] she replied. "There it was the children who, even before the adults, felt the need of doing something themselves about creating a different kind of future. The children took it upon themselves to start changing the city, without waiting for a decree from the authorities."

"Wow! Children again! And how did it all start?"

At the corner where the Nevsky Prospekt[2] crosses the Fontanka[3] embankment some workers had dug a trench. An eleven-year-old boy accidentally fell into it and injured his

---

[1] *Neva* (pron. *ni-VAH*) — the river that flows through the city of *St. Petersburg* into the Gulf of Bosnia and the Baltic Sea. The city was founded on the swampy delta of the Neva River by Emperor Peter the Great in 1703 as Russia's new capital and 'window on the West'. Partial to Western (especially Germanic) cultures, he gave the city a German-style name after his own patron saint. In 1914, at the onset of the First World War, the name was russified to *Petrograd*. The Bolsheviks who came to power with the 1917 revolution immediately moved the seat of government back to Moscow, and after Lenin's death in 1924 renamed the former capital in his honour. During World War II *Leningrad* endured a 900-day siege and blockade by the Nazis but was never captured. After the collapse of the Soviet Union, a vote by the city's residents in 1991 restored its original name.

[2] *Nevsky Prospekt* (Nevsky Avenue) — the principal thoroughfare of St. Petersburg, stretching more than four kilometres from the Admiralty to the Alexander Nevsky Monastery. Named after Grand Prince Alexander Nevsky (1220–1263) who defended the territory against attacks by Swedish

leg. While he was recuperating, he spent a long time sitting at the window of his flat at No 25, Fontanka Embankment. But his apartment windows looked out not onto the river, but onto an interior courtyard. The view included a shabby brick wall and the rusty spots covering the roof of the house it was attached to.

One day the boy asked his father:

"Papa, isn't our city supposed to be the best in the country?"

"Of course," the father replied, "it's one of the best in the world!"

"And why is it the best?"

"What d'you mean, *why?* It's got a lot of different kinds of monuments and museums, and the architecture in the city centre is world-famous."

"But we live in the city centre too, and all we can see from our windows is a shabby wall and the rusty roof of the building next door."

"A wall... Well, yes, we didn't do so well with the view."

"Are we the only ones?"

"Maybe a few others, but anyway..."

———————

armed forces and German knights, the street dates back almost to the founding of the city itself. It was designed by French architect Alexandre LeBlond under commission from Peter the Great, and over the years has figured prominently in the writings of major Russian authors, including perhaps its most famous resident, Dostoevsky. Today, lined by cathedrals, museums and hundreds of shops and apartment houses with neo-classical façades, the Nevsky still forms the axis of the city's business and cultural centre.

[3]*Fontanka* — one of the several channels of the Neva River flowing through the delta on which the city of St. Petersburg is built. Embankments on both sides give it more the appearance of a canal (the city boasts about fifty canals and a hundred islands). Nevsky Prospekt crosses the Fontanka on the architecturally unique Anichkov Bridge (built in 1715) — each of its four corners is adorned with a bronze sculpture of a horse, all executed by Russian artist Piotr Klodt (1805–1867) in the mid-nineteenth-century.

The boy took a snapshot of the view from his apartment windows and when he was able to go to school again, he showed the photo to his chums.

Then all the children in his class took snapshots from their windows and compared the photos. The overall picture was not very pretty. The boy and his chums went to see the editors of one of the local papers and asked the same question he had earlier asked his father:

"Why is our city supposed to be more beautiful than others?"

They tried explaining to him about Alexander's Column[4] and the Hermitage;[5] they talked about the Kazan Cathedral[6] and the legendary Nevsky Prospekt...

[4] *Alexander's Column* (Russian: *Aleksandriyski stolp*) — a prominent column in the centre of Palace Square behind the Tsar's Winter Palace, erected in 1834. Auguste Ricard de Montferrand, a Russian architect of French descent, was commissioned by Tsar Nicholas I to design this monument commemorating his predecessor (and elder brother) Alexander I's victory over Napoleon during the War of 1812. Atop the column is a sculptural representation of an angel with Alexander's face, designed by Boris Ivanovich Orlovsky (real surname: Smirnov; 1796–1837). At 47.5 metres, the pink granite column is the tallest structure of its kind in the world, eclipsing both the Colonne de Vendôme (44 m) in Paris and the Trojan Column (38 m) in Rome.

[5] *The Hermitage* (Russian: *Ermitazh*) — one of the major art museums in the world, begun in 1764 by Empress Catherine the Great, who wanted a place to display (for family and invited guests) her own large private collection. The Hermitage comprises a series of five ornate buildings erected over a number of years along the banks of the Neva River, including the Tsars' Winter Palace, designed by Bartholomeo Rastrelli (1700–1771). Following the 1917 revolution, the whole complex was proclaimed public property and today draws millions of visitors each year.

[6] *Kazan Cathedral* (Russian: *Kazansky sobor*) — a large cathedral on Nevsky Prospekt, bordered on either side by double rows of columns in semi-circular formation. Built in the early 1800s by Russian architect Andrei Voronikhin (1759–1814), it is the burial place of Russian field marshal Mikhail Kutuzov who led the Russian army in its successful repelling of the Napoleonic invasion. During the Soviet period the cathedral was turned into the State Museum of Religion and Atheism, but is now once again under the jurisdiction of the Russian Orthodox Church.

"What makes the Nevsky so hot?" the boy enquired. "I think it looks like a stone trench with flaking edges."

They tried explaining to him about the architectural merits of the thoroughfare, about the sculptural mouldings on the building façades. About how the city at the moment didn't have enough funds to restore all the houses at once, but soon there would be money available, and then everybody would see how beautiful the Nevsky really was.

"But what's so beautiful about a stone trench, even if the façades are spruced up? Besides, it'll only get shabby again before long and they'll only have to refill the holes and fix up the parts that have fallen down."

The boy and his chums went around to various editorial offices, showing them their now considerable collection of photos and asking the same question over and over again. At first the journalists were irritated at his persistence. On one occasion a reporter with a youth newspaper told him:

"Oh, it's you again?! And now you're dragging your henchmen along with you — you've got more and more of them, it seems, all the time. You may not like the city, the view from the windows, but can't you do at least something about it yourselves? There's enough criticising going on without you kids adding your two cents' worth. Go back to your homes and stop interfering with our work!"

This admonition was overheard by a veteran journalist, who after seeing the group of children make their way out of the newspaper offices, spoke thoughtfully to the young reporter:

"You know, their audacity reminds me of a particular fairy tale."

"A fairy tale? Which one?" the reporter enquired.

"*The Emperor has no clothes!* Remember those words in the story?"

After that the boys stopped bothering the editors with questions and showing the huge collection of pictures they carried around in a backpack. The school year ended, and come September another began. And it didn't take long for the news to spread through the newspaper offices: *the boy and his chums are back again*. The veteran journalist exclaimed to his colleagues at the journalists' club for the umpteenth time:

"He's back... Yes, indeed... And just think, he finally managed to get a hearing. And he wasn't alone. They all sat quietly waiting together in the reception room for about three hours. I agreed to see them. I warned them to talk quickly, as I had set aside only two minutes to hear what they had to say. They came in and spread out a huge sheet of drafting paper across my desk. I looked at their masterpiece and was dumbfounded. I kept looking, not being able to take my eyes away, or even to say a word. Two minutes must have gone by, for I heard the boy say to everyone:

"'It's time for us to leave. We've outstayed our welcome.'[7]

"'What's that?' I called after them, just as they were on their way out the door. He turned around, and I felt the look of another age descend upon me. Yes, indeed... There's a lot we still have to think through, make sense of... Yes, indeed!"

"Well, did he say anything?" asked a colleague.

Others, too, became restless and asked:

"Don't keep us in suspense — did he say he was coming back?"

Whereupon the veteran editor replied:

"He turned around and answered my question like this:

"'That's *our* Nevsky you've got in front of you. For now it's only on paper. But eventually the whole city will be that way.' And then the door closed."

[7] *We've outstayed our welcome* — the original Russian phrase (*Vremia zdes' uzhe ne nashe*) can also be interpreted to mean: 'The age you live in here is no longer the age *we* live in'.

For the umpteenth time the journalists bent over to examine the design, and marvelled at its amazing beauty.

The design showed the houses along Nevsky Prospekt no longer one right smack up against the other, forming a continuous stone wall. Some of the old buildings were still there, but every other building had been taken down. In place of the razed houses there were now marvellous green and fragrant oases. Birds were shown nesting in the many birches, pines and cedars, and it seemed as though one could hear their song just from looking at the drawing. The people sitting on benches beneath shady trees were surrounded by beautiful flower-beds as well as raspberry and currant bushes. These green oases jutted out a little into the street, and the Nevsky no longer looked like a stone trench, but a splendid living green allée.

The building façades had a multitude of mirrors built into them. The thousands of splashes of sunlight reflected in the mirrors played with the passers-by, caressed the petals of the flowers and played in the streams of the little fountains set up in each green oasis. People were shown drinking water along with the splashes of sunlight and smiling...

"Anastasia," I asked, "did the boy ever show up again?"

"What boy?"

"You know, the one who kept pestering the editors with his question."

"The 'boy' was gone for good. He became a great architect. Together with his like-minded chums he created splendid cities of the future. Cities and villages, in which happy people began to live. But his first marvellous creation was the city he designed on the Neva."

"Anastasia, in what year will Russia's marvellous future appear?"

"You can determine the year for yourself, Vladimir."

"What d'you mean, for myself? Is time subject to Man's will?"

"What Man *does* in his time is definitely subject to his will. Everything created by a dream already exists in space. The dreams of many human souls — your readers — will turn the Divine dream into material reality. What you have seen may come about in three hundred years, or it could come right now, this instant."

"Right this instant? But you can't build a house in an instant, and a garden won't grow up even in a year."

"But if you, right where you are living at the moment, even if it is just a tiny flat, plant a seed in a little clay pot of earth, from which may grow a shoot of a family tree, this tree will eventually grow to maturity in your future family domain..."

"You yourself are talking about what *will be* — that's not the same thing as *right now*. In other words, a dream cannot materialise itself in a single instant."

"What do you mean, it cannot? After all, that material seed you plant — that is precisely the beginning of the dream's coming true. The shoot interacts with the whole Universe, it materialises your dream, and you will be enfolded by splendid bright energies, you will stand before the Father as the embodiment of His dream."

"Interesting, indeed. That means we should get started, right away?"

"Of course."

"Only where can I find the right words to get people to understand?!"

"The words will be found if you can be sincere and true to yourself in front of people."

"I don't know how, but I shall act. Your dream has sparked something in my soul, Anastasia. And I very much want to make the future I have seen come true."

CHAPTER FIFTEEN

Making it come true

First of all I had to determine whether there were any people willing to get involved in the building of an eco-community and then to work in it. I asked the Anastasia Foundation for Culture and Assistance to Creativity, based in Vladimir,[1] to circulate information on the building of an eco-village according to Anastasia's design. A scant two months later, one hundred and thirty-nine people had responded, declaring their interest in building the future community — including Russians who had emigrated abroad. Once this book is out, telling about the future of Russia and giving information on Russians' new lifestyle, that number may well rise a hundred or a thousandfold, and be spread over a number of regions of the country. Hence the organisational work of building the communities should be able to start in different regions at the same time. In regard to this, the Anastasia Foundation, which as an information clearing-house has reviewed the existing laws on the subject and suggested that any readers sharing Anastasia's views proceed as follows:

First: Start with your own region by organising a spearhead group that could eventually be given legal status in accord with prevailing legislation.

Some regions, possibly, already have readers' clubs or community organisations bringing Anastasia's readers together,

---

[1] *Vladimir* — here referring to the name of the city of Vladimir (see footnote 1 in Chapter 6: "A garden for eternity").

which could get the project off the ground there. But if you don't happen to know of anything like that in your region, you can get in touch with the Anastasia Foundation, which receives a lot of correspondence on this and can provide you with addresses. Overall, I have a lot of faith in entrepreneurs. They have more experience in organisational matters and so, even if community organisations are already set up in some areas, you should still try and get in touch with entrepreneurs.

You should appoint an authorised representative, at least temporarily or on a trial basis — someone who can act on your behalf in dealing with the authorities (submitting applications for land allotments, calling meetings when required, etc.). Provide a small honorarium for your chairperson. The representative's role can be filled either by an actual person or a corporate body.

In the latter case you might want to appoint, for example, a well-known construction company, which could subsequently enjoy priority rights in the awarding of contracts for erecting single-family houses, as well as infrastructure buildings. Such a major contract will be extremely profitable for the construction company, and so it may agree to take on the job of applying for land-use permits and compiling budget estimates.

Second: Submit a formal application to your region's local public authorities — and directly to the official at the top — for a single allotment of land with an area of no less than 150 hectares. The size of the allotment will depend on how many interested participants you have, as well as what kind of local resources are available.

You will need to consider that in the future your community will be home to quite a few families, and so it should include a school, club and medical facility, and these are best supported by a significant number of people. Small communities may not be in a position to create the required infrastructure.

Third: In applying for an allotment, you should contact land surveyors, architects and builders to draft blueprints for the settlement. Another important reason for this is that you will need to find out the depth of the water table under the allotment, with a view to drilling wells to supply each house with running water, to determine what depth house foundations should be as well as the feasibility of constructing a small pond in each domain. Drawing up a good overall plan for the community is also important in determining the location of the future school and play areas, as well as where the access roads should go.

The Anastasia Foundation has already commissioned competent specialists to work out a model plan, and if it is completed before you launch your spearhead group, you can consult with the Foundation — it will cost you less. But then you will have to adapt the model to your own locale, introduce your own modifications and share them with other spearhead groups. Successful proposals which have the greatest appeal will be adopted by other groups, and eventually we shall jointly put together a master design.

Fourth: After completing the design for the settlement — and this is something not only specialists but also future residents can participate in — you will receive a detailed set of schematics, including an overall plan highlighting the individual plots of at least one hectare each. Every participant should be formally assigned a plot of land, perhaps by drawing straws. Land use entitlement should be formalised with an appropriate legal document, drawn up in the name of the individual owner rather than the organisation, as was the case in the Auroville community in India.

And so here you are standing on your own plot, on your very own hectare of land. This is your kin's domain, the place where your descendants will be born and will live. They will fondly remember its founder, their family patriarch, and they may even rebuke him for certain mistakes in planning out the place.

Right at the moment the design of everything to be situated on the assigned plot is completely up to you. Where will you place your family tree — an oak or cedar, for example — which will keep on growing for as long as 550 years, and may be looked upon by the ninth generation of your descendants as they remember you?

Where will you decide to dig a pond, plant an orchard and a small grove of woodland trees, build your house and set up your flower beds? What kind of living fence will you create around the perimeter of your kin's domain? Maybe the one Anastasia described, or maybe it will come out even more fanciful and functional than the one depicted in my previous book. It can be started even now, even before you get the official documents, even before a spearhead group is organised among the people who share your vision. You can start the building process in your thoughts, pondering what will go in each corner of your future kin's domain.

You should remember that the house you build, even one of fairly solid construction, will last about a hundred years and then fall into disrepair. The living structures you set up, on the other hand, will only become better and stronger, thriving more and more as the ages pass. They will convey your living thoughts to your descendants for centuries, and perhaps even for millennia to come.

You can start building right away, and not just in your thoughts. Even now you can plant the seeds of your future majestic family trees in a clay pot on the windowsill. Of course you can also buy grown saplings ready for transplant at a specialised nursery, or dig up young shoots in the forest without damaging the growth around, especially in places where the forest growth needs thinning out. That is possible, of course, but I think Anastasia is correct here — it's better to grow the sapling on your own, especially when it comes to your future family tree. A sapling from a commercial nursery is like a baby from an orphanage. Besides, you need to grow not only one sapling, but several different ones. And before planting the seed in the pot of earth, you need to infuse the little seed with information about yourself.

I realise that support on a national level may be needed to overcome bureaucratic obstacles in certain regions. Or if not support, then at least an absence of opposition. Appropriate changes in legislative policies are required.

Instead of waiting around idly for this to happen all by itself, waiting for at least one of our existing political bodies to mature into a state where it will support such a project, the Anastasia Foundation, at my request, has worked out a draft constitution for a new political party, a party of land-users. This germinating social movement has been called *Co-creation (Sotvorenie)*. Its platform, which still has to be discussed and finalised, comes down to one central theme (as I see it): *The state should grant to every willing family one hectare of land for lifetime use, for the purpose of establishing their own family domain.*

This movement is still young, and nobody is really in control of it at the moment, but I think that in time we shall see literate politicians coming on board who are capable of working out a relationship to the new movement on the level of federal policy-making. For the time being the Co-creation Party functions mainly as an information clearing-house. A legal department will get started as soon as sufficient funds become available. For now the party's administrative affairs are being handled by the Anastasia Foundation for Culture and Assistance to Creativity.

The regional spearhead groups set up to organise new communities will be quite successful after they gain the support of the local public authorities. This should happen once the authorities see the substantive benefits which will accrue to their region. And these can be pinpointed right now. They do exist and they are indeed substantive. Try to get a discussion of the project going in the local press and see if you can get specialists — ecologists, economists and sociologists — to weigh in on the specific influences the project will have on your region.

In an effort to do my part to help — at least in some way — in getting land allotted for the purpose of setting up kin's domains, I have decided to publish in this book an open letter to the President of Russia.

CHAPTER SIXTEEN

Open letter

**To Vladimir Vladimirovich Putin,
President of the Russian Federation**

**From Vladimir Nikolaevich Megre,
Citizen of the Russian Federation**

Dear Vladimir Vladimirovich!

We live in a generation which must be very lucky indeed. We have before us a real opportunity to begin building a prosperous, flourishing state thoroughly protected from external aggressors, internal conflicts and crime. A state in which happy families will live in prosperity. Our generation has the opportunity of not only building a splendid country, but of actually living in it, provided there is enough good will among the legislative powers that be to grant to every willing family one hectare of land for the purpose of establishing thereon its own kin's domain. This simple action will suffice to call forth an impulse to creative endeavour on the part of the majority of people at various levels of society.

The land should be granted free of charge, for lifetime use, with the right of inheritance. The produce grown on these kin's domains should not be subject to any form of taxation.

You will agree, Vladimir Vladimirovich, that an abnormal, illogical state of affairs has now come about: every Russian is supposed to have a Motherland, but nobody can show exactly where his piece of this Motherland is. If every family receives one and transforms it into a flourishing corner of Paradise, Russia as a whole will become a magnificent land.

Current policies on national development do not inspire people into creativity, since it is not clear where or to what kind of future they are leading. The forging of a democratic, economically developed state on the Western model has been rejected — intuitively, perhaps — by the majority of the population. And I think this is all to the good. Common sense makes us ask ourselves: Why should any of us in particular, or we as a nation, waste our efforts on building a state which will only be racked by drugs, prostitution and gangsterism? All those things are part of Western society.

We used to think that the so-called developed societies enjoyed an abundance of food products, but now it is clear that this abundance has been achieved at the expense of applying all sorts of chemical additives and poisonous chemicals to the soil, as well as genetic engineering. We have seen that imported food products have nowhere near the taste quality of our own. In Germany, for example, people gladly buy potatoes brought in from Russia.

In a number of countries the government has become concerned over this situation and mandated special labelling of genetically modified produce. Scientists, too, are becoming more and more concerned. America and Germany are among those countries that have the highest per-capita cancer rates in the world. Do *we* have to go down the same path?

I don't think it is a path that inspires very many people. But our country has come to tolerate the promotion of foreign goods and the Western way of life. We have become resigned to the appearance in our midst of more and more diseases, to the fact that we can now drink water only out of bottles we buy at the store and that the population of Russia is decreasing by 750,000 souls a year. It's all just like in the West. After all, the birthrate has fallen in highly developed countries too. We are trying our hardest to be like them. But I have been hearing from people who live in these countries, hearing about their hopes — their hopes that Russia is searching for and will inevitably find its own path of development, and show the whole world a happier way of life.

Mr President, you, no doubt, have received various proposals for the future development of our country. If this new proposal appears questionable in comparison with others you have seen, I would ask you to test it on an experimental basis in regions where the respective governors can discern in it a grain of common sense.

You will find further details of this proposal in the series of books entitled *The Ringing Cedars of Russia,* of which I happen to be the author. I would not imagine that you have had the time to read them personally, caught up as you are in attending to a flood of affairs of state. Still, there are certain appropriate administrative bodies which are aware of these books and have already rendered their verdict.

They conclude that these books have engendered a new religion in Russia, which is "spreading like wildfire" — an opinion that is also being circulated in the press in a number of publications. Their conclusion came as a complete surprise to me. While I *have* expressed my feelings about God in these books, I never thought of creating any kind of new religion. I simply wrote books about an extraordinary and beautiful recluse living in the Siberian taiga and the fervent dream she entertains about what is splendid and beautiful in life.

One could say that the enthusiastic reaction on the part of people of different social backgrounds and the popularity of these books both in Russia and abroad bear some resemblance to a religious phenomenon. But I think this is quite a different story here. The ideas, philosophy and topical awareness of this Siberian recluse, not to mention the language in which she expresses herself, have all deeply stirred people's hearts.

It will probably be quite a while before scientists reach a unanimous conclusion on who Anastasia is and what is the full significance of the books containing her sayings, or how one should interpret the public reaction to them. Let them keep on trying to figure it out. I am only concerned lest their theoretical analyses overshadow the concrete proposals made by Anastasia.

Vladimir Vladimirovich, so that you may be personally persuaded of the effectiveness of Anastasia's proposals regarding the land, I invite you to authorise an experiment, regardless of who either Anastasia or Vladimir Megre may be, which will put some of her less significant statements to the test.

First: I suggest that your public officials will not be unduly burdened if asked to commission an appropriate scientific research institute to do a simple analysis of the effectiveness of Anastasia's proposal on cleansing the air in major cities from harmful dust pollution. The gist of this proposal was set forth back in my first book.[1]

Second: I recommend you authorise an analysis of Siberian cedar nut oil as a general remedial agent. Both data from ancient sources and modern research by scientists at the University of Tomsk[2] confirm Anastasia's statement that this natural product, provided it is obtained through a specific technological method, is one of the most effective remedies in the world for the cure of a broad range of diseases. You will not find anywhere else on the globe a vaster array of plantings than in Siberia, which is home to the nut-bearing cedar.

---

[1] See Book 1, Chapter 17: "The brain — a supercomputer".

[2] *Tomsk* — a city of a half-million residents in southwest Siberia, founded during the reign of Tsar Boris Godunov in 1604. The university was established in 1880.

The Russian federal budget could realise substantial profits from putting this product on the international market, as well as from its use within our own country. We need to have a state policy on the exploitation of Siberian flora. A policy aimed not at the establishment of large-scale industrial enterprises but at the unfolding of a network of small businesses involving people actually living in the remote regions of Siberia. The implementation of such a policy does not require a huge outlay of capital, only a legislative decision allowing the local residents to acquire land in the taiga on a long-term lease basis.

Moreover, Vladimir Vladimirovich, life inevitably confirms even the statements of Anastasia's that seem less plausible at first glance. Personally, I am absolutely convinced of our country's splendid future. It is only a question of whether those living today will accelerate its coming or slow it down. I sincerely wish you, Vladimir Vladimirovich, along with all of us alive today, the opportunity of being the creators of this splendid future!

Respectfully,

Vladimir Megre

CHAPTER SEVENTEEN

Questions and answers

Anastasia's design intrigued me. I wanted to think and talk
about it on a daily basis. I wanted to stand up for it at all
costs, defend it against ridicule and dispel the doubts of the
sceptics. I talked about it at the readers' conferences held
in the city of Gelendzhik[1] and at the Central Letters Club[2]
in Moscow. The majority of the participants at these conferences (there were more than two thousand in all, hailing from
various countries of the Commonwealth of Independent
States,[3] as well as from further afield) either supported this
design or at least expressed an interest. But in this chapter
I shall reproduce some of the basic questions and comments
by the doubters, along with my responses to them, based on
Anastasia's statements and my own convictions, as well as information I have managed to glean from other sources.

   Question. In today's world no nation's economy can survive independent of the global economic system. Today's

---

[1]*Gelendzhik* — see footnote 1 in Book 1, Chapter 30: "Author's message to
readers". On one of the readers' conferences in Gelendzhik, see Book 4,
Chapter 34: "Anomalies at Gelendzhik".

[2]*Central Letters Club* — in Russian: *Tsentral'nyi Dom literatorov* (literally: Central House of Literati).

[3]*Commonwealth of Independent States* — an organisation of countries comprising most of the former members of the Soviet Union. It was formally
launched at a conference in Alma-Ata (Kazakhstan) on 21 December 1991,
following the official dissolution of the USSR at a conference in Minsk (Belarus) earlier the same month.

economic processes point to the need to create large industrial structures, the need for specialised knowledge of today's
markets and how they are set up, as well as the major directions of capital flow. It does not appear that you have training
in economics. Your proposal involves emphasising small-scale
commodity production, which may take away from more important things and ruin the national economy.

Answer. It is true that I have had no training in economics.
But as to your point that large conglomerates are of prime
importance to the nation's economy, I am in complete agreement with you. I think you will also agree that a large factory,
say, is economically viable for the nation only when it oper-
ates to produce goods in high demand. When a large enterprise shuts down — and such cases are not infrequent in our
country, or in others — it inevitably means losses.

The state is obliged to pay workers unemployment benefits. Hundreds of thousands are forced to eke out a wretched
existence on the strength of this paltry allowance. They don't
know what to do, they're so used to relying on their produc-
tion-line job to feed themselves and their families. Given
these conditions, they could make better use of their new free
time working intensively on their own plots of land.

One's family domain is not just to provide a home base to
spend one's leisure time in. It can also serve as a profitable work-
place, more profitable, even, than in many enterprises, even major ones. In terms of the larger picture — on the national level,
that is — the state may be seen as not only made up of industrial
and financial conglomerates, both large and small, but its very
building-blocks consist precisely of these family nuclei.

For any family the domain can serve as a home base — an
insurance policy against any possible form of nationwide economic disaster. I don't see anything wrong with each family
being offered the opportunity to provide independently for
its own poverty-free existence.

I also believe that personal freedom is impossible without economic freedom. A working family, even one living in a modern city apartment, cannot be free, dependent as it is on an employer who determines one's salary, on utility companies with the power to supply or withhold heat, water and electricity, on the availability of groceries and on the prices of food products and consumer services. The family is slave to all of these, and the children in such a family are born into a slave mentality.

Question. Russia is an industrially developed country and a mighty nuclear power. And only as such will it be able to guarantee the security of its citizens. If all its residents do nothing but work the land, the country will be transformed into a purely agrarian state and thus become defenceless against external aggressors.

Answer. I don't think everybody's necessarily going to agree to work on their plots of land right off the bat. It'll be a gradual process, and the situation will unfold naturally, in an orderly manner. National power depends not only on possessing a sufficient number of nuclear warheads, but also on the overall economic state of affairs, including sufficiency and quality of food products. And when a state does not have sufficient food production to feed its people, it is then obliged to sell off not only its natural resources but its armaments as well, thereby strengthening the position of any potential aggressor.

The proposed design has the power to strengthen the economic position of the state as a whole, and as such offers the opportunity not only for more effective scientific and industrial development but also a more efficient combat-ready army.

In the near future, however, when this way of life has been adopted on a massive scale, I think — indeed, I am quite convinced — that it will provoke considerable interest among many citizens of other countries, including countries we don't currently get along with. And people in those nations too will want to reshape their lifestyle the same way many Russians have done. The adoption of this design in a variety of countries will signal the start of a whole new era of peaceful co-existence among peoples.

Question. The implementation of the proposal is feasible, of course, in the more trouble-free regions of Russia. But isn't it naïve to think of implementing it in an inherently crime-prone republic such as Chechnya?[4]

Answer. A significant lowering of social tensions, especially in the so-called 'hot spots', along with complete cessation of conflict through the help of the proposed project I see as something not only *not naïve,* but absolutely realistic. If you take the northern Caucasus, for example, and its most troubled region, Chechnya, it has recently become clear (and this has been reported in the press) that the basic conflict is centred around the struggle of a small group of people for control of the republic's oil reserves, as well as for money and power. This situation is typical of most of the 'hot spots' today — indeed, of most of the conflicts the world has known throughout the ages. That still leaves the question of why such a large part of the population, especially men, has been drawn into the Chechen conflict.

---

[4]*Chechnya* (pronounced *chich-NYAH*) — a small, predominantly Muslim republic of about 800,000 people in the Northern Caucasus area of the Russian Federation. With its capital at Grozny, Chechnya is situated to the north of Georgia (a former Soviet republic, now an independent country). Chechnya was forcibly annexed by the Russian Empire in 1859, and throughout history, a part of the Chechen population has fiercely resisted Russian rule. The Chechens' striving for independence has been constantly suppressed by the Russian Federation, and in the mid-1990s this led to a military conflict which has not been settled to the present day (mid-2006).

Chechnya used to have hundreds of illegal oil-refining operations, belonging to a small group of people. Tens of thousands of people from among the local population worked in these enterprises. When the government tried to restore law and order these people lost their jobs, leaving their families without any means of support. The principal aim of this class of people in joining the militants was to try and protect their jobs and the welfare of their families, minimal though it was. Besides, their participation in the rebel forces wasn't exactly volunteer work — they ended up earning quite a bit more than the unemployment benefit they had been getting. Consequently, for the majority of the ordinary fighters, taking part in the armed gangs was simply a job — no different from being a policeman or a Russian army officer, only better paid. As a result, many of these foot-soldiers don't see much in the way of hope for their families' welfare if military operations were to cease.

How can we possibly do away with unemployment in Chechnya if we can't completely do away with it in even a single region closer to home, especially one that is comparatively well off? Let's say the Government pours colossal resources into Chechnya and starts setting up all sorts of enterprises there to guarantee a job for everybody who wants one. But then another problem arises — the size of the pay packet offered. Say you offer a special raise for the Chechen population, then all of Russia will be working to support the Chechens, since the only way the raise can be implemented is on the backs of the Russian taxpayers as a whole. Even then, not all the money will reach its intended target, since the problem of getting allocated funds through to those who actually need them has not been resolved. In sum, we'd be faced with the same situation we have today, only with a significant increase in expenditures.

The Chechen Republic is a region favourable to agricultural production. Now let's suppose a law granting land for family domains is already in effect. Suppose that the state is able to protect these family domains from any kind of encroachment. So a Chechen family receives land for its kin's domain where everything they produce belongs exclusively to them and their future descendants, guaranteeing them a poverty-free existence and a life not ruled by bombs, and not as outlaws, but in their own splendid corner of the Earth — a piece of their Motherland which they have established themselves. I am certain that such a family will not oppose a government which has given them an opportunity like that — on the contrary, they will defend such a government more zealously than they now oppose it. They will defend such a government as passionately as they would defend their family nest. They will counter any attempt by agitators to separate Chechnya from such a government, or any attempt at racial discrimination.

I am convinced that if the government launched a campaign on a sufficiently large scale, introducing settlements like that into Chechen territory, even on an experimental basis, the 'hot spot' we call Chechnya will be transformed into not only one of the most stable regions of Russia, but one of the major centres of spirituality on the Earth. We shall see a complete hundred-and-eighty-degree turn. When Anastasia spoke of ways to eliminate crime, I too had a hard time believing what she said. But eventually, life inevitably kept bearing out the truth of her words. And as far as the Chechen Republic is concerned...

At the readers' conference in Gelendzhik there were more than a thousand people from all parts of Russia and the Commonwealth of Independent States. I was especially struck by the fact that a delegation had come from Chechnya. Nobody had invited them specially to the conference; the Chechens came all on their own. Later I spoke with several of them personally.

At the moment we are talking about Chechnya, but are other parts of our country free of crime? It's there all right,

and in just about every form you can imagine. One of the
causes of crime is unemployment, and the fact that people
are released from prison with no opportunity to rebuild their
lives in our society. Anastasia's project is capable of solving
this problem.

Question. If you give a hectare of land to everybody in Russia who wants one, there won't be enough land to go round.
Especially for the rising generation.

Answer. At the present time we are faced with a question
even more acute — namely, that there are not enough people
to work the land. And I'm not talking just about wasteland
and land unsuitable for farming, but arable land as well. As to
the rising generation, it is unfortunately the case that every
year more Russians are dying than are being born. According
to Goskomstat (the government statistics agency), the Russian population is showing an annual attrition rate of 750,000
people. So the current concern is over whether there will be
a rising generation at all.

At first I too was under the misconception that a family, or
even a single person, living, let's say, in a flat in a five-storey
apartment block, takes up less land than a family or person
with a private house and a garden plot. But, as it turns out, it's
not that way at all. Any person, no matter what floor he lives
on, consumes as food all sorts of things that grow on the land.
To get those growing things delivered to him, roads, trucks,
warehouses and stores are required, and all of these take up
land-space too. So at any given moment every individual is
being supported by his own plot of land. It supports him regardless of whether the individual has abandoned it or even
thinks about it at all.

Naturally I wasn't able to give a full answer to this question
right off, as I didn't have immediate access to all the figures,
but I looked them up later and can now include them here.

Russia's land: The total land mass of the Russian Federation comprises nearly 1,710 million hectares, of which only 667.7 million hectares are fit for agricultural production. Figures for the beginning of 1996 show 222 million hectares used for farming at the time, or 13% of Russia's total land resources. Of these, 130.2 million hectares (7.6% of the total) were classified as arable land.

At the present time Russia's population comprises 147 million people. Hence the 'problem' of allocating a hectare of land to any family wishing to have one simply doesn't exist, according to the statistics. Moreover, the real problem is quite the opposite: the population of our country is shrinking drastically. And here's what the analysts have to say in regard to the general state of the Russian population: if current trends continue, between 2000 and 2045 the number of children under 15 years of age will be cut in half, while the number of senior citizens will increase by 50%. The capacity of the population to reproduce itself will be pretty much exhausted.

Oh yes, and one more problem: the *quality* of the arable lands of our country.

Large areas of the nation are witnessing topsoil erosion. Specialists are of the opinion that these processes have already reached a critical stage at the regional and inter-regional levels. In all of Russia's agricultural zones erosion (or the threat of erosion) has affected 117 million hectares (or 63% of all agricultural lands). Over the last 50 years the rate of erosion has increased by a factor of 30; the rise has been especially steep since the onset of the 1990s. According to the UN's Food and Agricultural Organisation (FAO) experts, Russia is among the top ten countries of the world in terms of erosion rates, and by 2002 erosion will affect as much as 75% of our farmland. I could go on and cite even more detailed statistics about our country's land — they're all pretty miserable. I shall include them at the end of this book.

Now, after becoming familiar with the statistics cited above, I can confidently state that Anastasia's project is capable of stopping the drunken orgy our nation is indulging in with its land resources. To this day it is the only effective and feasible project in existence. It envisages the restoration of the soil's fertility through natural processes. It does not require additional capital outlays on the government's part, and yet with one fell swoop solves the problems of ecology, refugees and unemployment, and completely eliminates the problems we today are creating for our children by our attitude to the land.

Perhaps there is somewhere in Nature a more effective and feasible project. In that case, let it be brought forward. At the moment, all some agencies are doing is demanding more money for the restoration of agricultural production by outmoded means. The government does not have the money they require. But the saddest scenario would be for such plans to be realised by borrowing money abroad and having chemical fertilisers poked into the soil to its further detriment, since we do not have sufficient quantities of manure to go round.

That money will have to be repaid with interest, the condition of the land will deteriorate even further, and the whole problem will fall on the shoulders of the rising generation. I shall do all I can to promote Anastasia's project. Of course, government officials will hardly accept a recluse from the taiga as an authority, and I am no specialist in agriculture, and so it will be a challenge for me to prove its effectiveness before our worldy-wise politicos, but nevertheless I shall keep on trying with all the means at my disposal.

I will be most grateful to those readers who are familiar with the intrigues of the workings of our government if they can explain in a more professional language the effectiveness of Anastasia's project to our high-ranking government officials. Perhaps this book will find its way, too, into the hands of government agencies empowered to undertake such measures, and so I am appealing to them once more with a declaration on behalf of all willing participants. I don't know how many willing participants there are, but I am certain that their numbers are in the millions. On their behalf I make the following request, namely, that the Russian government...

...settle the land question on a legislative basis and grant each willing family in our nation one hectare of land free of charge, affording the opportunity to each willing family to establish its own kin's domain, dignify it and lovingly care for its own piece of the Motherland, thereby making the Motherland as a whole beautiful and happy — the Motherland, after all, consists of little pieces.

Question. In many regions of our country the ecological situation is extremely complex. One could even call it disastrous today. Wouldn't it be better to first direct our efforts toward the improvement of ecological conditions in general — as many ecological organisations are doing at the moment — before turning our attention to individual domains?

Answer. You yourself say that there are a lot of organisations focusing on the ecological situation, but it is getting worse. Doesn't this mean that simply focusing attention on it is not enough here, since the situation is continuing to deteriorate and even reaching disastrous proportions?

Let us imagine a beautiful garden, with all different kinds of trees growing in just one splendidly laid out domain. Just one little corner of Paradise! Only one hectare in size. Of course that's not sufficient for a global change, either for a country or the planet. But now let us imagine a million of such little corners and we shall see the whole Earth as a flourishing garden of Paradise. But still, it is up to each one of us in particular to start by setting up our own little corner. Perhaps then we shall be able to go from being totally focused on the subject to being totally involved in concrete actions.

Question. Do you believe that an unemployed family can get rich with the help of a single hectare of their own land? If you believe that, then tell me why today's rural areas are at a standstill? People in these rural areas have land but they're still going hungry.

Answer. Let's consider this phenomenon together, but first I want to add a few more questions to the one you asked.

Why do millions of people say that for them four or five hundred square metres of a dacha plot has been a significant help to them in financial terms, significantly increasing the amount of food available to them, and yet rural residents with 1500 to 2500 square metres call themselves poor and starving?

Why? In addition to other factors, doesn't the state of our well-being also depend on our level of conscious awareness? The majority of the rural population thinks that you can have a good life only in the cities, and that's why you've got so many young people leaving the rural areas altogether.

I think our own recent propaganda is at least partially to blame. I'm sure you remember those glowing articles in the Soviet press in the fifties and sixties — who were the heroes back then? Miners, lumberjacks, machine operators, aeroplane pilots, sailors...

Even paintings of cityscapes invariably featured a host of smoking chimneys from industrial giants. There was occasionally a condescending reference to the collective farmer, but a Man tending his own garden plot was always negatively portrayed. They even tried building city-type apartment blocks in rural areas, thereby depriving people of their own back yard and made them work only on so-called communal land. Just as with the Auroville community in India — you could live on the land and cultivate it, but you still couldn't have any land to call your own — all of which leads to some pretty sad results.

You hear constant talk from both politicians and the media of the widespread poverty in the Russian countryside today, just as in the majority of the population at large. There's so much talk about it that everybody *en masse* ends up convinced that if you live in the countryside you must be poor. There are hardly any examples cited indicating that your well-being largely depends on *you.*

It must be in somebody's interests to keep rehearsing the scenario: *Don't rely on yourself — I am the only one that can make you happy.* That's what you hear from a lot of religious leaders, as well as a lot of politicians gathering their own circle of voters around them. If you want to be poor and destitute, you can go right on believing them. I want to talk about not how to be poor, but how to be rich. When someone asks me if it is possible to live above the poverty line with one's own parcel of land, I answer: *Yes!* And here's a concrete example.

In 1999 an acquaintance of mine, a Moscow entrepreneur who had read *Anastasia,* invited me over for a visit. He intrigued me when he said that he could prepare a table almost identical to the one Anastasia had set before me in the taiga. When I arrived, his dining table was still empty. We sat down and chatted, and Andrey (that was the entrepreneur's name) kept looking at the clock, apologising for someone he was expecting being held up.

Before long his chauffeur arrived with two large baskets. The table was soon spread with tomatoes, cucumbers, bread and much else besides. The room was filled with tempting aromas. In a few minutes the women in Andrey's household had laid out a splendid table. No Pepsi-cola to drink, but some marvellous, fragrant Russian *kvass.*[5] Instead of French cognac there was home-made wine — on top of it all infused with

[5]*kvass* — a fermented beverage made from rye, barley or other natural ingredients.

some sort of herbs. The tomatoes and cucumbers were not as splendid as the ones Anastasia had in the taiga, but they were far tastier than what you could get at the supermarket or even at farmers' markets.

"Where did you get all this from?" I asked Andrey in astonishment, and this is what he told me.

At some point on their way back to Moscow from Riazan,[6] Andrey's chauffeur had stopped the jeep at a small roadside market. They bought a litre-jar of pickles and a jar of tomatoes. Turning in to a small café, they decided to have a decent meal. They opened the jars they had bought and took a taste.

After lunch Andrey told his driver to turn around and go back to the roadside market. He bought from the elderly woman behind the table everything she had, and offered to give her a ride home in his jeep. The woman lived all alone in a rather old-looking cottage with a small vegetable garden. Her lot was situated in a wee village about fifteen kilometres from the main road. Andrey's enterprising mind was already working quickly and here is how things unfolded.

Andrey purchased a house in the country with 2000 square metres of land, on the edge of a forest, about 120 kilometres from Moscow in an ecologically clean zone. He registered the house in the name of this woman, presented her with the documents and a contract obligating him to pay her a monthly amount of 300 US dollars, while the woman in turn was to give the produce from her garden to his family, except for what she ate herself.

The woman's name was Nadezhda Ivanovna,[7] she was 61 years old. And she really didn't understand documents or believe in them. Then Andrey took her to the local rural

---

[6]*Riazan* — a city (whose history dates back to the late 11th century) on the Oka River about 200 km south-east of Moscow, with a population of slightly more than a half million.

council and asked the chairman to read her the documents and assure her that they were in order from a legal standpoint. The rural council chairman read over the documents and said to the woman:

"What have you got to lose, Ivanna? Nobody's asking you to give up that tumble-down hut of yours. So if you don't like it, you can always come back." Nadezhda Ivanovna was finally persuaded to accept the offer.

For the past three years she's been living in a well-built house. Andrey hired workers to dig her a well and put in a heating system with a hot water furnace. They also dug and outfitted a vegetable cellar. They put a fence around the whole property, brought in all the furnishings she needed, along with a goat, some chickens and animal feed. As well as a lot of other things needed to set up a home.

Nadezhda Ivanovna's daughter and wee granddaughter came to live with her. Since Andrey has read what Anastasia had to say about vegetable-growing, he cultivates seedlings himself, but only with seeds he obtained from Nadezhda Ivanovna. Each summer Andrey's father, a retired restaurant manager, takes the seedlings out to her home and gladly helps the women with the garden work.

This arrangement has provided both Nadezhda Ivanovna and her daughter with work and a place to live. Andrey and his family (his wife, their two children and his father) are supplied all summer long with fresh fruits and vegetables which are really eco-clean, along with marvellous marinated produce during the winter. And all year long they have access to health-giving herbs whenever they need them.

---

[7] *Ivanovna* (pron. *ee-VAHN-av-na*) — a patronymic derived from her father's name *Ivan* (not a surname). In informal circumstances older people can be addressed by the patronymic alone, and the full form *Ivanovna* is nearly always shortened to something like *Ivanna*.

Maybe somebody will say that the example I have cited is an exception. Nothing of the sort! Ten years back, when I was president of the Interregional Association of Siberian Entrepreneurs, many of its members tried to set up their own household plots, either for their companies or just for their families. Today you can find such services advertised in the papers. Only there is one *but* — it is very hard to find any capable workers, or rather, anyone who is competent to do what Nadezhda Ivanovna did. And since such people are so hard to find, let's recall for ourselves what attitude *we* should cultivate toward the land. Let's share our experiences of how to be rich and happy on our own land, and not how to be poor.

Question. Vladimir Nikolaevich, I'm an entrepreneur. I too happen to know that many well-off people use the services of rural residents who are experts at cultivating and preserving agricultural produce, which is definitely superior in taste quality to what comes out of large-scale enterprises. But if everybody follows the same path, that will mean a saturation of the market, and then how is a family going to survive on income just from its own hectare of land, if it turns out that nobody needs the tomatoes and cucumbers they grow?

Answer. The land yields not just tomatoes and cucumbers, but much more besides. However, even if half the total number of Russian families have their own domains, they still won't be able to satisfy the demand for their produce over the next twenty to thirty years, since the demand will come not just from Russians but from many people abroad, especially in the rich, developed countries. The reason is that agricultural producers in most countries have got so caught up in the business of artificial selection and chemical treatment of crops that the original form of these crops has simply got lost — and I'm not just referring to how they look but to the fulness of their content. The example of cucumbers and tomatoes, though, gives everyone a chance to be convinced independently of the following:

Go into any average supermarket — or, better still, into an up-scale supermarket (there are quite a few these days in our big cities) — and you will see very beautiful imported tomatoes and cucumbers, priced from 30 roubles[8] per kilogram. They are uniform in size and a treat for the eyes, and sometimes they're sold with the little green stems left on. But there's no aroma and no taste. They're *mutants!* They're an illusion, a mock-up, only an external reminder of what ought to be there. Most of the world today feeds on such mutants. This is not my discovery — it's something people are concerned about in many of what we call the developed countries of the world.

A decree was passed in Germany, for example, mandating product labelling to include information about the presence of artificial additives, and people who can afford to are boycotting these products. Products grown in eco-clean regions, using only limited quantities of chemical fertiliser, cost a lot dearer in the West. Only the current Western agricultural system does not permit farmers to grow produce that is ecologically clean through and through. Farmers in Western countries are obliged to use not only hired labour but all sorts of technology besides, including weed-destroying chemicals and chemical fertilisers, in their efforts to maximise their profit margins.

Let's say a Western farmer, and there are some of these already, wants to grow eco-clean produce, and even take what Anastasia said into account. You may remember she said that it wasn't necessary to destroy all the weeds, since they

---

[8]*30 roubles* — at the time this book was written, 30 roubles in Russia was worth more than 4 US dollars in terms of buying power — a price far greater then that fetched by domestically grown produce.

too perform significant functions. But let's say a farmer still wants to grow this kind of produce, if only for his family and friends. Right off he's faced with a challenging problem: *seeds*. Artificial selection has done its work — the original varieties have long since disappeared in the West. And there are few of them left even in Russia. Especially after imported seed stock was allowed on the Russian market.

If people use their own seed stocks, the variety of vegetables will gradually see a restoration of their original properties — drawing from the soil everything needed by Man — but a complete restoration will take decades. In Russia, possibly thanks to both poverty and the abundance of small private plots, many people are using their own seeds, and this turns out to be their greatest asset, the effects of which will soon be multiplied a hundredfold in monetary terms.

We're talking about seeds, about the necessity of growing crops in eco-clean zones and the avoidance of chemical fertilisers — all this is very good, something they're talking about in a lot of countries... But that's it — only talk. There's still a very real shortage of healthful and tasty agricultural produce in the world, especially in the developed countries. But that's not all! The processing and preserving are of the utmost importance.

In spite of all the efforts of our technocratic world, our highly equipped technological complexes are unable to match many Russian grandmothers in their production of marinated tomatoes, cucumbers and cabbages of superior taste quality. What's the secret? Apart from the many pearls of wisdom, few people realise that once the tomatoes or cucumbers are plucked from the beds they have been growing in, no more than fifteen minutes should go by before they are sealed in preserving jars. The shorter this period the better. This is what preserves the marvellous aroma, the ethers and the aura. The same applies to the additives — dill, for example.

Water is extremely important. What good can we possibly derive from using chlorinated, dead water? We can boil it, steam the jars, but there are people who take spring water and add huckleberries, among other things... Would you like to try it yourselves? Just take a tumbler, fill it a third full of huckleberries, then fill it up with spring water, and you will be able to enjoy drinking this water even six months later.

You will also notice the strikingly distinctive, superior quality of the fruits and vegetables preserved for the winter, one jar at a time, by these many Russian 'crackerjacks'. These products' pre-eminence in quality of taste over produce from even the most well-known food companies in the world is something each one of us can confirm for ourselves by simply comparing the two.

Now let's say a family living in its domain has canned a thousand litre-jars of tomatoes and cucumbers. The result is first-class produce, surpassing all others in many respects. In terms of taste quality and eco-clean production there is none like it anywhere on the planet. This produce becomes a highly desirable commodity for the tables of many consumers in various countries of the world, including American billionaires and tourists at Cyprus' famed hotel resorts. And it will say on the labels: *From Ivanov's domain, From Petrov's domain, From Sidorov's domain,*[9] etc.

Of course entrepreneurs won't be interested in selling just a thousand litre-jars. But let's say there are three hundred family domains in a community, they would end up with three hundred thousand jars, and *that* would get a major business firm's attention. I would imagine that initially a jar would cost the same as one currently in the supermarket, somewhere around a dollar, but once people actually taste it, the price will go up, maybe as much as dozens of times.

[9]*Ivanov* (pron. *ee-va-NOFF*), *Petrov* (*pe-TROFF*), *Sidorov* (*SEE-da-raff*) — three common Russian surnames.

I mentioned cucumbers and tomatoes just as an example. There's a whole lot of things that a domain can produce — for example, wines, liqueurs, sweet berry wines — from currants, raspberries, blackberries, sweet rowanberries — and so much else besides. Each person can make up their own 'bouquet', improving it more and more as time goes on. And no super-expensive élite wines will be able to compete with them. There aren't any wine-making materials anywhere in the world like those you can get in Russia. Besides, wines can be prepared using herbs according to ancient recipes, and can be made healthful and vitamin-enriched.

Anastasia says that soon the hand-embroidered Russian *kosovorotka*[10] will be considered the most fashionable garment in the world. So this is another line to think along. During the winter months families can prepare hand-made wood-carvings.

It all comes down to the folk saying: *If you want to be happy, be it.* You could also say: *If you want to be rich, be it.* The main thing is: not to program yourself for poverty. You should attune your expectations to wealth. It makes a lot more sense to think about how to become wealthy, and not to constantly tell yourself it's impossible.

Question. Anastasia maintains that it is a lot easier for young couples to hold on to their love for each other in a domain such as you describe than in a typical apartment. Please tell me whether you have discussed this point with psychologists or people who research family problems, and if so, what do they have to say about this, and what makes it happen?

Answer. I haven't talked about this with any academics. Just what precisely makes the love last longer is not something

[10] *kosovorotka* (lit. 'skewed-collar') — a Russian men's shirt with an off-centre buttoned opening near the top and embroidered collar, cuffs and hem.

that frightfully interests me. The main thing is that it hangs in there. The fact that it happens is something you could possibly confirm for yourself after thinking it over. Consider where you would like to see your own son or daughter living — in a city flat, which is like a sack made of stone, or in a house surrounded with a magnificent garden?

Consider what you would like to feed your daughter, or son, or grandchildren — tinned goods or fresh, ecologically clean produce? And in the long term, do you want to see your children living healthy lives or living off the local pharmacy? Ask any young woman who, other things being equal, she would prefer to marry — someone who had set up his life and his future family nest in a concrete apartment block or in a house with a splendid garden? I think the majority would choose the latter.

Comment. The regeneration of any country can begin only on the basis of its spiritual rebirth. Certain members of our government, including the President, have realised this and started talking about spirituality. Anastasia is considered by a majority of readers to be a highly spiritual individual, living according to the laws of God the Creator. She speaks of spiritual values, while here you are leading people astray, calling them in particular to get involved in business on their own plots of land, thereby leading them away from spirituality.

Response. In the long term, I think that nobody will ever be able to lead mankind away from true values. It's good that our leaders today are talking about spirituality. As for Anastasia's sayings, even though I didn't always understand them myself at first, yet later they would still spill over into some kind of concrete reality. Concrete reality is more meaningful to me than philosophical musings, and so here I am talking about concrete things, which I consider most important on the spiritual plane as well. The world probably has a great many concepts of spirituality and God.

After talking with Anastasia and trying to make sense out of what happened, such concepts started coming together for me too. For me God is a person. A good, smart and life-affirming person. A person aspiring to a happy existence for people, His children, to all alike and to each Man in particular. God is the Father, loving and caring for each one of us. Yet to each Man He has given complete freedom of choice. God is the wisest person, striving every moment to do only good for His children. And His Sun comes up each day, the grass and the flowers grow. Trees grow, clouds sail by and water gurgles, ready at any moment to quench any Man's thirst.

And I don't believe, and nothing can ever make me believe, that our wise Father could ever think spirituality is something to be attained only by incessant talk about it without specific concrete actions.

Ever since the so-called Iron Curtain fell, our country has been flooded with hordes of all sorts of people passing themselves off as religious preachers, and quite a few home-grown ones have popped up as well. All trying to tell us what God the Father wants of us. Some say we need to eat a special way, others teach us the best words to use in addressing God. Still others — the Krishnaites, for example, maintain that you have to jump up and down and chant mantras from morning 'til night. For me, all that's balderdash. I can imagine no way of paining God more than through antics like that — all that jumping up and down and wailing. Any loving parent tries to see to it that his son or daughter carries on his father's work, taking part in conjoint creations with him.

God's first-hand creations are all around us. And what can be a higher manifestation of our love for God than a caring attitude to them, or building our lives, our own well-being and that of our children with the help of these Divine creations?

All these antics and meditations have not made us any happier — either our country as a whole or any of its citizens individually. And the reason they have not made us happier is that they are leading us in exactly the opposite direction — away from truth, away from God. Their efforts have been intense and constant, tossing out all sorts of new variations in their antics as truth. Doctrines come and go. Some of them which have been around for ages now only provoke mirth, while others pop up for a few years and then disappear without a trace like a flash in the pan, leaving only a trail of dirt, garbage and ruined lives in their wake.

To my question as to why we are constantly compelled to listen to various rantings about God from all sorts of preachers, and why God does not speak His own words to us directly, Anastasia replied:

"Words? The peoples of the Earth have so many words with different meanings. There are so many diverse languages and dialects. And yet there is one language for all. One language for all Divine callings. It is woven together out of the rustlings of the leaves, the songs of the birds and the roar of the waves. The Divine language has fragrance and colour. Through this language God responds to each one's request and gives a prayerful response to prayer."[11]

God talks with us every moment, but is it not our spiritual apathy that makes us unwilling to hear Him? *All I have to do,* comes the thought, *is chant a mantra or jump up and down and heavenly manna will fall my way which will make me happy and choose me as ruler over all.* Presto — no sooner said than done! And here *we* have to spend years setting up our Paradise, waiting until our trees grow and bear their fruit and our flowers blossom... Yet if we don't do that we are not only rejecting God, we are actually insulting Him — degrading Him with our antics and pompous verbalisations.

[11]Quoted from Book 4, Chapter 11: "Three prayers".

Of course you can refuse to listen to Anastasia, and especially to me. But ultimately, at some point you will walk into a springtime forest or garden, where you will stand still and listen to your heart. Many people's hearts will most certainly hear the Father's voice. As to the question of what God can do in the face of the energies of annihilation holding sway on the Earth, to say nothing of so many people taking His name in vain even as they strive to gain personal power over others, the Father (according to Anastasia) has replied:

"I shall come up as the dawn at the inception of the on-coming day. By caressing all creations on the Earth without exception, the rays of the Sun will help My daughters and sons understand that each one in their own soul can hold conversation with My Soul."[12]

He believed — and still believes — in us, affirming:

"There is one main defence against all the many and varied causes leading one into dire straits, against all the barriers that a lie can throw up in one's face — namely, the fact that My daughters and sons aspire to the conscious awareness of truth. A lie inevitably has its limits, but truth is limitless — it will impart itself as a conscious awareness to the hearts of My daughters and sons."

So, there is no excuse for tardiness in retrieving from one's heart the conscious awareness of God's son — not of a slave or some half-crazed bio-robot jumping up and down to the jingling of a bell.

But how much can one ask of the Father — "Give me!" "Grant me!" "Set me free!"? Isn't it time we ourselves did something pleasing for our Father? And what *could* be pleasing or bring joy to Him? In response to a question like this, Anastasia once referred to a simple test we can make use of

[12]This and the following quotation are taken (with slight variations) from Book 4, Chapter 6: "First encounter".

to verify the authenticity of the many religious concepts and tendencies we are faced with. She described it this way:

"When your heart is stirred by something someone says, claiming to speak in the Father's name, take a look at how the preacher lives his own life, and then imagine what the world would be like if everybody started to live that way."

This simple test can help verify a lot of things. I tried imagining what mankind would be like if everybody to a man started chanting mantras from morning 'til night the way the Krishnaites do, and the immediate result was the end of the world. Now imagine how it would be if every Man on the Earth started growing his own garden. The Earth, naturally, would be transformed into a blossoming garden of Paradise.

As an entrepreneur — all right, a former entrepreneur, but still one at heart — I like specifics, and perhaps that's why I consider 'spiritual' someone who can take actions which will be beneficial to the Earth, his family, his parents and, consequently, God. If someone who calls himself spiritual cannot happify either himself or the woman of his heart, or his family or children, then that is a false spirituality.

Question. Anastasia spoke of a fundamentally different approach to education for children, and a new school. Is this something feasible only in the kind of community she has designed, or in our major urban centres too? What does Shchetinin[13] think about this? Back in your first book you quoted Anastasia as saying she considers raising children a top priority and was always trying to bring up the subject,

[13] *Mikhail Petrovich Shchetinin* — a well-known Russian educator who founded an alternative school at Tekos in the Caucasus based on ideas similar to Anastasia's. For a description of the school — where pupils cover the 11-year Russian school curriculum in only two years — see Book 3, Chapter 17: "Put your vision of happiness into practice" and Chapter 18: "Academician Shchetinin".

whereas you seem to be constantly avoiding it — it almost never comes up in your books. Why?

Answer. Mikhail Petrovich Shchetinin set up his boarding school in the forest. As soon as the foundation is laid for the first community consisting of families' own domains, we shall have to ask Mikhail Petrovich to work out a special programme for the future school. And if he cannot teach in it himself, I shall ask him to at least send his best pupils to it, and select appropriate instructors from among those currently teaching.

I don't think setting up a school like that in today's urban centres is really feasible. Anastasia's sayings aside, let's just think back to our own schooldays. You hear one thing at school, another in the street and still something else at home. While you are trying to figure out where the truth lies, trying to get a complete picture of the world, half your life goes by. I think we have to try and start living a normal life ourselves before trying to educate our children. And once we have got a life set up that's worthy of human existence, then we can take care of our children in partnership with the school, working in harmony, complementing each other.

Anastasia, indeed, often speaks about bringing up children, but she doesn't talk about anything resembling a system scheduled according to days, hours and minutes. And quite often what she says is not all that clear. She says, for example, that a child's education begins with your own education, with setting up a happy existence for yourself, with your own attempts to get in touch with God's thoughts. And one of the principal points in this education is precisely the setting up of a splendid kin's domain.

Chapter Eighteen

The philosophy of life

I visited this man three times in all. He lives in a prestigious dacha community not far from Moscow. His two sons, who hold some sort of fairly high positions in the government hierarchy, built their ageing father a large two-storey mansion and hired a housekeeper to look after both the house and their father. At best they come to see their father once a year on his birthday.

His name is Nikolai Fiodorovich,[1] and he's already in his seventies. His legs ache, and so almost the whole time he sits in his imported wheel-chair. His huge mansion is designed in the best European style, with half the ground floor taken up by his study with its multitudes of shelves home to a considerable collection of books in a variety of languages. Most of these books are on philosophy, in expensive leather bindings.

Before his retirement, Nikolai Fiodorovich taught philosophy at a prestigious Moscow university, and has several academic degrees. In his more senior years he settled into this mansion, and spends almost all his time in his study, reading and reflecting.

I got to know him thanks to the persistence of his housekeeper Galina, who came to one of my readers' conferences. I am grateful to her for introducing us.

---

[1] *Fiodorovich* — a patronymic derived from the Russian name *Fedor* (also spelt *Fiodor* in English, which is closer to the actual pronunciation). Similarly, the feminine patronymic *Nikiforovna* (to be encountered presently) is derived from *Nikifor.*

152   BOOK 5: WHO ARE WE?

Nikolai Fiodorovich had read the books about Anastasia, and he was a most interesting chap to talk with. In spite of his academic degrees, this old fellow could explain in simple, straightforward terms things that had not always been clear to me in Anastasia's sayings, as well as reveal new aspects he had discovered in them.

After the publication of my third book, *The Space of Love,* the office of the Anastasia Foundation forwarded several letters to me written by the leaders of various religious denominations, aggressively denouncing Anastasia, calling her a fool and a scoundrel. One of them even wrote a long letter replete with obscene language.

I was at a loss to understand why Anastasia had suddenly started provoking such unmitigated aggression among certain religious leaders, and so I decided to send some of these letters along to Nikolai Fiodorovich for his opinion. Two months later his housekeeper Galina came to see me, having looked me up at my hotel. She was very distraught and pleaded with me to come see Nikolai Fiodorovich right away, as she was concerned about his health. It was hard to resist Galina's insistence.

Galina had a gorgeous, solid physique. Not fat, she was simply a large and physically strong Russian woman in her early forties. She had spent her whole life in some Ukrainian village, driving trucks and tractors and looking after cows. She was an excellent cook with a good knowledge of herbs, and was extremely neat. Whenever she got excited she would lapse into her thick Ukrainian accent.[2]

---

[2]*Ukrainian accent* — a 'softer' and more relaxed pronunciation by comparison with the terser manner of speaking in north and central Russia (not unlike the difference between the American Southern drawl and the more clipped Canadian speech). In Ukrainian (and some south Russian dialects), the name *Galina* would sound more like *Halina.*

I have no idea how Nikolai Fiodorovich's sons happened to find her and set her up as a nursemaid to their father, but it was curious to see this ageing intellectual, a philosophy professor, talking with a country woman of limited educational background. Galina had been allocated a room of her own in the mansion. It would have been fine for her simply to look after the household affairs — she did this quite well — but she couldn't help listening to what Nikolai Fiodorovich and I were saying to each other. She would invariably think up something that needed doing in our presence and start dusting a particular spot over and over again, all the while commenting aloud on what she was hearing, as though talking to herself.

This time Galina had come to collect me in the Niva,[3] which Nikolai Fiodorovich's sons had purchased so she could go grocery-shopping in the town when necessary, or drive into the woods to gather herbs, or fetch medicines for their father. I dropped what I was working on and went with her. Driving through the streets of Moscow, Galina was very quiet — she looked tense behind the wheel, and I even noticed drops of sweat on her face — until we got past the outer ring road. Once she found herself on a familiar route, she breathed a noticeable sigh of relief. Now she was much more relaxed behind the wheel and started quickly telling me about all her concerns in her mixture of Ukrainian and Russian.

"He was sure quiet back then. The man would sit the whole livelong day jest quietly in his wheel-chair, readin' books and thinkin' to hisself. I'd make up hominy grits or oatmeal for 'im every morning, I'd feed him and I could then go to the market or mebbe into the woods to get some herbs — for his health, ya know. I could go with a clear conscience, see, knowing he'd

---

[3]*Niva* — a Russian make of four-wheel-drive sports utility vehicle, produced since 1977 by the Volga Automobile Factory in Toliatti, which also makes the Zhiguli — see footnote 1 in Book 4, Chapter 22: "Other worlds".

be sittin' in that chair of his thinkin' his thoughts or readin' a book.

"But now it's all different. I brought him the letters you sent. He read 'em. Jest two days after that he says to me: 'Take some money, Galina Nikiforovna, go an' buy some of those Anastasia books, an' then go to the market, no need to hurry home. Stay there at the market an' watch the people. As soon as you see somebody who looks sad or sick, give 'em a book. I did this once, even twice, but there was no way he'd quiet down. 'Don't worry about my dinner, Galina Nikiforovna,' says he, 'I'll make do myself, if I get hungry.' But I still always made it home in time for dinner.

"But the other day when I got home from the market I went into his book room as usual to give 'im some herbal tea. An' hey, his chair's empty, and if he ain't lying there face down on the carpet! I rush over to the telephone and grab the receiver to dial the doctor's number, jest like his sons told me to. They even gave me a special number, not the one everybody uses. So I call up and cry 'Help!' into the telephone. An' jest then he lifts his head an' says to me: 'Cancel the call, Galina Nikiforovna, I'm okay... I'm jest doin' some exercises... push-ups.' So I dash over to him, pick him plumb up off the floor and set him back in his chair. How'd he ever get hisself up off the floor with those achin' legs of his?

"'What kind of exercise is it,' I says to him, 'when someone jest lays on the floor?' And he replies: 'I'd already done my exercises an' was jest restin'. No need for you to worry yer little head over.'

"The next day he'd gotten out of his chair again onto the floor to do his exercises. So I went out and bought him some dumb-bells — not dumb-bells, exactly — something called an *ex-pan-der*. With handles and elastic bands — you can hook up jest one band to make it easier, four when you've got a bit more strength. I bought him this expander, see, but he still keeps tryin' to get up out of his chair, jest like a kid who don't know any better. His heart ain't any too young. An' seein' it ain't too young, he shouldn't try things too heavy all at once, he has to do it one step at a time. But he's just like a foolish child.

"It's pretty near five years I've been workin' for him now, an' nothin' like this ever happened before. An' I haven't a clue myself as to what's goin' on in my heart. You have a talk with him, tell him to at least go easy on his exercises if he likes 'em so much. Tell him to go easy."

When I entered Nikolai Fiodorovich's spacious study, the hearth was cheerily ablaze. The old philosophy professor was not sitting in his wheel-chair as usual, but at his large desk, writing or sketching out something. Even his outward appearance told me that something was different about him. He was not wearing his customary dressing-gown, but sported a proper shirt and tie. He greeted me with more vigour than usual, quickly invited me to take a seat and, bypassing the traditional "How-are-you's", started in talking. Nikolai Fiodorovich spoke fervently, passionately:

"Do you know, Vladimir, what marvellous times are coming upon our Earth? I don't want to die — I want to live on this kind of Earth. I read the letters with all those obscenities directed at Anastasia. Thank you for passing them along to me. In many respects it was a real eye-opener. They call Anastasia a taiga recluse, an enchantress, a sorceress, whereas in fact she is a warrior *par excellence*. Indeed, just think about it, Anastasia is a warrior *par excellence* for the forces of light. Her significance and greatness are something that will be appreciated by future generations.

"The human consciousness, mind and feelings expressed in the sagas, folk tales and legends that have been passed down to us were incapable of even imagining the greatness of this warrior. Only please don't be surprised, Vladimir, don't get

touchy as you usually do about Anastasia. Yes, she is Man...
she is a woman endowed with all — and I mean *all* — of human nature, with all the feminine weaknesses and virtues, designed to be a mother, but at the same time she is also a great
warrior! Right this moment!

"I shall try to express myself not quite so abstrusely. It all
comes down to the philosophical concept. You see, Vladimir,
on the shelves of my study there are a great many books.
These are philosophical works of thinkers of different times
and from different parts of the globe."

Pointing to his bookshelves, Nikolai Fiodorovich listed
them off one by one.

"That's ancient rhetoric, talking about the living, animat-
ed body of the cosmos. Next to that is what's been written
about Socrates — he himself didn't write anything. Over to
the right you see Lucretius, Plutarch and Marcus Aurelius.
A little lower down are five epic poems of Nizami Ganjavi.[4]
Further along there are Arani,[5] Descartes, Franklin, Kant, Laplace,[6] Hegel and Stendhal.[7] All of these men attempted to
learn the central essence of things, to fathom the laws of the
Universe. It was people such as these Durant[8] was referring
to when he wrote:

[4]*Nizami Ganjavi* (also spelt *Giandzhevi*) (1141–1209) — one of the most celebrated historical Persian poets from the region of Azerbaidzhan. He was
learned not only in Arabic and Persian literature, but also in a variety of academic disciplines, including mathematics, geometry, astronomy, medicine,
Islamic law and theology, history, philosophy, music and the visual arts.

[5]*Dr Taghi Arani* (1904–1940) — Iranian Marxist intellectual, arrested and
tortured for his communist sympathies.

[6]*Pierre-Simon Laplace* (1749–1827) — French mathematician who used mathematics to study the origin and stability of the solar system, an early con-
tributor to the theory of probability.

[7]*Stendhal* (real name: Marie-Henri Beyle, 1783–1842) — French realist writer
known for his detailed analyses of his characters' psychological make-up.

"'The history of philosophy is essentially an account of the efforts great men have made to avert social distintegration by building up natural moral sanctions to take the place of the supernatural sanctions which they themselves have destroyed.'⁹

"Great thinkers," Nikolai Fiodorovich continued, "have attempted, each in their own way, to get closer to the concept of the Absolute. Their philosophical concepts gave rise to religion-like philosophical tendencies which in turn passed into history. Eventually, having defied all the timid counter attempts, the dominant concept in our lifetime has turned out to be, to put it concisely, the concept of subjection to some kind of Supreme Mind. Its precise location is unimportant, be it in the infinite spaces of the Universe or localised in the essence of a particular human soul. Much *more* important is the fact that the concept of subjection or inclination dominates over everything else. After that come the particulars — subjection to a teacher, a mentor or a ritual.

"My collections also include Nostradamus' prophecies. Taken as a whole, they constitute a philosophical concept, namely that man is perishable, corruptible and insignificant, and that he has a lot to learn. This concept is precisely what distorts and destroys the soul of Man. No one who adheres to this concept can be truly happy. Not a single person on the Earth can be happy as long as such a concept is dominant in Man's consciousness.

"It weighs equally upon the philosopher and the one who has never gone near philosophy in his life. It weighs equally

---

⁸*William (Will) James Durant* (1885–1981) — American philosopher, historian and writer, of French-Canadian heritage. Two of his best-known works are the eleven-volume epic *The story of civilization* (1935–1975) and *The story of philosophy* (1962).

⁹Will Durant, *Philosophy and the social problem*. New York: Simon & Schuster, 1928, p. 7.

upon the newborn and the aged. It weighs upon the fœtus in the mother's womb. Many adherents of this concept are living today. They have been around at different times, and today their followers are proselytising human society with their beliefs in the frailty and insignificance of Man's essence. But no! Other times are upon us! Anastasia's words from God were like a flash of light to me. You wrote them down, Vladimir, I remember them. When Adam asked God:

"'Where is the edge of the Universe? What will I do when I come to it? When I myself fill everything, and have created everything I have conceived?'[10]

"And God replied to His son, replied to us all:

"'My son. The Universe itself is a thought, a thought from which was born a dream, which is partially visible as matter. When you approach the edge of all creation, your thought will reveal a new beginning and continuation. From obscurity will arise a new and resplendent birth of you, and it will reflect in itself your soul, your dreams, your whole aspirations. My son, you are infinite, you are eternal, within you are your dreams of creation.'

"What a perfect, philosophically comprehensive, precise and concise response that explains it all! It stands head and shoulders above all our philosophical definitions taken together. You can see for yourself, Vladimir, the vast collection of books on my library shelves, but the one Book which is worth far more than all the volumes ever published on philosophy taken together is missing. Many have seen this Book, but few are afforded the opportunity to read it. The language of this Book is not one that can be studied, but it can be felt."

"What language is that?"

---

[10]Adam's questions and God's reply are quoted from Book 4, Chapter 8: "Birth".

"The language of God, Vladimir. May I remind you of how Anastasia described it:

"'The peoples of the Earth have so many words with different meanings. There are so many diverse languages and dialects. And yet there is one language for all. One language for all Divine callings. It is woven together out of the rustlings of the leaves, the songs of the birds and the roar of the waves. The Divine language has fragrance and colour. Through this language God responds to each one's request and gives a prayerful response to prayer."[11]

"Anastasia can feel and understand this language, but what about us?... How can it be that we have let it go unheeded for centuries? Think of the logic! Cold logic dictates that if God created the Earth and the Nature that lives all around us, then every blade of grass, every tree and cloud, the water and the stars can only be His materialised thoughts.

"But we simply pay no attention to them, we trample them, break them, disfigure them, all the while talking about our faith. What kind of faith is that? Who are we really worshipping?

"'The parade of worldly rulers, no matter what grand temples they might have built, will be remembered only by the filth they have bequeathed to their descendants. Water will prove to be the criterion, the measure of all things. Every day that passes, water seethes with more and more contamination."[12] That's how Anastasia put it. That could only have been said by a consummate philosopher, and it behoves all of us to ponder that statement.

"Just think, Vladimir, anything we construct, even if it is for worship, is temporal, just like religion itself. Religions come

[11] Quoted from Book 4, Chapter 11: "Three prayers".
[12] Quoted from Book 3, Chapter 24: "Who are you, Anastasia?" (only with a different sentence order).

and go, along with their temples and philosophies. Water has
existed since the creation of the world, just as we have. After
all, we too are composed, by and large, of water."

"But Nikolai Fiodorovich, why do you think Anastasia's
definitions are the most accurate?"

"Because they are taken from that one Book that covers
everything. And their logic, Vladimir, is the logic of philosophy. There's one preceding statement, given in God's name,
in which God answers the question 'What do you so fervently
desire?', and His answer is directed to every single entity in
the Universe:

"'Conjoint creation and joy for all from its contemplation.'[13]

"Just one brief sentence! Only a few words, that's all! Just
a few words to express God's aspiration and desire. None of
the great philosophers have been able to give a more precise
and accurate definition. 'One must perceive reality through
one's self,' says Anastasia.[14] So any parent who loves their children should determine whether this may not be what they are
really dreaming about. Who among us, being the son or the
daughter of God, would not desire conjoint creation with our
children and joy from its contemplation?

"What consummate power and wisdom are contained in
these philosophical definitions of Anastasia's! They are absolutely crucial for mankind! They are effective. The hosts
of doomsayers have lined themselves up against them. They
will continue to manifest themselves — not just in the form
of cursing Anastasia in correspondence, but in a variety of

---

[13]Quoted from Book 4, Chapter 2: "The beginning of creation".

[14]An approximation of Anastasia's words in Book 2, Chapter 8: "The cherry
tree": "To perceive what is really going on in the Universe one need only look
into one's self." See also Anastasia's grandfather's advice in Book 4, Chapter 33: "School, or the lessons of the gods": "Decide what's real by yourself."

ways. Many small-minded preachers will gather a fistful of
followers around them and look as if they are preaching truth
to people — people who are too lazy to think for themselves.
Anastasia has already said about these:

"'Woe unto you who call yourselves teachers of human
souls! Cool the passions of your heart, and may everyone now
know: the Creator has given all to each one right from the
start. The Truth has been there right from the start in each
one's soul. And we need only refrain from hiding the Creator's great creations under the murky domain of dogma and
conventions, the murk of inventions for the sake of one's own
selfish interests.'"[15]

"These are the people who will try to pounce on Anastasia. Because Anastasia is utterly destroying their philosophy.
With her own philosophical concept she is actually forestall-
ing the end of the world. And this is our reality today: we are
witnessing and participating in the greatest deeds of all time.
Here we are at the threshold of a new millennium, and we
are entering upon a new reality. We are already living in this
reality."

"Wait, Nikolai Fiodorovich. I didn't get what you said
about reality and deeds. Let's say one — or maybe two — philosophers said something. And Anastasia says it, too — what
have reality and deeds got to do with it? It's all just words.
Philosophers talk, and life goes on unfolding in its own way."

"The life of any human society has always been constructed, as it is today, under the influence of philosophical concepts. The Jewish philosophy was one way of life, the cru-
saders' philosophy was another. Hitler had his own philosophy, and we under the Soviet régime had ours. Revolution,
after all, is only one philosophical concept taking the place of

---

[15]These phrases are quoted (though not in the original order and with slight
variations) from Book 3, Chapter 24: "Who are you, Anastasia?".

another. But all that amounts to details determined by local conditions. What Anastasia has accomplished is much more global in scale. It has an impact on human society as a whole and on each member of society in particular. She said she would transport mankind across the dark forces' window of time.[16] She has done this, Vladimir. She has set up a bridge over the abyss which everyone may cross, and each one is free to decide whether to go across it or not.

"I am a philosopher, Vladimir. I can now see this very clearly. What's more, I can feel it. Her philosophical concept shines like a clear ray of light on the threshold of a new millennium. And each one of us, at any given moment, acts this way or that depending on our individual philosophical convictions. If these change, then our actions change accordingly. As I was sitting in my study, for example, and reading through various philosophical works, I pitied all mankind, inevitably moving toward its doom. I wondered where I would be buried, and would my sons and grandchildren come to my funeral, or whether it would be too much trouble for them to come see their grandfather. I pitied all mankind, and thought of my own death. And then along came Anastasia, with an entirely different philosophical concept, and my actions took an about turn."

"How would you do things differently now, for example?"

"Well, I'll tell you. Now... Now when I get up in the morning I start acting in accord with my new philosophical concept."

Nikolai Fiodorovich got up, bracing his arms against the table. Then, holding on first to the chair, then a bookshelf, he managed to make his way on his aching legs over to one of the bookcases. He looked at the titles on each spine, then pulled out one book in an expensive leather binding and headed

[16]See Book 1, Chapter 27: "Across the dark forces' window of time".

over to the fireplace, leaning on various pieces of furniture as he went. Tossing the book into the blazing hearth, he explained:

"Those are the prophecies of Nostradamus about all sorts of cataclysms and the end of the world. D'you remember, Vladimir, Anastasia's words on this? You should remember them. She says:

"'The dates you gave, Nostradamus, for fearful cataclysms on the Earth, were not predictions. You created them out of your own thought and persuaded people to accept their implementation. Now they are still hovering over the Earth, still frightening people with their sense of despair."[17]   This could only have been said by a consummate philosopher and thinker, one who understands that a prophecy is nothing more than an attempt to set a direction for future developments. The more people believe in universal doom, the greater will be the number of thoughts attempting to outline the image, and it will come to pass.

"It can come to pass simply because human thought is material and creates what is material. And whole sects immolate themselves in different parts of the world — that is, the ones who believe in doom immolate themselves, while the ones who have faith in the future live. And she is fearless in the face of despair. She completely destroys any notion of the end of the world when she declares:

"'But now they will no longer come true. Let your thought join in fray with mine. I am Man! Anastasia I am. And I am stronger than you.' And again she says: 'All anger on Earth, leave your deeds and make haste to me, join fray with me, try your utmost.' And again: 'With my Ray I shall take but

---

[17]These and the following quotations concerning Notradamus' prophecies are drawn (in fragmented order and with minor modifications) from Book 3, Chapter 24: "Who are you, Anastasia?".

a moment to burn up the murk of age-old dogma.' She alone has gone out to fight against the countless hordes. Against the millions who outline an image of mankind's total doom. And she doesn't want to involve *us* in this fight. She only wants us to be happy, and so she says in her prayer addressed to God:

> *In your bright dream the coming ages all will live and share.*
> *It shall be so! I wish it so! I am a daughter of Yours.*
> *My Father, You are present everywhere.*[18]

"And she will get her wish. Her philosophy is extraordinarily potent. And the coming ages will indeed live in the Divine dream, in splendid gardens of Paradise.

"And she will not distract anyone with memories of herself. People will not build monuments to her nor reminisce about her when it is clear to everyone where true humanity lies. People will simply drink in the Divine nature, they won't be thinking about her. But flowers will bloom in various gardens, including one splendid flower named *Anastasia*.

"I am old, but I am willing to serve as her foot-soldier even today. You say, Vladimir, that philosophy is just a bunch of words. But these words, spoken somewhere in the far-off taiga, have been enthusiastically taken in by my heart, and here you have first-hand evidence of concrete material actions: it is not mankind that is perishing in the flames, but predictions of the doom of humanity. That is why the doomsayers are all stirred up and have set their forces in array. Anastasia has stirred up people who have built their philosophy on such a scenario and manipulated mankind for their own purposes with the threat of the 'inevitable' end of the world."

"Hasn't anyone before Anastasia come out against the notion of the end of the world?"

---

[18]Quoted from Book 4, Chapter 11: "Three prayers".

"There have been a few timid — but ultimately insignificant — attempts, but they've hardly received any attention. Nobody, but nobody, has spoken out as she has. Nobody's words have been accepted so readily and joyfully as hers, in any human heart. And not a single philosophical concept has ever taken hold of people this way. But hers has taken hold. It is burning up the murk of age-old dogma.

"How she does it — well, that's not for us to grasp at the moment. There is an extraordinary rhythm in her words, and a consummate logic, possibly something else. Possibly... No, undoubtedly! 'The Creator,' she says, 'has shone forth with some kind of new energy! An energy that tells us anew about something we see around us every day...'[19]

"Undoubtedly a new energy has made its appearance in the Universe, and more and more people in our time are starting to possess it day by day. The fact is that decades and possibly even centuries, as a rule, are required to spread a significant philosophical concept. And here it's only taken *her* a few years... Amazing!

"You surmised, Vladimir, that her words were simply words. But her words are so strong that — you see these hands?" He raised one of his hands, looked at it and added: "Even these old hands of mine are materialising her words. And the whole prospect of the end of the world is burning up in flames. And life will go on. These hands can still help life go on. The hands of one of Anastasia's foot-soldiers."

Holding on to the furniture, Nikolai Fiodorovich made his way over to the table and picked up a pitcher of water. Bracing himself with one hand against the wall, he headed over to the window. It was a challenge, but he made it. On the windowsill stood a beautiful flower-pot, in which a green shoot, still very young, was sprouting up from the earth.

---

[19] Quoted from Book 4, Chapter 13: "To feel the deeds of all mankind".

"Look, my baby cedar's come up at last. And now my hands will water it, materialising the words that are close to my heart."

Bracing one hip against the windowsill, Nikolai Fiodorovich grasped the pitcher with both hands and said:

"The water isn't too cold for you, my dear?" After a moment's thought, he took a swallow of the water, held it in his mouth for a little while and then, resting his hands on the windowsill, let a thin stream of water spew from his mouth onto the earth beside the green shoot.

Galina was in the study during our conversation. She was always thinking up some excuse to be in his study. She would bring tea, or start dusting, all the while muttering quietly to herself, commenting on what she had heard and seen. These last actions of Nikolai Fiodorovich evoked a rather louder comment than usual:

"Now what's the point of that? Any decent person might wonder. Here he goes doin' tricks like that in 'is old age. He won't ride in his wheel-chair, he goes an' tortures his agein' legs, makin' 'em walk like that. An' somehow people ain't satisfied. Here it is nice an' warm an' comfy at home, but it ain't enough for them, jes' ain't enough!"

I remembered Galina being concerned about Nikolai Fiodorovich's health and asking me to warn him about something, only now I couldn't figure out what there was to warn him about, and I asked him:

"What have you thought up this time, Nikolai Fiodorovich?"

He was a bit emotional, but said distinctly:

"I have a big favour to request of you, Vladimir. I ask you only to respect an old man's wishes."

"Go ahead. I'll be happy to oblige if I can."

"I've heard say you're planning to get people together who want to start building an ecological settlement. You want to see about having a hectare of land granted each family to set up a kin's domain."

"Yes, I do. The Anastasia Foundation has already submitted a proposal to several regional administrations about this. But there's been no decision on land grants as yet. They've offered a few small allotments, just for a handful of families each, but unless we have a minimum of a hundred and fifty families, we shan't be able to afford the cost of any infrastructure."

"They'll grant the land, Vladimir. Most definitely they'll grant it."

"That would be good. But what about this favour you want?"

"When they start handing out land for kin's domains, and they'll definitely be doing this all over Russia, I would ask you, Vladimir, not to forget about an old man. Please, don't forget to count me in. I too want to establish my own piece of the Motherland before I die."

Nikolai Fiodorovich started getting more and more excited, his words came quickly and with passion:

"To establish it for myself. For my children and grandchildren. See, I'm growing my own baby cedar in this pot, so I can plant the seedling in a piece of my Motherland with my own hands. I shan't be a burden to anyone. I'll set everything up on my own hectare of land, I'll put in a garden and plant a living fence. I'll be able to help my neighbours. I have some savings, and I keep receiving honoraria for various articles. My sons — whatever else you say about them, they never refuse any financial help. I'll build myself a little house there and I can help finance construction for my neighbours."

"Now that'll be a fine sight to see!" Galina was muttering even louder than before. "People don't stop to think of it — how you can plant a garden when your legs don't move. And here he is plannin' on helpin' his neighbours. Oh, if decent

folk could only hear that! What would decent folk think?
Here his sons have built 'im a house like this — he should jest
live and be happy, and thank his sons and God for it. But people jes' can't sit still. They've gotta keep thinkin' up things like
that right into their old age. What might decent folk think
about people like that?"

Nikolai Fiodorovich heard what Galina said, but didn't pay
any attention to her, or at least pretended to ignore her, and
went on:

"I realise, Vladimir, that my decision may be treated as ex-
cessive emotionalism, but that's not how it is. My decision
is the fruit of extensive reflection. I may appear to enjoy a
fine life, but that's only an appearance. I have a mansion fully
equipped — practically a palace... I've got a housekeeper to
take care of it... My sons have done pretty well for themselves... But you know, before learning about Anastasia I was
as good as dead.

"Yes, Vladimir, dead. Look, I've been living here for over
four years now. I spend most of my time in my study. I'm
useful to no one, and there's literally nothing I can have an
impact on. And the same fate awaits my sons and grandchildren. It's the fate of experiencing your death while you're still
alive.

"They call Man dead, Vladimir, when he stops breathing,
but that's not the case. Man dies the moment he stops being
useful to others and is no longer in charge of anything.

"The neighbours' houses around here aren't quite so grand,
but I don't have any friends among them. And my sons have
asked me not to announce my name even to the neighbours.
There are a lot of jealous types about, wondering whose house
this is — a house that's practically a palace. Once they find
out, they'll splash my name all over the media, enquiring how
I managed to finance this set-up. They'll never believe it was
my own hard-earned money. The way I sit here, I may as well

be in prison, or even dead. I just sit here in my study, never go upstairs — there's no reason for me to. Certainly I have a lot of philosophical publications to my name, but after finding out about Anastasia...

"I'll tell you right off, Vladimir — and please don't take what I say as a fantasy of old age — I'll prove to you what I'm about to say is true. You realise, Vladimir — right now, right this very moment, God's judgement is coming to pass."

"Judgement? But where and how? Why doesn't anybody know about this?"

"You realise, Vladimir, for so long we've imagined this judgement to be the coming of some kind of terrible Being from on high, with its terrible entourage. And this Supreme Being is supposed to tell each of us where we've been right and wrong. Then this Supreme Being is supposed to mete out punishment in due measure, sending whoever's being judged to either heaven or hell. How primitively we've pictured God's judgement!

"But God isn't some primitive creature. He can't judge that way. He has given Man eternal freedom, and any kind of judgement is a violation of one's person, it's a deprivation of freedom."

"Then what did you mean when you said something about God's judgement coming to pass right this very moment?"

"And I'll say it again: God's judgement is coming to pass right this very moment. Everyone is given the opportunity to judge himself.

"I realise now what Anastasia's done. Her philosophy, power and logic are speeding up the processes. Just think, Vladimir, many people will believe her, and bring the idea of these splendid Divine communities to fruition. Once they believe, they'll find themselves in a garden of Paradise. Others won't believe and will remain where they are now. Everything in the world is relative.

"At the moment we are not in a position to compare our life with any other, and so we think our lifestyle is tolerable. But when it is put side by side with another kind of life, when the unbelievers finally believe, they will see themselves in hell. Some people count themselves happy simply because they don't know how unhappy they really are. God's judgement is coming to pass right before our eyes, but it is strange to our way of thinking.

"This isn't just *my* discovery. I know of this psychologist in Novosibirsk who's undertaken a study of how various population groups react to Anastasia's sayings — she's said practically the same thing. I don't know her personally — I've only read her conclusions in print, and they're similar to my own.

"People in various cities and towns are feeling and realising the majesty of what's been taking place. Professor Yeriomkin, whose poems have been published in the people's collection,[20] is another one who's described the Anastasia phenomenon in magnificent verse. I'd like to remind you, Vladimir, of these lines he dedicated to Anastasia:

In you I have beheld a Man quite clearly,
Possibly from the end of another era,
Where, midst goddesses, my own grandchildren too
Will be an embodiment of you.

"I memorised these beautiful lines. I want my grandchildren, too, to live among the goddesses, and therefore I want to provide this opportunity for them, I want to begin establishing for them a piece of our splendid Motherland. Just to

[20]*people's collection* — a reference to the 544-page volume of readers' poetry, art and letters published in Russian under the title: *V luche Anastasii zvuchit dusha Rossii. Narodnaya kniga* (The soul of Russia sings in Anastasia's ray. A people's book).

buy a piece of property, even more than one hectare in size, is no problem for me, but it is important to me who my neighbours are. And so I want to set up my property in a circle of people who share my way of thinking. To set it up for my grandchildren. One of them will most certainly want to live there. And my sons will want to come and rest there in their father's garden from the bustle of daily life. At the moment they come and see me only on rare occasions. But they *will* come to the garden I shall set up. I shall ask that I be buried in this garden. My sons will come...

"I'm talking about my grandchildren, my sons, but above all I need to create something inherent in the essence of Man, otherwise... You see, Vladimir... All at once I have acquired the desire to live and be active. I can do it. I shall become a foot-soldier and enlist in Anastasia's cause."

"You can live jest as well right where you are. Why don't you jes' live out a good quiet life right here?" Galina enquired.

This time Nikolai Fiodorovich took it upon himself to reply. He turned to her and said:

"I can understand your concern, Galina Nikiforovna. You're afraid of losing your job and a roof over your head. Please don't worry — I'll help you build a little house nearby, you'll have your own little house and your own plot of land. You'll get married — you'll find the one meant just for you."

All at once Galina straightened up to her full height, threw her white rag down on the side-table — the rag she had been pretending to dust with all during our conversation — and placed her hands on her solidly built thighs. She looked as though she wanted to say something, but couldn't, as though her emotional state had cut short her breath. Then, mustering up her strength, she managed to pronounce quietly:

"Well mebbe I don't like the idea of bein' close to a neighbour like you... Anyways, I can build my own house, jest as soon as I get my land. When I was a kid I helped my father build a log cabin. And I've saved up a pretty penny. Besides, workin' around here ain't so pleasant. Who is there to clean up for day after day upstairs? Nobody ever goes upstairs, yet here I am, cleanin' up like a damn fool after nobody. I don't want to live in a neighbourhood if the neighbours don't have their head screwed on right!"

Galina did a sharp about-turn and quickly headed off to her room. But presently the door of her room opened, and Galina re-appeared in the doorway, holding in her hands two little pots with green shoots just like those in Nikolai Fiodorovich's fancy pot. She walked over to the window and put her little pots down next to his on the windowsill. Then she returned to her room and brought out a large basket filled with a whole lot of little cloth bundles. She placed the basket at Nikolai Fiodorovich's feet and said:

"Them's seeds. Real ones, 'cause I gathered them meself all summer long and right through the fall. They're from real medicinal herbs. The ones they sow in the fields to sell at pharmacies, they ain't got the power of these here. Jes' scatter 'em with your own hand on your land — they'll multiply your health and strength — when they're growin', and when you make a herbal tea with 'em and drink it in the wintertime. 'Sides, that baby cedar of yours, it's gonna be lonely — well, there's some friends an' a brother for it."

Galina pointed to the windowsill, where the three pots with little shoots were now standing, and then walked slowly to the front door, calling over her shoulder:

"Good-bye, philosophers! Maybe you already know the philosophy of death. But as for the philosophy of life, you've still got a lot to learn."

As far as anyone could tell, Galina had been deeply offended by something, and she was walking away for good. Nikolai Fiodorovich took a step to follow her, but stumbled. He then tried to catch himself by reaching out for the back of a chair, but the chair fell over. Nikolai Fiodorovich started to sway back and forth, flinging his arms out to the side. I jumped up to offer him a hand, but I was too late. Galina, who by this time had already reached the door of the room, turned at the noise of the falling chair and saw Nikolai Fiodorovich swaying back and forth.

Quick as a wink she was at his side. With her strong arms she managed to grasp the old man whose legs had already given way beneath him, and stood there holding him to her bosomy breast. Wriggling one hand free, she picked up Nikolai Fiodorovich by the legs and carried him like a child to his wheel-chair. She sat him down in it, then took hold of a plaid rug and began covering his legs, gently chastising him:

"Some soldier of Anastasia's you are! You ain't no soldier, jest a green recruit!"

Nikolai Fiodorovich put his hand in Galina's. Fixing his gaze on this drooping woman now sitting at his feet, he said, switching to the familiar form of address[21] for the first time:

"Forgive me, Galya. I thought you were laughing at my aspirations, and here you are..."

"I'm the one laughing? You think I'm crazy?" Galina blurted out. "Every night I sit and think only soul thoughts. 'Bout how I'm gonna plant herbs — real medicinal herbs, 'bout how I'm gonna use 'em to feed this bright-eyed falcon[22] here, to help

[21]*familiar form of address* — similar to using *tu* instead of *vous* in French (see footnote 1 in Book 1, Chapter 2: "Encounter"). The informal form of address is reciprocated by Galina in addressing Nikolai Fiodorovich.

[22]*bright-eyed falcon* (Russian: *sokol yasny*) — a reference to a Russian folk-tale about a falcon named Finist. When Marya, the daughter of a rich merchant, is brought a falcon feather by her father at her request, she waves it in the air, whereupon a falcon appears and later turns into a handsome young man. The two fall in love. Injured, however, thanks to the trickery of Marya's wicked elder sisters, Finist flies off and eventually recovers, but Marya must set out on a long quest to find him, and rescue him from a palace where a sly princess has her own designs upon him. The tale ends, of course, with Marya and Finist marrying and living happily ever after.

'im get his strength back. I'll make some real soup from fresh cabbage that don't smell of chemicals. I'll give him some real cow's milk to drink, not that fancy pasteurised stuff. An' jest as soon as this ol' bright-eyed falcon gets hisself straightened out, mebbe I'll even bear him a child. Me, I wasn't laughin', not one little bit. I's just *sayin'* that to see how firm a decision he'd made, to see whether he might change it in midstream."

"It is firm, Galina, I'm not going to change it."

"Well, if that's how it is, then don't chase *me* out to the neighbourhood. Don't hand me over to some other suitor."

"I wasn't chasing you out, Galya. It's just that I had no idea you wanted to be with me some place other than this well-appointed mansion. I am happy to accede to your wishes, Galya. I am immeasurably grateful to you. I simply had no idea..."

"What's there here to have no idea about? What woman would turn away from such a determined soldier as yourself? Oh, I've read about Anastasia, how I've read about her!... Took me a long time, it did — had to read syllable by syllable, but still I got it right off. All us gals today need to become like Anastasia. So I've decided to be a little bit of Anastasia to you. All us gals need to become a little bit like Anastasia. She ain't got too many soldiers jes' yet, only a bunch of green recruits, still wet behind the ears. Us gals are gonna make 'em strong, an' make 'em well!"

"Thanks, Galya. That means, you, Galina Nikiforovna,[23] have read the books — and pondered them during your evenings?"

"For certain. I've read all the books on Anastasia an' thought about them during my evenings. Only please don't address me as a stranger any more. I've been meaning to ask you for a good long time now. Just call me Galya."

---

[23] *Galya / Galina Nikiforovna* — Nikolai Fiodorovich's alternation of familiar and formal forms betrays his temporary uncertainty as to how he should address this woman.

"Okay, Galya. I was intrigued by what you said when you were offended — really intrigued. You said we already know the philosophy of death. But as for the philosophy of life, we've still got a lot to learn. What a concise formulation of two contrary philosophical tendencies. A succinct definition indeed: the philosophy of death and the philosophy of life. Simply amazing! Anastasia is the philosophy of life. Yes! Of course, of course! Just amazing!"

Stroking Galina's hand excitedly and tenderly, Nikolai Fiodorovich exclaimed:

"You're a philosopher, Galina — I had no idea!"

Then he said, turning to me:

"There's absolutely no doubt there is so much more we need to figure out, both from the philosophical point of view and through the help of esoteric definitions. I am trying to evaluate Anastasia as Man — a Man such as we must all become. But there are certain unexplainable abilities she has which prevent us from fully appreciating her as a Man like us.

"Vladimir, I remember your describing an episode in which she saved people at a distance from being tortured. She saved them, but she herself, if you recall, lost consciousness, went white all over and even the grass turned white around her.[24] What kind of device was operating here, to make both her and the grass turn white? I've never heard of anything like that before, even though I've tried asking esoterics about it. It's not something either philosophers or physicists — or esoterics — know anything about."

"Whaddya mean, they don't know 'bout it?" Galina burst into the conversation, still sitting on the floor at Nikolai Fiodorovich's feet. "An' what's there to think about, when we need to scratch their eyes out?"

[24]This incident is described in Book 1, Chapter 28: "Strong people".

"Whose eyes, Galya? Do you have your own opinion on this phenomenon?" Nikolai Fiodorovich enquired in surprise.

Galina was only too ready and willing to provide an answer: "It's as plain as the nose on your face! Jest as soon as a Man is attacked by somethin' rotten, by some sort of wretched news or threats, or cussed in anger, he goes all white. Turns pale, you know. He turns pale when he don't return that anger, but burns it up within 'imself — meaning he gets all shook up, and burns up the anger within 'imself, and this makes 'im go all white. You see lots of examples like that in life. Anastasia too can take this rot and burn it up within herself, and the ground goes all white, tryin' to help her, and as for me, well, I think you gotta scratch its eyes out — the eyes of any kind of rot, I mean."

"Wow! Really! Many people turn pale," Nikolai Fiodorovich exclaimed in surprise, fixing his gaze on Galina, and then added: "but Man truly turns pale when he does not reciprocate someone's insult, but tries to keep a stiff upper lip and hold it within. He burns it up within himself, as it turns out. Why, that's true! How simple it all turns out to be! Anastasia burns up within herself the energy of aggression aimed at her. If such energy were reciprocated, it would fail to dissipate in space but would go off and find some other target.

"Anastasia doesn't want anyone to be a target. Just think of all the filth that will be aimed at her! So much has been building up over centuries, and is being produced even now by the adherents of the philosophy of death. Who is strong enough to withstand such an onslaught? Tell me, who? Stay the course, Anastasia! Stay the course, noble warrior!"

"And stay the course she will," Galina chimed in. "We're gonna help her now. I've started givin' away your books down at the market, and the gals that have been readin' 'em now stand around on a street-corner in klatches. I gave 'em some cedar seeds too. They planted 'em. An' I told 'em about the

healin' herbs too. The gals say: 'We've gotta do somethin'!'
Sure, we ain't gonna beat up our husbands, like one of 'em
there on the corner suggested. But we better think about
who we're gonna have a child with."

"What are you talking about, Galina?" Nikolai Fiodorovich
asked in surprise. "Don't tell me you have your own activist
group already?"

"No way! What kind of 'activist group' might that be? We
jes' stand around on the street a bit an' chit-chat about life."

"And where did the idea of beating up on men come from?
What arguments motivated that?"

"Whaddya mean, what arguments? How come our men
don't come through for us? They want us to give 'em a child,
so we give 'em a child, but then there ain't no nest for our
young 'uns. An' if you can't make a nest, why ask for a child?
What gal's gonna be happy with her man when her kid jes'
wanders around aimlessly right before her very eyes?

"Teacher's come to us twice already. Teacher says some sort
of psych factor stops 'em from gettin' ahold of themselves —
it's all because of some kinda loan they're waitin' for from
some foundation overseas. It's a 'syndrome', she says. Lack
of self-confidence. An' this psych syndrome digs up all sorts
of reasons to avoid buildin' a nest.

"An' the teacher went an' told the gals that these loans have
to be paid back in a certain number of years. Maybe twenty,
maybe thirty, I don't remember. I only know, they need to
pay back a little bit more than they've been given. So it's like
a man today ends up sellin' his own kids?"

"Why would you make a comparison like that, Galina?"

"Whaddya mean, *why?* The men we've got today, they've
been foolin' around, lookin' to borrow money. An' who will
have to pay it back? For certain that'll be their kids — the kids
that are still jes' young 'uns. Yeah, an' the kids who ain't even
born yet. And our kids'll have to pay back even more than

their dads have borrowed! When the gals began graspin' this picture of the future, they started goin' crazy over concern for their kids — they felt like bashin' their men's snouts in. As for me, I thought we better not wait for help from anywhere, it's time we ourselves started helpin' these poor men of ours.

"I once tried a taste of that overseas sausage, an' my heart broke out in tears, an' I really wanted to send a piece of our Ukrainian bacon to whoever made that sausage, along with some of our own home-made sausage. Oh my dear God! People in those countries have no idea how sausage should taste!

"There's no point in takin' loans from people like that — that's bad money, it's no good at all, it'll bring us nothin' but harm. As for beatin' up, I told you only one gal proposed whippin' all them men, the other gals didn't go along. What's the point? So you can knock the last bit of sense out of 'em? Even so, the gals tell each other how miserable their men have made their lives. And I boast a bit, I say *my* man's come to 'is senses. He's already started makin' a nest."

"*Your* man? Who is he?"

"Whaddya mean, who is he? I've been tellin' 'em about *you*. How you've gone an' planted a baby cedar, how you sent me to buy you a draftin' board with a large ruler — the one on the table over there," Galina indicated, pointing to the drafting table next to Nikolai Fiodorovich's desk. "I told 'em how you asked me what trees are best to plant around the hectare, and made drawin's on sheets of paper at your desk, and sketched out a loverly community, where good people can live. You didn't have enough room on your sheets of paper, so you asked me to bring you bigger sheets, an' the board an' the ruler too.

"I told the gals 'bout that, an' we all went together to choose the drafting board. We chose the biggest and best we could find, an' it sure cost a lot. The gals said to me: 'Don't be stingy, Galina.' They helped me, an' I could see the envy in their eyes. The bitches were jealous that my child would be born in a marvellous garden, in his own native ground, with good people all around. An' I ain't mad at them for bein' jealous — after all, everybody wants to be happy.

"They pooled their money together an' bought me a camera so's I could take a picture of your sketch. So I took the camera, an' they showed me what button to press and where I should look through to take a snap. Only I never got the courage to ask your permission so I never pressed the button."

"You did the right thing, Galina, not taking a photo of my design without permission. When I've finished, then perhaps I shall publish it as one proposal for the new settlement."

"That's gonna take you a long time, and the gals right now can't wait to see this loverly, beautiful future, at least to sneak a glimpse. You've managed to come up with a lovely drawin' on one of them large sheets."

"What makes you think I shan't soon complete it? Everything's almost all ready to be published — I have the plans, and colour drawings too."

"That's what I said — you already have a beautiful picture. For certain it shouldn't be published for people to use, but you could still show it to the gals — the ones I meet with — an' I'll just say it's not quite right yet."

Nikolai Fiodorovich quickly wheeled himself over to the drafting table. I followed. There on the table lay plans, done in coloured pencil, of several domains of the new settlement. The drawings showed little houses, and gardens, and a living fence made out of various kinds of trees, and ponds too... The overall impression was a fine, beautiful arrangement of everything.

"Where did you notice a mistake or an inaccuracy?" enquired Nikolai Fiodorovich of Galina, who had by now joined us at the drafting table.

"You didn't put any Sun in the picture. An' once you get the Sun in, you have to put in shadows too. An' if you're goin' to put in the shadows, you'll see that you can't plant any tall trees along the eastern fence — they'll give too much shade on the plant beds. The trees should be planted on the other side."

"Really? Maybe you're right... I wish you'd told me earlier. But this is only a draft so far... Anyway, Galina, did you say you're going to have a child?"

"Well, it's like this. You keep on doin' your exercises for now. But once you stand on your own native ground, you'll crawl out of your catacombs. An' I'll feed you with what grows in your native soil, an' give you a healin' tea to drink. An' spring'll come, you'll see, an' everythin' on that native ground's gonna come alive, and bloom. An' you'll feel your own strength again. *That's* when I'm gonna have my child."

Once again Galina sat down on the carpet at Nikolai Fio-dorovich's feet and put her hands on one of his arms resting on the side of his wheel-chair. Even though she wasn't exactly a spring chicken, Galina had a strong, powerful and attractive body — she could even be called tender and beautiful. Their conversation became more and more friendly in tone, as though they were immersing themselves in some kind of philosophy of life, while I stood around slightly stupefied, feeling like a third leg. So I managed to get a word in edgewise:

"Excuse me, Nikolai Fiodorovich. It's time for me to be going. I don't want to be late for the plane."

"I'll have some pies ready for you in a flash," said Galina, getting up. "An' some preserves for your trip — I'll get you back to Moscow in a jiff."

Nikolai Fiodorovich slowly got up from his chair. Bracing himself with one hand against the table, he extended the other to me in a gesture of farewell. His handshake was firm, it no longer felt like that of an old man.

"Give my greetings to Anastasia, Vladimir. And please let her know that the philosophy of life will definitely triumph here. Our thanks to her!"

"I'll tell her."

CHAPTER NINETEEN

Who controls coincidences?

Right from the very first appearance of the Anastasia book there have been quite a number of articles written by various scholars on the 'Anastasia phenomenon'. Many of them included references to me. Whenever I heard or read unflattering remarks about myself, even if they temporarily upset me, it wasn't for long — maybe a day or two, a week at the most. My insides would get stirred up a bit, but then it was history. But this time...

At a meeting in Moscow one of my readers handed me an audiocassette. He said it was a recording of a talk given at an academic conference by the leader of a scholarly research group which was studying the 'Anastasia phenomenon'.

I listened to the cassette a few days later. What I heard was beyond belief. Its message (once it had sunk in) not only knocked me off the rails, it seemed it was going to do me in for good. Really do me in — especially in my own self-esteem. Before listening to it, I was planning to head off again to the taiga to see Anastasia and my son, but after hearing it I put my plans on hold. Here's what I heard (slightly abbreviated):

My respected colleagues, I should like to present you with some of the conclusions and arguments worked out by a research group I head on the basis of over three years' investigating the phenomenon we shall call *Anastasia*.

In my report I shall use the name *Anastasia* not just for the sake of convenience, but because the subject of our investigation has presented itself under that name. This does not rule out the possibility of giving it a more specific and characteristic definition in the future. It is difficult to do that at the moment, since I am persuaded that we are dealing with 'something' that surpasses the boundaries of traditional academic disciplines and possibly modern science on the whole.

We began by defining three research questions: (a) the truthfulness of the events described by the author Vladimir Megre in his books, (b) Megre's books themselves and (c) public reaction to Megre's books.

By the end of the first six months it was clear that the truthfulness or untruthfulness of the events described in the book was an irrelevant question. The wild emotional reaction of most readers who have had contact with Megre's books has nothing to do with whether the events described are real or not. Public reaction is determined by a different set of factors entirely. However, the time and resources and intellectual potential we spent pursuing this question led to what is, in my opinion, a rather interesting conclusion — namely, that the tendency of individuals, including sociologists and academic circles in general, to cast doubt on Anastasia's existence is in fact a contributing factor to the very phenomenon we are studying.

It is this very hoopla surrounding the question *Does she or doesn't she exist?* that has enabled the phenomenon to penetrate unhindered into all levels of society today. The denial of the existence of Anastasia has actually served to neutralise any opposition to her designs. If she doesn't exist, after all, then it follows that there is no object to study, nothing to oppose. On the other hand, the public reaction to Anastasia's sayings attests to the vital necessity of research to determine her significance and intellectual capabilities.

As to the truthfulness of the events set forth in the books, we can state the following:

In describing these events, the author not only presents himself under his own name, but does not shield anyone else connected with these events. He makes no effort to change the real names of people or places, or to cover up embarrassing facts about himself.

For example, the episode described in the first book — where Megre, in the presence of the captain, flirts with the local country girls visiting the ship during a pleasure cruise[1] — has been fully documented as fact. Crew members have also confirmed the presence that evening of a quiet and taciturn young woman with a kerchief tied around her head. Megre showed this woman around the ship, then spent some time alone with her in his cabin. From the book we learn that this was the first appearance of the Siberian recluse Anastasia on Megre's lead ship, the one that served as his headquarters. It was the entrepreneur's first encounter with the Siberian recluse, and their first conversation together.

The chronology of many of the events described in the book has been confirmed by documents and eyewitness accounts. Not only that, but other situations even more extraordinary have come to light which the author for one reason or another did not describe in his books. A notable case in point is Megre's stay in a Novosibirsk city hospital, where medical records indicate the progress of his illness, medical test results, the prolongation of his illness, *and* his remarkable recovery.

We have determined that his recovery immediately followed the doctors' application of cedar oil which was left at the hospital by an unidentified woman!

I shan't deny that, carried away as we were in our pursuit of the truth of the events described in the book and with access to criminological facilities, for example, we were in a position to prove or disprove a great deal. We were halted in this pursuit, however, by the public's wild and extraordinary reaction to Megre's books, or, more specifically, to Anastasia's sayings therein recorded. The details of Megre's intimate relations

[1] See Book 1, Chapter 24: "A strange girl".

were not a drawing card for most people — they were excited instead by Anastasia's monologues.

Even our initial investigations of this reaction — and especially its latest manifestations — clearly indicated that 'something' calling itself Anastasia is exercising an unmistakable influence on today's society.

Her sphere of influence continues to increase in size even today. And we need to pay greater attention to even the most improbable arguments — try to discern them and follow them up. In all probability, the phenomenon known as Anastasia possesses powers and abilities which our mind and consciousness are not in a position to fully make sense of.

In Megre's very first book, in the chapter entitled "Across the dark forces' window of time", the phenomenon predicts not only the appearance of the book, but also how and by what means she will capture people's minds and consciousness. In her monologue Anastasia affirms that she has collected from various ages the best combinations of sounds to be found in the Universe, and that they will have a positive influence on people. She affirms that this action is quite simple:

"As you can see, it is simply a matter of translating the combinations of signs from the depth of eternity and infinity of the Universe — exact in sense, meaning and purpose."[2]

Our group as a whole reached a unanimous conclusion: this particular saying is an invention. This conclusion was based on the following logical and (as we believed) irrefutable argument: Even if certain unusual combinations do exist in the book, then they cannot exercise any influence over the reader, since there is no instrument to reproduce them. The book cannot utter sounds, and consequently cannot convey to our hearing the 'sounds of the Universe' said to have been collected by Anastasia.

Later, however, Anastasia did give the following answer:

[2]Quoted from Book 1, Chapter 27: "Across the dark forces' window of time".

"You are right, a book does not make sounds. But it can serve as a score, like a musical score. The reader will involuntarily utter within himself any sounds he reads. Thus the hidden combinations in the text will resonate in the reader's soul in their pristine form, with no distortion. They are bearers of Truth and healing. And they will fill the soul with inspiration. No artificial instrument is capable of reproducing what resonates in the soul."[3]

In his third book, *The Space of Love,* Megre sets forth Anastasia's dialogue with the scholars. But for some unknown reason he abbreviates it. Or, if we assume that the phenomenon itself participated in the book's appearance, then it is possible that it deliberately omitted the continuation of Anastasia's response to the scholars. What for? Possibly to leave the unbelievers in their state of inaction? The fact remains that proofs of Anastasia's incredible declaration do exist.

Here is the continuation of Anastasia's dialogue with the scholars. To her adversary's statement that the blending within Man of certain sounds not part of human speech has never been anywhere established as fact,[4] Anastasia replied as follows:

"It has been established. And I can give you an example."

"But it must be an example everybody can relate to."

"Fine. Ludwig van Beethoven."

"What about him?"

"His *Ode to Joy.* That was the name he gave to his Ninth Symphony. It was written for a symphony orchestra and mass choirs."

"Okay, but how can that prove your statement about the evocation of sounds within the reader's mind? Sounds that nobody's ever heard?"

---

[3]Quoted from Book 3, Chapter 4: "Chords of the Universe".

[4]See Book 3, Chapter 4: "Chords of the Universe".

"Sounds evoked within the mind of the reader of a book are heard by the reader alone."

"There, you see? By the reader alone. That means there's no proof. And your example with Beethoven's symphony isn't convincing."

"At the time he wrote his Ninth Symphony, *Ode to Joy*, Ludwig van Beethoven was deaf," responded Anastasia.

This fact is attested by Beethoven's biographers. Not only that, but the deaf composer himself conducted the first performance of his symphony.

In the light of this particular historical fact, Anastasia's next saying no longer raised any doubts:

"Every letter or combination of letters from any text, being uttered, can be transformed into sound. A page of text can be compared to a page from a musical score. It is simply a question of who is able to set forth the note-letters and how. Will they comprise a great symphony or simply audible chaos? And another question: does everyone have an instrument of sufficiently high quality within themselves to reproduce the full orchestration?"

The researchers in our group subsequently came to the following conclusion:

Anastasia's sayings in respect to the derivatives of explosion,[5] transportation by creating a vacuum, purification of the air, agrotechnical methods, the significance of cedar oil in the treatment of many diseases, the energy of Man-produced thought, as well as many other phenomena, deserve the most meticulous study by scientific circles.

[5]*derivatives of explosion* — see Anastasia's declaration to Vladimir in Book 1, Chapter 16: "Flying saucers? Nothing extraordinary": "The functioning of all your machines, every single one of them, is based on the energy of explosion."

In arriving at this conclusion, our group does not make any claim to be the first to discover it. Scholars in Novosibirsk came to it at the same time or even a little ahead of us, as may be seen in a presentation by the leader of the Novosibirsk Scholars' Circle, Sergei Speransky.[6] In a published paper entitled "It's more useful to believe", the Novosibirsk psychologist Nina Zhutikova came up with the following conclusion on the basis of her sociological research:

"One's relationship to Anastasia is not dependent on the presence or absence of academic degrees, but very much depends on a Man's character, his scale of values, on his conscious and subconscious mindset — i.e., on a Man's personality and all its elements; it depends on whether this Man wants Anastasia to be real or not; it depends on how open a Man's consciousness is, on the degree that it is ready to accept amazing phenomena that go beyond the bounds of commonality. What is revealed to us and how — this depends on the characteristics of our time and corresponds to the level of our own self-awareness."

Possibly the Novosibirsk researches could have gone even farther than ours, but the Siberian branch of the Russian Academy of Sciences declined to finance them. Today our group, having received a commission — and consequently prearranged funding, — is already in a position to state with confidence and the support of evidence the following fact:

Our civilisation has witnessed a phenomenon never before subject to scientific measurement nor, consequently, to scientific definition. Our research must attract not only representatives of modern scientific disciplines — especially physicists and psychologists — but esoterics too. The processes taking place in our society today under

---

[6] *Sergei Vladimirovich Speransky* — see footnote 1 in Book 3, Chapter 19: "What to agree with, what to believe?".

the influence of the Anastasia phenomenon are evident and ac-
tual, and we cannot — in fact, we do not even have the right
to — leave them unstudied.

Some of the events described in Megre's books indeed look
like fiction at first glance, and we have endeavoured to treat
them with scepticism. Nevertheless, the subsequent events
that happened to the author but are not described in the
books are even more incredible. But the incredible has happened. And we find ourselves obliged to draw conclusions
which are difficult even for *us* to believe.

One of these conclusions is that Vladimir Megre does not
exist, and that there's no point in studying his biography for
an explanation of what has happened.

What appears at first glance to be a rather far-fetched
conclusion removes and explains a whole host of improb-
abilities — namely: how did it happen that an ordinary Siberian entrepreneur suddenly became capable of writing a
book — a series of books, now, which has become one of the
most popular in Russia? The speculations put forth in the
press, upon closer inspection, turn out to be unfounded:

*A bankrupt entrepreneur decides to settle his affairs by becoming
a writer.* But we have a lot of bankrupt entrepreneurs. Yet not
one of them has ever become a famous writer.

He managed to think up a sensational story-line. But the story-
line has nothing to do with it. Our esoteric press does nothing but publish sensational stories about unusual phenomena
week after week — superhealers, flying saucers and aliens —
yet the public hardly bats an eyelid. And these stories are prepared by professional writers and journalists.

Megre's books have a powerful publicity engine working for them.
Just the opposite: many publications are now trying to promote themselves on the back of Megre's books. We have established beyond a doubt that Megre's first three books were

published without even any exposure in bookstores — not by a publishing firm with a large distribution network but by Moscow Printshop Number Eleven which doesn't deal in the book trade at all. And yet here people have been standing in queue for Megre's books, and wholesalers have been paying advances up front to carry them, even before they're published.

In the minds of many book dealers, the popularity of Megre's books flies in the face of all book business norms, and goes against experts' predictions concerning consumer demand.

So what is the result? Did Vladimir Megre miraculously become a genius out of the blue? Nothing miraculous about it. I repeat: Vladimir Megre — the entrepreneur who was well-known in Siberia — simply does not exist today. Evidence in support of this argument may be found through a careful reading of Anastasia's sayings back in the first book. Let's recall her words addressed to Vladimir:

"You will write this book, guided only by feelings and your heart. You will not be able to do otherwise, since you have not mastered the technique of writing, but through your feelings you can do *anything*. These feelings are already within you. Both mine and yours."[7]

Note carefully Anastasia's last words cited here: *These feelings are already within you. Both mine and yours.* This means that Vladimir Megre's own sense-perception of the world has been supplemented with that of Anastasia's. We shall not examine how and by what means this supplementing was effected. We shall accept it as a fact which engenders the following logical conclusion: if to one defined magnitude another is added, then the aggregate of the two magnitudes engenders a third independent magnitude.

Hence the present Megre's date of birth cannot be determined by the date registered on his official birth certificate.

[7]Quoted from Book 1, Chapter 27: "Across the dark forces' window of time".

There is more justification in considering his birthdate to be in 1994 — i.e., the moment he met Anastasia.

Even though the outward appearance of the new individual corresponds to the former Megre, the radical difference between the two is all too apparent. This includes, for example, both his literary talent and his ability to hold an audience's attention for an extended period of time — five hours or more — as has been twice attested by witnesses to his appearance at a readers' conference in the city of Gelendzhik in the Krasnodar region.[8] This fact is reflected in accounts in a number of national magazines.

Many researchers and journalists have got caught up in comparisons and investigations of events connected with the activities of Vladimir Megre, just on the basis of the descriptions in the books. They have been attempting to prove, either subconsciously or openly and aggressively that *this cannot be so!*

My dear colleagues, I am inclined to believe, and not without some justification, that the following communications will convince you that such a feeling is nothing more than a defence mechanism found in those whose mind or consciousness is incapable of making sense of what is really going on.

Vladimir Megre himself — or, more accurately, part of his own *self* — is even less capable than that of making sense of the events he is involved in. It is just that he has gradually become accustomed to them, and is beginning to categorise even the most incredible phenomena as normal or commonplace — which has also served to keep him from having a nervous breakdown. I think that, like many readers, he did not pay any special attention to what Anastasia said to him back at that first meeting with him in the taiga. When Megre protested: "I shan't even make an attempt to write anything," Anastasia responded: "Believe me, you shall. *They* have

[8]Described in Book 4, Chapter 34: "Anomalies at Gelendzhik".

already created a whole network of circumstances that will make you do this."[9]

This dialogue is given right in Book 1, but in Megre's subsequent books there isn't even an attempt to return to this question: who in fact are these mysterious *They*? Upon receiving specific information, the members of our group once more delved into the dialogues reproduced in the first book to select all the references to this *They* scattered over its pages. I shall cite these references in Anastasia's words:

"If it had not been for *them* — and for me too, a little — your second expedition would not have been possible."

"I want you to be purified. That is why I thought back then about your trip to holy places, about the book. *They* have accepted this, and the forces of darkness are always fighting with them, but never have the dark forces scored a major victory."

"My plan and conscious awareness were precise and realistic, and *they* accepted them."[10]

"*They* are answerable only to God."[11]

The following conclusion can be drawn from Anastasia's sayings: some indeterminate forces will set in place for Megre some kind of network of circumstances compelling him to carry out action somebody's pre-programmed for him. And if that is so, then Megre's role as an individual in his creations amounts to *nil*, or at least something very insignificant. Everything is simply being handed him on a platter through this network of supposedly coincidental circumstances. This also means that the individual of the past known as Megre has evidently been violated.

[9]These and the following passages (except as otherwise noted) are quoted from Book 1, Chapter 26: "Dreams — creating the future".

[10]Quoted from Book 1, Chapter 27: "Across the dark forces' window of time".

[11]Quoted from Book 1, Chapter 24: "A strange girl".

We decided that if we succeed in establishing certain anomalies in Megre's behaviour — or, rather, the presence of a network of circumstances or so-called coincidences, such a presence could confirm or disprove (a) the reality of what happened in the taiga, (b) the degree of participation of Megre as an individual in the events taking place in society surrounding the publication of his books, and (c) the existence of some kind of forces capable of producing coincidences influencing Man's destiny.

The episode in Megre's life which we have managed to examine in the greatest detail, right down to individual nuances, is his behaviour on Cyprus in June 1999, during the time when he was working on his fourth book, *Co-creation*. It would even be more accurate to say that he was in the process of figuring out the meaning of his dialogues with Anastasia (which he had already transcribed) about the creation of the Earth and Man. What we discovered on Cyprus can only be summed up in one short phrase: *What is it?* Let me acquaint you with certain events that took place there.

At the end of May 1999 Vladimir Megre took a Transavia[12] flight to Cyprus, but not as a member of a tourist group. There was nobody he knew on Cyprus. He did not know any of the languages spoken on the island. The Cyprus travel agency, Leptos,[13] placed this individual Russian tourist in a single room on the second floor of a small hotel. The room had a balcony overlooking a fair-sized pool, where tourists (mainly from England and Germany) would lounge around and have fun.

---

[12] *Transavia* — an international airline company, part of the Dutch-based KLM Group.

[13] *Leptos* — a large conglomerate headquartered in Paphos (Cyprus) that includes both tourist services and property development.

Megre's Russian travel agent had informed the manager of Leptos that this particular tourist was a Russian writer. But that was hardly news to a major travel firm like Leptos, accustomed to hosting world-famous celebrities. As far as they were concerned, Megre was just an ordinary tourist. Nevertheless, on the second day of his stay he was approached by the senior company manager responsible for the Russian tourist market with an offer to show him around the city, including the estates the company itself had developed. They brought along a Russian-speaking interpreter employed by the firm. I am now going to quote, my friends, from a transcript of the statement provided to us by the Leptos interpreter, Marina Pavlova,[14] during an interview:

> I accompanied Nikos, the manager of Leptos, and Megre, and interpreted during their conversation. Megre distinguished himself from most Russian tourists by his uncompromising attitude, which bordered on tactlessness. For example, we were standing on a mountain with a terrific view of the sea and the city of Paphos.[15] Nikos was giving the usual spiel:
> "Look at all this natural beauty around us. What a fantastic view!"
> I translated the sentence, but Megre responded:
> "It's a depressing view. Nice and warm... The sea... But look, the vegetation's all stunted, just an occasional bush here and there. So unnatural in a climate like this."

[14]*Pavlova* (pronounced *PAHV-la-va*) — a Russian surname (feminine form).

[15]*Paphos* — a bustling seaport on the south-west coast of the island, which before the time of Constantine served as the capital of Cyprus. An even earlier settlement by the same name (with ruins dating back to 3000 B.C.) is located some 16 km to the southeast. The Paphos District covers the whole western tip of the island and according to local legend is the birthplace of the goddess of love, Aphrodite.

Nikos began to explain:

"Earlier the island was covered with cedar forests, but when the Romans invaded, they cut down the forests to build their ships. Besides, there is very little rainfall here."

To which Megre retorted:

"The Romans were here many centuries ago. Over that time new forests could have grown up, but you have not been planting them."

Nikos tried to explain that there is very little rainfall on the island, and even drinking water must be collected in special reservoirs.

But Megre sharply responded:

"There is no water because there is no forest, and the wind carries the clouds on past the island. If there were a forest, it would slow down the movement of the lower air currents, as well as the movement of the higher-altitude clouds. It would rain more often on the island. I think the reason they don't plant a forest is that they are trying to sell all the land for development."

Having said this, Megre turned aside and became lost in thought. We didn't say a word. An oppressive pause hung over us. There was nothing anyone could say.

The next day, as we were having lunch at a café, Nikos enquired as to what he might do to make Vladimir's stay more comfortable. Megre replied in all seriousness:

"There should be more Russian spoken on the island. The restaurants should serve proper fish, instead of some kind of perch. The hotel rooms should be quieter. Besides, I'd rather have a forest around me than people who smile when they don't mean it."

Then there was the meeting between Megre and the head of the Leptos agency. How this came about I have no idea. The CEO has never met with any tourists in person, and even many of his employees have never seen his face.

I was present at the meeting as an interpreter. But even here Megre said the company should change the layout of the sites where it was constructing its new estates. Each site should be no less than a hectare in size, a place where people can plant trees and look after them, and that way the whole island will be transformed. If this doesn't happen, it won't be long before the island becomes an undesirable tourist destination, and Leptos will see a significant decline in business.

After a moment's pause, the CEO began expounding with considerable aplomb on the island's legendary tourist sites and the most famous site of all, the Baths of the goddess Aphrodite.[16] He concluded by offering Megre an opportunity to suggest anything that might make his stay more comfortable. While the CEO of Leptos might have been able to satisfy the wishes of many Western millionaires, what Megre said to him in response completely threw him for a loop — it sounded like a joke, as though Megre were making fun of him. Megre in all seriousness replied:

"I need to meet with the granddaughter of the goddess Aphrodite."

I tried translating this sentence as a joke, but nobody laughed. The shock of the remark left everybody speechless.

By and by news of this Russian tourist's eccentricities reached the ears of the hotel staff where Megre was staying, and they began to make fun of him. Nikos told me in conversation that there was something abnormal in Megre's behaviour.

---

[16]*Baths of Aphrodite* — a serene, shady grotto and pool near Polis on the Akamas Peninsula, about 50 km north of Paphos, where the goddess Aphrodite, according to legend, was wont to take her baths.

Nikos and I made regular morning visits to the hotel on administrative matters, and each time Nikos would jokingly ask the clerk on duty at the main desk whether Aphrodite's granddaughter had checked in yet. The clerk would laughingly respond that she hadn't arrived yet, but there was always a room waiting for her!

Megre evidently felt the mocking glances of the hotel staff whenever he came down to the bar from his room in the evening, or to breakfast in the morning. It seemed to bother him. As a Russian, I too felt uncomfortable about seeing my fellow-countryman being ridiculed, but there was no longer anything I could do.

On the morning of the last day of Megre's scheduled stay on Cyprus, Nikos and I went to the hotel as usual. Nikos wanted to say good-bye to Megre. Once again he greeted the desk clerk with his customary jocular enquiry, but this time the clerk's usual response was not forthcoming. The clerk, in a rather emotional frame of mind, told Nikos that Megre had not spent the night in his room and was not in the hotel at the moment. He went on to report in all seriousness, without even the hint of a smile, that the evening before, Aphrodite's granddaughter had come to the hotel in a motorcar and collected Megre along with his things.

She had told the clerk on duty in Greek that there was no need to be concerned, that Megre would not be returning to the hotel and so his room could be reassigned as needed, and that they need not bother booking Megre's return flight to Moscow. She also asked him to tell Nikos that she would bring Megre to the hotel at ten o'clock the next morning to say good-bye. The clerk repeated that Aphrodite's granddaughter had talked with the hotel staff in Greek but with Megre in Russian. Without a clue as to what was going on, Nikos and I seated ourselves in two of the comfortable armchairs in the lobby and silently waited for the appointed hour to arrive.

At ten o'clock on the dot the big glass doors of the main entrance swung open, and we saw Vladimir Megre accompanied by a beautiful young woman. I had seen her before. She was Elena Fadeyeva,[17] a Russian who lived and worked on Cyprus as a representative of a Moscow travel firm. I told you I recognised her, but not right away. This particular morning Elena Fadeyeva looked exceptionally beautiful. Wearing a long light-weight dress, she sported an attractive hairdo and had a cheery sparkle in her eyes. The slender young woman accompanying Megre immediately drew the attention of the hotel staff in the lobby. Bartenders, maids and clerks froze in their tracks, their eyes fixed on the approaching pair.

In talking with them Nikos and I learnt that Megre had decided to extend his stay on Cyprus by a month. When Megre temporarily withdrew to see about something at the bar counter, Nikos remarked on Megre's fussiness, saying he was making demands which neither he nor the Leptos CEO could possibly fulfil. Whereupon Elena responded: "I have fulfilled all his wishes. I think I shall be able to fulfil any others, too, that may arise."

Nikos continued to question Elena as to how she was able to do the impossible in just twelve hours. How could she make Megre's favourite Siberian freshwater fish appear on Cyprus, or cause cedars to grow on the island in just twelve hours, or make all the Cypriots suddenly be able to understand Megre speaking Russian? Where could she have found a place for him to stay where nobody could interrupt the solitude he so desired?

Elena replied that everything Megre needed just simply appeared as though by coincidence. She put Megre up

---

[17]*Fadeyeva* (pron. *fa-D'AY-a-va*) — a Russian surname (feminine form). The first name *Elena* is pronounced *ye-L'EN-a*.

at her own villa, which just happened to be vacated at the right moment. The villa was located not far from Paphos at the edge of the village of Peyia,[18] where nobody could possibly disturb him. She provided him with transportation by hiring a motorscooter especially for him. It turned out that her Russian friend Alla who was also working on Cyprus just happened to have some Siberian freshwater fish on hand. And cedars grow on a hillside not far from her villa. Besides, Megre had brought with him two little Siberian cedars, and she put them in pots right at the villa's entrance. The language barrier would present no further problem for Megre, since there are telephones in all the places he wants to visit, including shops and cafés, and she always has her own mobile phone with her and that way she can interpret for Megre whenever necessary — i.e., whenever he has something he wants to say to someone.

As Elena and Vladimir were already making their way toward the door under the fixed stares of everyone present, I reminded Nikos that he had forgotten to ask how Elena would be able to fulfil Megre's request concerning the granddaughter of the goddess Aphrodite. Nikos looked at me in surprise and replied:

"If that Russian girl isn't the living embodiment of Aphrodite or her granddaughter, then for certain the spirit of Aphrodite is present in her at this moment."

My dear colleagues, after hearing Marina Pavlova describe these events of Vladimir Megre's life during his stay on Cyprus, the question naturally arose: whence came this chain

---

[18]*Peyia* — one of the four municipalities in the Paphos District of Cyprus, close to the tourist resort of Coral Bay — a picturesque village of whitewashed houses hugging the steep Mediterranean coastline. A quiet haven in comparison to the bustle of Paphos, Peyia also features the remains of two Christian basilicas on its outskirts.

of coincidences which fulfilled all Megre's stated demands in the blink of an eye? Was it really just coincidence, or was someone — like Anastasia, or the mysterious *They* she talks about — somehow shaping these coincidences? Note how immediately after the people around Megre at his hotel began to wonder what was going on, a situation turned up to remove him from the curious observers' field of vision — he retired to Elena Fadeyeva's villa.

As far as the people back at the hotel were concerned, this ended the unusual chain of coincidences. But we wondered whether it had really come to an end, and so we reconstructed subsequent events in as much detail as we could, thanks to the help of what we were told both by Fadeyeva personally and by people who know her. And what did we learn? It turned out that not only did the series of extraordinary coincidences not stop, but they became even more mysterious. I'll cite just a few excerpts from our records.

So — here we have Vladimir Megre staying all by himself in Fadeyeva's small but cozy villa. He was most probably in the process of deciphering Anastasia's sayings about God, about the creation of the Earth and Man, and Man's destiny. He had just finished working on this part of the book. But he didn't understand everything himself yet. And true to his nature, before publishing the book, he wanted to find somewhere (or in some thing) at least a modicum of confirmation of Anastasia's unusual sayings. From time to time he would ring up Elena and ask her to come and see him, to take him somewhere in the car. And each time the young woman would drop whatever she was doing at the moment to fulfil Megre's request, even if it meant reneging on a commitment to greet people arriving from Russia. Twice she had to reassign her duties to one of her colleagues, losing part of her income in the process.

So, where did Megre go? We established that, apart from the usual tourist spots, he paid a visit to two churches, which none of the other tourists went to, along with a monastery not on the tourist circuit and a vacant castle in the Troodos mountains.[19] On several occasions he climbed the ridge not far from Fadeyeva's villa. He would take solitary walks among the cedars growing on the ridge while Elena waited for him down by the road.

We were also able to establish that all Megre's visits to the churches and monasteries were spontaneous — i.e., not planned in advance. More specifically, they formed part of the same chain of coincidences. Here is what Elena Fadeyeva told us about Vladimir Megre's night-time visit to one of the churches:

I went to see Vladimir at around nine p.m., directly after he called. He told me he simply wanted to go for a ride around the city. He got into my car and we headed for Paphos. Vladimir seemed absorbed in his own thoughts and scarcely offered a word of conversation. We drove for about an hour or so. As we passed by all the cafés along the embankment, I suggested we stop for something to eat, but he declined. When I asked where he would like to go, he said he felt like visiting some vacant church.

I turned the car around and headed full speed (I'm not sure why I was in such a hurry) to a little village. I knew there was a church there that hardly anybody visits. We drove right up to the entrance and got out of the car. Not a soul around. The night-time silence was broken only by the roar of the waves. We walked up to the main door. It was dark, but just below the door-handle I could feel a large

---

[19]*Troodos mountains* — the largest mountain range on Cyprus, spread across the western end of the island and capped by Mount Olympus (1,952 metres high). The range is home to a number of monasteries and Byzantine churches; nine of the latter are listed as UNESCO World Heritage sites.

key sticking out. I turned it and opened the door. Vladimir went in, and for a long time stood in the middle of the floor below the dome. I stayed by the entrance. Then Vladimir went through the archway the priests come out of and must have lit a candle or something. Anyway, something there began emitting a bright glow, and the whole church interior brightened a bit. I stood for a while longer and then went out to the car. Some time later Vladimir appeared and we left.

Here is the second incident Fadeyeva told us about:

I wanted to show Vladimir a village way out in the country, so he could see how the local people lived. There were so many turns going off the mountain road we were travelling and somehow (probably by mistake) I took a wrong turn, since instead of ending up at the village, we presently found ourselves in front of the gates to a little monastery. Vladimir wanted to go in at once and asked me to go with him to interpret with the monks, but I said I couldn't. I was wearing a rather short skirt and had no head covering, and that's not permitted in a monastery. So I stayed outside.

I watched as Vladimir walked across the courtyard. All at once he noticed a young monk in front of him. They stopped to face each other and began conversing. Then they came over to me. I could hear the young monk speaking with Vladimir in Russian, and presently Vladimir was approached by an older grey-haired man — the Father Superior — and the two of them sat and talked for the longest time on one of the benches in the courtyard. The monks and I were standing a little distance away, and we couldn't hear what they were talking about.

Then the Father Superior and the monks gathered to see us off. But on his way out the gate Vladimir stopped, and everybody else stopped, too. Vladimir turned and headed across the courtyard to the church. Nobody followed him. We were still waiting at the gate when he came out of the vacant monastery church.

And so the chain of coincidences continued. Just to remind you, Vladimir Megre was working on deciphering what Anastasia had said about God. Was it just a coincidence that at the very moment when he wanted to visit a vacant church, there at his side, coincidentally, was Elena Fadeyeva, who just happened to know about such a church? Was it just a coincidence that a key was sticking out of the door of this vacant church? Was it just a coincidence that Elena made a wrong turn and ended up taking Megre to a monastery hardly anybody goes to? Was it just a coincidence that he encountered a Russian-speaking monk? We are dealing here with a chain of events, real-life situations, practically a series of seeming coincidences, sequentially arranged, all leading to some kind of predetermined end.

Now that we know about such coincidences, can we still talk about the philosophical conclusions Megre comes to in his books as being purely random or coincidental? Perhaps it was in some of these churches where Megre (as we now know) stood alone under the dome, that God's words became consolidated in his mind, afterward to appear in his fourth book, *Co-creation?*

Time and again we have tried to trace in detail the sequence of the coincidences surrounding Megre. Among a great many others there was one that interested us in particular — namely, how Megre just 'happened' to meet Elena Fadeyeva. We shan't speculate as to whether this young woman was actually imbued with the spirit of the goddess Aphrodite. We'll leave such speculation to the esoterics. But let's consider just why this girl dropped what she was doing at the very first call and rushed to Megre's side, made him borsch and carted him around Cyprus in her motorcar? Why did she change so radically, even in her appearance, after meeting Megre? Why did her eyes suddenly begin to sparkle upon meeting Megre (as claimed by people who know her)?

Perhaps it was just from meeting a celebrity? But as a representative of a travel agency affiliated with Mosèstrada,[20] Elena gets to meet much bigger celebrities than Vladimir Megre.

Money, perhaps? But Megre couldn't have had much money — otherwise he wouldn't have booked into a three-star hotel to begin with.

There is only one conclusion to be drawn from all this: *Elena Fadeyeva fell in love with Megre.* This is confirmed by something she said to one of her acquaintances. When the acquaintance asked her:

"Well, Lena, you haven't fallen in love with this Megre chap?"

Elena responded:

"I don't know — it's a rather strange feeling... But, if he asked me..."

And so we have yet another incredible coincidence before us: here's a twenty-three-year-old woman — slender, warm and outreaching, independent and pragmatic, not lacking in a fair share of attention on the part of the many men around her, suddenly falling in love at first sight with a forty-nine-year-old man. I think you will agree that such coincidences are extremely rare indeed.

We've tried analysing in still greater detail — even moment by moment — the first meeting between Vladimir Megre and Elena Fadeyeva. We spoke with the employees at the Maria Café who witnessed it first-hand. From what we were told

[20] *Mosèstrada* (in full: *Moskovskaya èstrada* — lit. 'Moscow Musical Stage') — a large Moscow-based entertainment enterprise. In Soviet times it was in virtual control of Moscow's pop-music entertainment sector.

by Elena herself and by the people who know her, we have reconstructed the day of that meeting. As a result we have been presented with yet another coincidence — but this time what a coincidence! It could explain Elena falling in love with Megre a few minutes before she met him for the first time! A kind of coincidence that can have an effect on both Man's consciousness and his subconscious simultaneously.

Picture to yourself Elena Fadeyeva driving her car on the way to the Maria Café in a resort town. One of the waiters had rung her up and asked her to come to the café if at all possible, as there was a Russian man sitting at one of the tables and getting very nervous. The café's sign featured its name in Russian, as well as names of Russian dishes, all of which promised a Russian-speaking waiter — but, as it turned out, this person did not happen to be on the premises at the time.

Elena at first declines, but then a little break happens to come up in her work. So she gets into her car and heads for the café where some kind of Russian man is waiting. Along the way she takes care to powder her sun-tanned nose, picks an audiocassette at random and slips it into the player in her car. The car's speaker system fills the interior with the words and melody of a Russian popular song.[21]

I am now going to remind you of the words of that song, and you, my dear colleagues, can draw your own conclusion. Here are the words Elena heard resonating from her car speakers just moments before her encounter with Megre in the café:

I myself am a rather young god,
My experience? Perhaps there's not much to say.

---

[21]*Russian popular song* — these are the words to the song "Don't let him go" (*Ne daj emu uyti*) by the well-known St. Petersburg singer-songwriter Maxim Leonidov (1962–). The third stanza shown here is actually the song's refrain and is repeated at the end.

But still, my dear girl, I just know I could
Help you, and shine sunlight upon your dark day.

No moments to spare — you're in a crunch.
You've a break coming up, hardly any time at all.
So you powder your nose, and head off to lunch
To meet him *at a café — at a table by the wall.*

Somewhere far away trains are flying through the wood,
And 'planes are off course — just why, we don't know.
If he *should take off, he'll be gone for good,*
So the answer is simple — just don't let him go.

Why are you suddenly quiet, my dear?
Just look into his eyes and do not be shy.
I've been closing this circle for many a long year...
The one who has brought him to meet you is I.

And she, or someone acting through her, did *not* let him go. And she, or someone acting through her, fulfilled all his wishes, providing more and more information to confirm his philosophical conclusions. He returned to Russia and submitted the manuscript of his fourth book, *Co-creation,* to the publishers.

Thus Vladimir Megre's life really turns out to be like the life of Ivan the Fool[22] in the Russian folk tales, the only difference being that the events that happened to Megre are absolutely real.

---

[22]Ivan the Fool (Russian: *Ivan-durak*) — the main character of many Russian folk tales: in their more recent versions, Ivan is a simpleton who invariably wins considerable favours through no effort of his own. In the older versions of the same tales he is portrayed as a wizard able to control natural forces. The term *durak* is based on the ancient root *ra* signifying the Sun, but which over the centuries has been perverted to take the opposite meaning of 'fool'.

Faced with the reality of such phenomena, we cannot deny the existence of some kind of forces capable of purposefully influencing the destiny of an individual Man. This begs a number of questions: are these forces capable of influencing the destiny of all mankind? How active have these forces been in the past? Have they become more active in our century? What kind of forces are they? The events we have witnessed suggest the need to pay more careful attention to Anastasia's sayings.

My dear colleagues, the majority of our research group is inclined toward the following conclusion: *the Siberian recluse Anastasia, while leaving the governments of the different countries in position for the time being, is actually taking personal control of the whole human civilisation.* Note the distinction — not 'seizing power', but 'taking personal control'.

Upon coming into contact with Megre's books, the majority of readers experience a desire to change their way of life. His readers already number more than a million, and their numbers are steadily growing. Once they have reached a critical mass, they will be capable of influencing the decisions of the world's governments. But even today in these governments there are to be found enthusiastic supporters of the conclusions reached in the books.

In other words our society as a whole will become just as controllable as Vladimir Megre himself. I hope there is no longer any doubt in your minds, my dear colleagues, that this Megre is an entity completely under the control of some kind of forces. I believe it is incumbent upon us, through our joint efforts, to figure out just who this Siberian recluse Anastasia is. Where is she, anyway? What are her capabilities? What kind of forces are helping her? Where are they trying to lead our society? These are the questions that modern science must answer.

CHAPTER TWENTY

Breakdown

I listened to the unknown speaker's report on the audiocassette a second time. It made absolutely no difference to me who this person was. The conclusions he reached had such an effect on me that not only did I not have any desire to continue writing, but my life itself began to seem meaningless.

Anastasia's concept of Man's significance was actually starting to grow on me — about how each Man is the beloved child of God, that he can be happy right here on the Earth. One only needs to gain a proper understanding of one's purpose. I believed Anastasia and believed in the possibility of changing our life today for the better by transforming our lifestyle and building new communities.

But all my faith collapsed after hearing what was on the cassette. The thing was that the facts cited by the speaker regarding the coincidences that had happened to me — which, in his words, formed a pattern — were spot on. Everything he said actually happened, and more. There were other things I knew about besides — things they hadn't been able to establish.

It all did happen the way he said, and that means that I've simply been a puppet in somebody's hands. It doesn't really matter whose — Anastasia's, or some kind of forces or energy — that's not important. What matters is that I, as a Man, am nothing — I don't exist. What exists is my flesh, which is so easily controllable by someone through arranged 'coincidences'. It would be all right if I were the only one who could be controlled. But there may very well be other people under someone's control from above, or maybe someone on high is controlling all humanity, and all humanity is just a plaything for an invisible someone, someone imperceptible to our human minds.

I didn't want to be anyone's plaything, but the facts cited in the report argue incontestably that I'm nothing, I'm being controlled — and this is clearly manifest. I can see it backed up by facts I know all too well myself.

Whatever happened to me on Cyprus wasn't bad — quite the contrary, it was good! But that's not the point! If an invisible someone has arranged a chain of wonderful coincidences, then tomorrow it may come into somebody else's head to arrange another, not so wonderful chain of coincidences. This is relegating Man to the status of a plaything. And what about mankind as a whole? How could I not have realised before that some kind of forces are playing with all mankind, like children with toy soldiers?!

When Anastasia talked about God and co-creation back in the taiga, it was as though some kind of curtain had parted as a result of her words.

For the first time in my life I pictured God not as some kind of amorphous, incomprehensible being or an old man sitting on a cloud — but as a Person, capable of feeling, experiencing concern, dreaming and creating. My impressions from what Anastasia told me were more vivid and more comprehensible than anything I had ever heard or read before on the subject. And that wasn't all! When she spoke, my heart felt good and not so lonely. Which means: *He exists!* He can be understood and He acts. He is wise and good. And this is confirmed by His creation all around us — the cedars, the grass, the birds and the beasts. There in the taiga, in Anastasia's glade, they are all somehow kindly, not aggressive.

We're so accustomed to taking His creations for granted — we hardly pay any attention to them, but we try to appreciate

Him through something else instead. Through some kind
of secret doctrines. And we wander the planet looking for
hidden sacred places, looking for teachers, looking for teachings. Now if that isn't truly absurd! A complete absence of
logic! If we talk about God as our good Father, then how can
we assume that He will conceal something good from His
children? There is nothing He has hid or concealed from
people — His children. On the contrary, He always endeav-
ours to be right beside them. What power is it that opposes
Him? What power has so mesmerised us that we through our
lifestyle have placed the whole planet — this splendid Earth
which He has given us — under the threat of global disaster?
What power is toying with us?

Every evening we see the glow emanating from the windows of our many-storeyed apartment blocks. Behind every
window people's lives are unfolding. And how many of them,
how many of these lives are really happy in this world? We
talk about morality, love and culture, we all try to present an
appearance of decency. But in reality? But in reality, even
by the most conservative estimate, every other man, though
outwardly decent, is fooling around with women on the sly —
unbeknownst to his family, which still presents a decent appearance.

What is one of the most lucrative sources of our national
government's income? Vodka and cigarettes. The State still
maintains a tight hold on its monopoly here. But who does
the drinking? The winos lolling about our fences and apart-
ment-block lobbies? Well, of course, they drink, too. But
they don't have the financial clout to sustain the hundreds of
our flourishing factories spewing out rivers of spirits. No, it is
the outwardly decent and respectable folk who constitute the
bulk of the consumer market here.

We maintain huge police forces, not to mention personal
security services and private investigative teams. What for?

To round up all the winos and philanderers? Nonsense! With the forces at its disposal Internal Affairs[1] could go and collect them all in a single day. It's not them they're after, but outwardly decent folk.

Just think — here we have a whole army of "special services", and believe me, they do not sit around with time on their hands. Which means there must be a whole army out there working against them! Which means that here a constant warfare is being waged, and we are all sitting right on the border between the warring parties, financing both sides. We attempt to improve the technical capabilties of one of the belligerents — namely, our organs of law enforcement, yet at the same time the other side is also upgrading its own technical prowess, and financing it from our pockets, too. After all, money has only one source — human labour. And the war is being waged on an ever more technically advanced level.

And it's not just a one-year or two-year conflict. It's all been going on for millennia. And nobody knows where it all started or who can put an end to it. And we're right in the midst of the action, and not one of us is neutral — we're all participants. We're all participants in a never-ending war. Some of us are directly involved in the fighting, some finance it willingly or unwillingly, others manufacture the arms for it. But we all proceed under the mask of decency, talking about science, technology and culture.

As an intensively developing, intelligent civilisation, we make ourselves look smart and utter the slogans of scientific and technical progress. Well, you smart civilisation, what about all the stinking water coming out of your taps? How did you ever think up, especially with that smart appearance

[1] *Internal Affairs* — the Russian ministry in charge of national security, including the "special services" branch which deals with any perceived threats against the State.

of yours, this business of forcing people to *buy* their drinking water in bottles? Water which gets more expensive day by day?

We are unwilling to take off our masks of decency. But why? Why do we inevitably complicate our lives this way year after year? Why are we moving so inexorably toward some stinking cesspool? And we *are* moving toward it, even if we don't want to admit it to ourselves. Why is nobody stopping this movement?

We have religious denominations aplenty. But not one of them can stop this movement. What if they can't stop it completely, but just slow it down? If so, then that would be a form of sadism, only prolonging the period of torture. We go on thinking of ourselves as being a smart and decent civilisation, but why, in this smart civilisation, are women losing interest in having children? Statistics are already showing us that our nation is dying out. What kind of forces are making a complete nutcase out of Man?

For a whole week I was depressed and apathetic about everything. I simply lay in bed the whole time and hardly had a bite to eat. Toward the end of the week I was suddenly overcome by fits of anger — even rage. I felt like doing at least something to counteract these forces. It didn't matter what kind of forces they were — dark or bright. Just to spite anything that was trying to control us... To show them that Man is capable of coming out from under their control.

But what could I do to spite them? If they — or Anastasia along with them — wanted me to write, then I would refuse to write. If meat was off limits, then I'd eat meat, and smoke and drink too. Judging by their actions, they wouldn't like that. Well just let them try and stop me!

I drank every day for a whole month. The stupor relieved me temporarily, but then came the sobriety of the following morning, and all the bad thoughts flared up in me once more. Why had I been writing? I was trying to be honest, while all along I was simply becoming a toy of amusement in good-ness-knows-whose hands.

At night-time, after getting thoroughly drunk, I would make my way along the wall to my bed. And how I wanted to cry out — cry out so that my grandchildren and great-grand-children could hear! So that they could hear and understand! Understand!!! I'd been writing because I couldn't take the lie of the mask any longer! I was trying to find a way out!

CHAPTER TWENTY-ONE

Attempt at deconditioning

Occasionally in the morning I would feel a desire to break free of my drunken stupor. And then I would head for the bathroom to shave off my several days' growth of stubble. Remembering Anastasia, I tried not to think of bad things, but of the good she had managed to accomplish. I tried to convince myself that she was doing something good, but life kept on tossing more and more destructive arguments my way.

And so on one particular morning, as I was routinely trying to come out of my stupor, a good friend of mine rang the doorbell of the flat I was renting. It was still early, and I hadn't finished shaving yet. I still had shaving cream on my face as I opened the door.

Vladislav was in some kind of emotional state. After saying hello he announced:

"We gotta talk. Go finish your shaving while I start."

I did so, and he began telling me that he had finally read the book. He was excited about it, and could agree with Anastasia on a lot of things. He thought her logic was ironclad, but there was something else that he was even more concerned about.

"So, because of this meeting with her, you broke up with your family and lost your business... You don't feel like carrying on with business any more, eh?"

"That's right."

"And you tried to organise a commonwealth of entrepreneurs with purer thoughts, like she suggested?... So, are you writing your next book?"

"I'm not writing at the moment. There's something I'm trying to work out."

"That's just it — you've got to work it out. Tell me, just what have you accomplished after five years' acquaintance with this recluse — what do you have to show for yourself?"

"What d'you mean, what? I'll give you an example. Here in the Caucasus you can already see the first glimpses of a change in people's attitude toward the dolmens.[1] You can imagine how many scientific papers had been written about them earlier, but they never made anyone excited about them. People just plundered them and carted things away.

"But what Anastasia said had an immediate effect. In just the *Druzhba* sanatorium[2] alone they had no sooner read my book than the employees got together and went to the nearby dolmen to lay flowers. And in other places too, people are changing their attitude toward their forebears, they're thinking about —"

"Stop! I completely agree with you. Her words *are* having an effect. And the fact you mentioned just now not only confirms this, but something else too. She's turned you into a zombie — you're not really yourself any more."

"What makes you think that?"

"It's simple. You're an entrepreneur who even back in the early days of *perestroika* was able to build up major commercial enterprises from scratch — even without any starting capital. You were the President of the Association of Siberian Entrepreneurs. And all of a sudden you stopped doing business, and now you're doing your own washing and cooking — hey, you're a completely different person!"

---

[1] *dolmens* — ancient megalithic tombs; see footnote 1 in Book 1, Chapter 30: "Author's message to readers".

[2] *Druzhba sanatorium* — the name *Druzhba* means 'Friendship'. This incident is described in Book 2, Chapter 33: "Your sacred sites, O Russia!".

"I've heard these arguments before, Vladislav. But what Anastasia said got me excited. She has a beautiful dream: 'Carry people across the dark forces' window of time'. She believes in it. She asked me to write a book. I promised I would. She's alone, after all, waiting and dreaming. She probably somehow associates the book with that dream of hers. You said yourself that what Anastasia says in the book can have a tremendous influence on people."

"That's just it — another illustration confirming her interference in things. Judge for yourself. An unknown author, an entrepreneur, all at once writes a book. And about what? About the history of mankind. The Cosmos. The Mind of the Universe. The raising of children. She's beginning to have an effect on people in their day-to-day real life, she's influencing their behaviour."

"But it is a positive influence."

"Possibly. But that's not the point. Haven't you ever thought what made you suddenly able to write a book?"

"Anastasia taught me."

"How did she do that?"

"She took a stick and outlined the letters of the alphabet on the ground.[3] And she said:

"'Here are the letters which you know. All your books, both good and bad, are made up of these letters. It all depends on how and in what sequence these 33 letters are arranged. There are two ways of arranging them.'"

"So that's it? All you have to do is arrange those 33 little letters in a specific sequence? You just arrange them, and then whole groups of people will head into the mountains to lay flowers at the dolmens? That's preposterous! Too much of

---

[3]Described in Book 1, Chapter 15: "Attentiveness to Man". There are 33 letters in the modern Russian version of the Cyrillic alphabet (see footnote 2 in that chapter).

a stretch for an ordinary mind. It has to be the presence of some power we can't fathom yet. Whether she's zombified you, or reprogrammed you, or hypnotised you, I don't know. But she's done something."

"Whenever I called her a witch or used words like *mysticism, fiction* or *incredible,* Anastasia herself would get very upset and start claiming that she was just an ordinary human being, an ordinary woman — it was just that she had a lot of information in her. But it's only a lot by our standards. She says that back in the days of our pristine origins anybody might have abilities like that. But later... And, after all... She bore me a son."

"And where's your son now?"

"In the taiga, with Anastasia. She says that it would be more difficult to raise a child in the conditions of our technocratic world and make him into a real Man. Because the little one can't comprehend artificial objects. They only lead him away from the truth. We can't show them to him until he's already assimilated this truth."

"And why aren't you in the taiga? Why aren't you with her, helping raise your son?"

"A normal Man can't live in those conditions. She's not even willing to light a fire. She's got her own way of eating. Besides, she says... that I shouldn't communicate with my child for the time being."

"So, she's not able to take it here in our normal living conditions. You can't live there. Then what's next? Ever thought about it? Here you are alone, without a family. What if you fall ill?"

"I'm not ill at the moment. I haven't had anything for well over a year now. She cured me."

"Does that mean you're never going to fall ill again?"

"I'll probably get ill at some point. Anastasia said that all one's little aches and pains will try to come back again, since there's a lot of the dark and harmful stuff in Man, and of course in me, just like in everyone else. You see, I still smoke. I've started drinking again. But that's not the main thing. She says people don't have too many bright aspirations and thoughts. And they're the principal defence against one's aches and pains."

"In other words, it's unlikely you're going to have the same kind of future us normal people have. Anyway, I've come to you with a business proposal. I'll dezombify you, dehypnotise you, and then, once you're back to a normal state, you'll be able to help me. You can help me get my firm back on track. After all, you've had experience, and you were a talented entrepreneur. You've got connections."

"I shan't be able to help you, Vladislav. I'm not thinking about business at the moment. My thoughts are occupied elsewhere."

"It's quite clear you're not thinking at the moment. You've got to pull out of this first, get back to a normal state of mind. Just believe me. I'm asking you as a friend. You'll thank me for it by and by. After all, once you get back to a normal state, you'll be able to evaluate what's happened for yourself."

"How can you define what is the most normal?"

"It's very simple. You live a normal, natural human life at least for a few days. You have some fun with girls. And then you take a look back at the past few years of your life. If you like what you see, you can go on working and living as you are now. But if, from a normal state of mind, you see that you were hypnotised, you can get back into business again. It'll be good for you, and you can help me."

"I can't go out with prostitutes."

"Who says anything about prostitutes? We'll take up with those who want it themselves. We'll have a party and enjoy some music and other people's company. We can have it at a restaurant or out in nature. I'll get everything organised, all you have to do is go along."

"I need to work out things within myself first. I need to think."

"Come on, enough with the thinking! Look at my proposal as an experiment. I'm asking you as a friend — just give me a week, and then you can think."

"Okay — let's go for it..."

The following day we went by car to a neighbouring town, where some nice girls (as Vladislav put it) lived — girls he said he'd known for a long time.

CHAPTER TWENTY-TWO

Our reality

The woman who opened the door for us was attractive and alluring. Thirty-something, feminine and shy, pleasingly plump. No, she wasn't fat. Her body preserved and even accentuated all the man-enticing curves — which were hardly obscured under the sheer gown she was wearing. Her childlike voice and welcoming smile at once made us feel at home.

"Hello there, travellers! Come on in, come on in. Svetlana told me about you. She said you'd like to see the town, and then go to a restaurant and have a great time!"

"That's just the ticket! We want to do all that, and of course with you, my lovelies," Vladislav blurted out. "And how's my dear Svetlanka — still out partying, eh what?"

"Now when would we have time to go out partying, and who with? Seems the rest of us have to wait a lifetime..."

"Why wait? See here, I've brought a pal along. He's from Siberia, and he's one-hundred-per-cent entrepreneur!"

She straightened her tight-woven braid and raised her timidly lowered eyelids to reveal a sparkling pair of eyes that looked as though they could be full of passion and desire. She offered me her hand.

"I'm Lena.[1] Hello!"

"Vladimir," I introduced myself, shaking her cream-puff hand.

While Lena got some coffee ready for us in the kitchen, Vladislav and I washed up and then took a look around her

[1]*Lena* — like *Lenka,* an informal form of *Elena.*

two-room apartment. I really liked her flat. The layout was pretty much like any other flat, but hers looked especially clean and cozy, well cared for. Everything was arranged in place, no clutter. The bedroom featured turquoise flowered wallpaper and matching curtains with frills. This colour, also picked up by the rug and the counterpane on what looked like close to a king-size bed — together with the tidiness of the room — had a soothing effect. The bed especially was truly inviting.

We sat ourselves down in comfortable armchairs in the other room, which was a little bigger. Vladislav switched on a rather expensive-looking tape player, and asked me:

"Well, what do you think of her?"

"Jolly good. I'm just wondering, how come she's not married?"

"How come millions of other women aren't married? Haven't you heard? There's not enough of us — men, that, is — to go round!"

"Sure I've heard it, but she's not just everyone. She's really nice, and she's managed to make a cozy nest for herself here."

"Yes, she has. She gets a decent salary. She's a top hairdresser. Not just a hairdresser — a stylist to boot. She goes in for competitions, and as for her clientèle — let's just say she has more than one wealthy lady waiting to pay good money for her services."

"D'you think she sleeps around?"

"No way. Svetka[2] said that back when they were in school together, Lenka took up with this dim-wit from the next class up. Then after they finished school she dumped him, but he kept after her for the longest time, and picked a fight with anyone who tried to go out with her. There were quite a few lads he and his pals left in a pretty bad way — right before her eyes. He even got hauled up on delinquency charges. She felt sorry for him and never testified against him. She always claimed she wasn't fully conscious and couldn't remember. So

[2] *Svetka* — like *Svetlanka,* an informal form of *Svetlana.*

they were only able to get him once — for beating up on some lad who had a high-placed daddy."

"Then maybe she's frigid — maybe she doesn't need a man?"

"Frigid? I should say not! Didn't you notice the way she looked at you with those eyes of hers? Like a boa-constrictor sizing up a rabbit! She was ready to jump into bed with you right off!"

"Don't exaggerate."

"Now don't you go with your faultfinding, just enjoy yourself. *Carpe diem!* We agreed we were going to relax and have a good time, so let's just relax and have a good time."

Lena brought in cups of coffee on a beautiful tray. She had changed into a body-hugging sun-dress and had put on a bit of makeup. Looking even better than before, she suggested:

"If you're hungry, I can throw something together."

"No," replied Vladislav. "We'll eat at a restaurant. Ring up one of the better places here and reserve a table for four."

While we sat and drank our coffee, Lena telephoned a restaurant and reserved a table with some manager she apparently knew quite well, as she used the familiar form of address,[3] instructing him:

"Try to find a good spot — I'm coming with some very nice gentlemen."

That evening, Lena took us on a ride in her car to see the sights of the city and its environs, ending up at the restaurant.

An obliging doorman in a richly adorned uniform opened the door for us with a gallant sweep of his hand. The Maitre D' escorted us to a table on the far side of the dining room. It was indeed a nice spot, on a slightly raised floor, with a good view of the whole restaurant and the stage. The dining room with its beautiful plaster mouldings on the walls and ceilings, indicating a rather expensive establishment, was already

---

[3] *familiar form of address* — similar to *tu* instead of *vous* in French.

almost filled to capacity. Probably only the wealthy could afford to enjoy a meal here. We decided we would hold nothing back — we ordered the most expensive hors d'œuvres, some good wine and a bottle of vodka for me.

The orchestra struck up a dance tune — some kind of tango. Vladislav immediately suggested we all take to the dance floor, and we started off. Lena's womanly body swayed cozily and comfortably in my arms. Already a wee bit tipsy, I was even more intoxicated by the fragrance of her perfume, not to mention those sparkling eyes of hers. Her lowered eyelids lifted from time to time to reveal a tender gaze, burning, as it seemed, in anticipation of forthcoming passion. And then they lowered once more, as though embarrassed all of a sudden.

By the time we got back to our table, all my sense of being a seeker on the straight and narrow vanished out the window. I felt good and light-headed, and I was grateful to Vladislav and Lena and everything in general. So, it *was* possible to live a good life, as long as one didn't dig into it too deep, but simply enjoyed its benefits.

I poured everyone a glass of wine, vodka for myself. I was just about to propose a toast when Vladislav interrupted.

After dancing with his Svetlana he looked very nervous for some reason. He immediately lit a cigarette, carelessly dropping the ashes into his salad. Without waiting for anyone else he took a large gulp of wine and didn't say a word, only fidgeted in his chair. I was on the point of picking up my glass and proposing my toast when he started muttering:

"Wait, something's come up... Something serious. Let's step out for a bit. We gotta talk." And without waiting for my reply he rose sharply from his seat. "You birds stay here and swap a bit of gossip. We'll be right back."

We went out into the spacious restaurant lobby. Vladislav beckoned me over into a far corner by the fountain and in a sour, muffled voice spat out:

"She's a bitch! You were right... A damned bitch!"

"Who's a bitch? If you've had a falling out with Svetka, then don't spoil the evening for others."

"Not Svetka... Lenka's set us up, or rather set *you* up, though I'm in for it, too. I'm gonna stick with you."

"D'you mind telling me just how she could set me up, or set us up? Who or what for?"

"Svetka told me while we were dancing. I'd been telling her all about you, and she felt sorry for you... As soon as she saw you... And while we were dancing she told me the whole story."

"What story?"

"Lenka's a bitch. Some kind of sick masochist. A pervert. You can see how men fall for her, she flirts with them, and then she takes them to this restaurant. She invariably gets a table reserved through her friend there, and that lackey right off contacts this mafia bloke."

"What mafia bloke?"

"That dim-wit over there, the one she got to know in school. I was telling you how even when he was younger he and his chums would beat up on anyone taking her out. And now he's making like a kind of local gang boss, running some sort of racket. Anyway, she knows that as soon as she asks for a certain table through her pal there, he'll automatically contact this mafia bloke. And right here in the restaurant, or more often afterwards in some secluded spot he'll lie in wait with his thugs and beat Lenka's companion half to death. The whole business is supposed to take place right before her eyes. She gets a real high from it, maybe even starts to 'come'. Svetka says it's already a disease with her. She once admitted to Svetka that these scenarios can even sometimes give her an orgasm."

"And the dim-wit, what does he get out of it?"

"Who knows what he does it for! Maybe he loves her like he did before. Maybe he too gets some perverse pleasure from it. Svetka says Lena pretends she's 'out of it', and then after the scene's over he takes her home and spends the night with her. And goodness knows what they do there in her flat."

"So why doesn't he just go ahead and marry her?"

"What difference does it make to *you* why they don't get married? I tell you, it's like Lenka's sick! Like she doesn't want to let go of her youth. You get married, and all you've got is humdrum everyday life. This way she gets her high, but what high would she get in married life? She's sick, Svetka says. What's it to us? We gotta think of ourselves, how to get outta this now."

"Let's just leave the restaurant, since you say they might contact that mafia jerk."

"Too late. He's already here with his henchmen. Watching us... Svetka says the first thing he'll do is come over to our table, and very politely ask to have a dance with Lenka. If her companion says okay, they'll have a dance. Otherwise, he'll calmly walk away. But it all ends up the same — they lie in wait and then beat him half to death. If there's any valuables, his henchmen will grab them. I've already given my Rolex to Svetka. If you've got anything like that, let me give it to her too for safekeeping."

"I don't have any valuables. Tell me, how come they're not afraid of the cops?"

"Listen, I tell you they've got it all set up... He's got a lawyer... Not only that, but they can make the whole situation look like they were protecting the woman from a rapist."

"And that means Lena won't testify?"

"She'll shut up, the bitch, fake a memory lapse, like she was in shock or had a fainting spell... It's all my fault. We've landed in this pile of crap, but I think I have an idea. I've got an idea. Let's pretend to start something, pick a fight, get into a row with each other, so the police will come and take us away. Better to spend a night in the drunk tank and pay a fine than end up scarred for life!"

"No, no way. I'm not going to punish myself for their sakes. Can't we go out through a back door, then you could ring up Svetka, order a taxi to go and collect her?"

"We shan't make it — they're already sitting out there. If we leave, they'll only come after us and bring us back. We'll get it doubly hard in that case. And then they'll claim we were trying to run off without paying our bill."

"If there's no escape, then let's go all out — sky's the limit! At least play on the nerves of these bastards. It's a shame the evening's spoilt — I was having such a good time."

"How're we gonna 'go all out'? Tell me, how?"

"We'll go and get really soused, then we shan't have a care in the world. Let's pull out all the stops, while we still can. Only don't let on that you know — don't get nervous in the meantime."

"What d'you mean? I'm not afraid for myself — I'm worried about you."

"Let's go."

We returned to our table. The spacious and luxurious restaurant sparkled with the grandeur of the ladies' refined attire, and the jewels adorning them were to all appearances genuine. A lot of the still very young beautiful girls in the company of their suave escorts also sported fancy jewellery. These were the so-called 'new Russians' out for a good time.

But *they* are Russia too. Which meant that here was Russia herself out for a good time in a way she alone was capable of. With daring and pizzazz. And the pizzazz will most certainly show itself in due time, even if for now everything is done with decorous grandeur and luxury.

As soon as we sat down at our table, I filled our wine-glasses to the brim and proposed a toast:

"Here's to satisfaction! Let each of us sitting here tonight bring at least a moment's satisfaction to those around us. To satisfaction!"

Vladislav and I emptied our glasses, while the women drank half of theirs. I edged my chair right up to Lenka's, put my arms around her right away, rested my hand on her half-exposed cleavage and whispered in her ear.

"You're beautiful and cute, Lena. You'd make a terrific wife and mother!"

Initially feigning embarrassment at my embrace and my hand upon her breast, she made an attempt to withdraw, but not a serious attempt. On the contrary, she began inclining her head toward me. Thus the game was afoot — playing by their (or her) rules. And I played along as best I could, without really thinking about why I was doing it, as though rushing headlong, ever closer to a sad result for someone's (or some dark forces') sport. And the result came.

From a table beside the stage rose a stout-looking fellow with a neck like a bull's. He stood there for some time, staring at us. Directly the music began he buttoned his jacket and confidently strode over to our party's table.

But half-way across the floor he suddenly stopped and began to stare just as hard in the opposite direction. And throughout the room many heads turned in the same direction. A number of couples even got up from their chairs in astonishment. I too followed their gaze, and nearly fainted from shock.

There, making her way from the main entrance to the stage was none other than Anastasia! And not a single person could be left unastonished at her sprightly — I would have to say: defiantly sprightly — step, not to mention her outfit!

And what an outfit it was! She was still wearing her old but clean cardigan, skirt and mother's kerchief, but this time they looked as though the world's most celebrated fashion designer had come up with a super-ensemble especially for her, outshining all the other women's attire that had seemed to me so refined and fashionable up 'til now.

Perhaps it seemed that way on account of the fact that her usual clothing was supplemented by some rather unusual jewellery, or perhaps it was her posture, or the manner in which she carried herself?

From Anastasia's earlobes hung (as though clipped on) two little green twigs with fur-like needles. Her head was encircled by a garland of grasses woven into a braid, keeping in place a thick golden shock of hair. Over her forehead a little flower, burning bright as a ruby, had been woven into the band. And she was wearing makeup — there was just a tint of green shadow above her eyelids.

She had on the same skirt as before, but with a slit almost to her thigh. Around her waist was a belt made from a kerchief and tied with a knot. The incredible ensemble was topped off with an extraordinary, superfashionable purse, into which she had transformed her bundling cloth. Folding the cloth in half, she had tied two of the corners to one end of a bark-covered stick and the other two corners to the other end, and then used a little grass belt she had woven to fasten it all together into a kind of hippie-style handbag. And to top it all off she strode with a freedom and confidence that models and supermodels could only dream of.

Upon reaching the dance-floor, where a few couples were launching in to some kind of a quick-paced dance, Anastasia all at once spun gaily around several times in time with the music, whereby every limb of her supple body bent and twisted with beautiful, fluid movements. Then she arched her arms over her head and clapped her hands with a delightful laugh, and all the men in the room responded in enthusiastic applause.

As she then headed for our table, two alert waiters approached her enquiringly, and I could see her gesturing in our direction. One of them picked up an elaborately carved wooden chair and followed her. As she walked past Lenka's friend with the bull neck who had been about to head over to our table, Anastasia paused for a bit and looked him straight in the eye. It almost seemed as though she gave him a wink before heading over to us.

There I was sitting with my arm around Lena, watching the proceedings with open-mouthed astonishment. None of us were talking, only staring.

Anastasia approached our table as though nothing unusual had happened, and greeted us as though she were an expected guest:

"Hello and good evening! Hello, Vladimir! If you will allow me... You will not mind if I join you for a bit?"

"No, of course not, Anastasia — do sit down!" I began, recovering from the shock of her arrival. I rose to offer her my seat, but the obliging waiter had already put the additional chair in place. The second waiter moved my plate to one side and, setting a clean plate in front of Anastasia, offered her a menu.

"Thank you," she responded. "But I am not hungry at the moment."

Reaching into her hippie-style purse, she brought out a cluster of berries wrapped in a large leaf — huckleberries and cranberries. Putting them on a plate in the middle of the table, she invited us to help ourselves.

"How did you happen to show up here all of a sudden, Anastasia?" I asked. "Have you been taking in the restaurant scene lately?"

"I came to visit you, Vladimir. I had a feeling I would find you here, and so I decided to come. I am not imposing on you?"

"You're not imposing at all. Only what's with the fancy get-up? And the makeup?"

"At first I did not have any makeup or fancy clothes, but when I tried to enter the restaurant, the doorman would not let me in. He let others in, and bowed to them as he held the door open for them, but he told me:

"'Outta here, sister, this ain't your local greasy spoon!'"

"I stepped aside to a more shaded place, and watched to see how others managed to get in. I realised they were wearing different attire and did not walk the same way I did. I caught on to it all quite quickly. I found two twigs handy that had fallen from a nearby tree, split them with the ends of my nails and attached them to my ears as decoration. Look!" Whereupon Anastasia turned sideways to me and showed me her invention. "What do you think — did they turn out well?"

"Very well indeed."

"So I quickly made myself a purse, and a belt out of my kerchief, and some makeup from leaf and flower sap. Pity, though, I had to tear a slit in my skirt..."

"You didn't have to make such a huge tear, practically to your thigh! Just to your knees, that would have been enough."

"I wanted everything to be as perfect as possible, so they would let me in."

"And where did you get the lipstick? That's real lipstick you're wearing!"

"That I obtained here. When the man at the entrance opened the door for me, I went over to the mirror in the lobby to see how I looked. Naturally, I was curious. There were some women standing in front of the mirror, looking at me. One of them came over, all excited, and asked me where I got my outfit from. She offered to do a 'full swap' — said she would give me her ring and costume jewellery. She even offered me some 'greenbacks'.[4]

"I explained to her that it would not take her long to put together a dress like this on her own. I started by showing her the clip-on twigs. The other women looked on, and one of them kept saying 'Oh, wow! Oh wow!' Another started asking me where she could find magazine pictures and descriptions

---

[4]*'greenbacks'* — American banknotes have commonly functioned for many years as a second currency in Russia, though not always legally.

of such fashions. And the first one said that if I wanted to 'turn tricks' here, she was the Madam and wouldn't allow any pimps, since her girls are free agents and she's quite capable of smashing any protection racket."

"That must have been Anka-putanka,"[5] said Sveta. "She's one tough cookie — they're really afraid of her. If anyone crosses her, she can come up with all kinds of schemes and arrange an 'incident' where so many heads will be banged together they'll really be sorry."

"'One tough cookie'..." Anastasia echoed moodily. "But her eyes are full of sadness — I feel sorry for her. I wanted to do at least something for her. When she started to sniff me over and ask about my perfume, I gave her a little twig containing the essence of cedar oil and showed her how to apply it. She at once daubed it on herself and on her girlfriends, and in return she gave me some lipstick and a pencil to highlight the edges. I could not get it right at first, and we had a good laugh over it. Then she helped me put it on, and said anytime I needed anything, I could come to her. She offered to have me join them at their table, but I said I had only come to see my —" Anastasia paused in mid-sentence, then continued after a moment's thought: "to see you, Vladimir, and the rest of you.

"Vladimir, could we take a little walk outside? There is a breeze blowing off the sea — the air is better there. Or would you like to stay here a little while longer with your friends? I can wait until you have finished. Or I — Are you certain I am not imposing?"

"Not at all, Anastasia!" I replied. "I'm really happy you came. It's just that I was so surprised to see you at first."

---

[5] *Anka-putanka* (pron. *ANN-ka poo-TAHN-ka*) — a play on words derived from the rhyme of *Anka* (derivative of the name *Anna*) and *putanka* (hooker). Two other variants of *Anna* which will be encountered later are *An* (highly colloquial) and *Ania* (endearing).

"Indeed? So, perhaps you and I could take a stroll by the sea? Just the two of us, or all together? Which would you prefer?"

"Let's go, Anastasia. Just the two of us."

But getting out of there wasn't all that easy. Elena's friend was heading our way. He too, it seemed, took a while to recover from the unexpected arrival of Anastasia. *We should have left earlier — right off,* I thought to myself, but now it was too late. They had already set their dastardly scenario in motion. And Elena, as though getting herself mentally prepared for it, began sitting up straight, lowered her eyes and made a show of smoothing out her hair.

He came over to our table, but instead of approaching Elena, he went directly to Anastasia. With a slight bow of his head he began addressing her, taking no notice of anyone else. Elena's jaw dropped in surprise at hearing him ask Anastasia:

"Miss, allow me the pleasure of asking you for this dance."

Anastasia rose, smiled and responded:

"Thank you so kindly for the invitation. Please, have a seat in my chair. They will miss your company otherwise. As for me, I really do not care to dance at the moment. My... my gentleman friend and I have just decided we would like to go for a walk in the fresh air."

In obedience to her suggestion he sat down in her chair, not taking his eyes off her for a moment. Anastasia and I headed for the exit.

My plan was to get as far away from the restaurant as possible, go for a bit of a walk as Anastasia wanted, then grab a taxi and go back to my flat. It was around ten o'clock at night. We walked through a shady allée and then down to the rocky seashore.

We hadn't yet reached the water's edge when I heard the screech of brakes. I turned around to look. From a jeep parked at the side of the road up above, five tough-looking lads were heading in our direction. As four of them encircled us, I recognised the fifth as the dim-wit with the bull neck — he took up a position just a little distance away. But it was he who kicked off the conversation:

"Hey, pal, you'd better get back to the pub. Your lady's missing you."

With no response from me, he started up again:

"Hey, you deaf or what? We say you'd better go back to your lady. But you got this lady mixed up with another and split. We're gonna help you back — right this instant."

The oversized lad standing nearest me took a step closer, and I made a decision.

"Run, Anastasia!" I cried, and decided to let him have it first, and keep them at bay as long as I could so that Anastasia could get away. I tried to land the first blow on the chap approaching me, but he seized hold of my arm, punched me in the solar plexus, and then *wham!* — right in the face. I tumbled to the ground, right on the rocks. I would probably have landed right on my head, but Anastasia reached out her hand and cushioned my fall.

My head was spinning and I could hardly breathe. I lay there and watched the big fellow's feet — shod in steel-reinforced boots — come right up to my face. *Uh-oh, he's going to use his foot on me next!* the thought flashed through my mind. Now he came *really* close and lifted his leg...

Only right at that point Anastasia did what just about any woman would have done under the circumstances — she screamed. But what a scream! It was a regular scream only for a split second. The sound associated with it quickly vanished, and her inaudible scream rose wildly in intensity to the point of shattering one's eardrums. I could see the lads around us letting some kind of objects fall from their hands as they grabbed hold of their ears. Three of them collapsed to the ground and began writhing on their knees in pain.

Anastasia, having covered my ears with her own hands, kept refilling her lungs with fresh breaths of air and screaming again. Her scream was evidently something akin to ultrasound, causing all our would-be attackers to writhe in pain. They had no idea what was happening, or where this piercing, unbearable sound was coming from. Through her hands I could feel the sharp penetrating sensation — maybe not as strongly as the others, but it still hurt.

Then I noticed a group of women running down toward us from the road. Anastasia stopped screaming and took her hands off my ears, I sat up on a rock. I could see the two *Zhigulis*[6] the girls had arrived in standing beside the jeep.

The women were armed — one was carrying a bottle, another a tyre iron, a third brandished a policeman's truncheon, while the fourth held a massive candlestick in her hands. Out in front was Anka-putanka, holding in her hands the neck of a broken champagne bottle, while following behind, slowly, came yet another — a plumpish woman clad only in a nightgown, who had apparently come straight out of bed and hadn't had time to get dressed. Somehow the Madam-in-charge had managed to sound the alarm and rope all her 'workmates' into the task at hand.

The fearsome, dishevelled Anka stopped just a few metres from our little group, which was now picturesquely sprawled over the rocks. Anastasia was the only one of us standing, and Anka spoke to her:

"How now, friend! You've got so many lads after you — they wouldn't be botherin' you, would they now?"

"I just wanted to have a talk with one of them," Anastasia calmly replied.

"And the rest of them — what are *they* doin' here?"

[6]*Zhiguli* — a car produced at Toliatti on the Volga River (see footnote 1 in Book 4, Chapter 22: "Other worlds").

"They followed us for some reason. I have no idea what they want."

"*You* have no idea? *I* know what those scumbags want," replied Anka and burst into a torrent of expletives in the direction of Lena's friend. "How many times have I told you, muttonhead, not to lay a hand on me girls?!!"

"*She* isn't one of yours," the 'dim-wit' responded gruffly.

"She's my 'professional colleague'. That means she's mine. Got it, you overgrown school-kid? If I see your pimp-snout so much as anywhere *near* one of me friends, I'll smash the livin' daylights outta you an' your cronies. Just remember that! I'm not puttin' up with a single pimp on my territory — not a single scumbag will I allow. You're not satisfied with sucking blood from the suits? You wanna be pimpin' for us too?"

"You've gone crazy. She's *not* yours. She's a novice. I just wanted to have some fun with her myself. This time, Anka, you've gone too far. What's all the fuss about her? What's she to you?"

"She's me friend. Got that? An' you've got your hands full with that sadist of yours."

"You've gone bonkers! Before you know it every last bird's gonna be your friend — eh what?"

The leader's voice in him was now no longer stifled by fear. And I realised why: while Anka was talking with him, his henchmen had come to, and the short, stocky fellow standing beside the leader was holding a gun in his hands, aimed right at Anka. A second man had his own gun trained on the group of hookers standing behind her.

Here was this group of young women, armed with whatever they could lay their hands on, standing directly in the path of the thugs' guns. The situation, as it now turned out, was far from being in their favour. One thing was absolutely certain: another moment and their morale would be broken and their bodies maimed, not to mention the loss of their freedom and income. I really felt like doing at least something to influence the proceedings and head off the inevitable dreaded result.

Anastasia was standing beside me, intently observing the situation. I jerked her arm. Putting my hands over my ears, I quickly said:

"Scream, Anastasia! Scream as quick as you can!"

Lowering my arm, she enquired:

"Why scream, Vladimir?"

"Eh? Don't you see what's going on? These women are about to get their heads bashed in, maimed for life. Their bluff's been called. It's all over for them."

"Not for all of them. The spirit is still fighting in three of them."

"But what can the spirit do against guns? They're done for."

"They are not 'done for' yet, Vladimir. As long as their spirit is still fighting, nobody should interfere. Outside interference may take care of the situation at hand, but it will weaken their self-confidence, and mean that a whole lot of other situations in their lives will not turn out favourably for them. They will come to rely on outside help."

"Stuff that philosophy of yours, at least for now. Can't you see the situation's hopeless?" I fell silent. It was clear Anastasia's mind was made up. And I thought wistfully: *Oh, if only I could scream like that!*

Seeing his cronies ready and alert, Lena's boyfriend (the pimp) spoke up — it was clear from the tone of his voice that he was already feeling he had the situation well in hand.

"I told you, Anka-putanka, you've gone too far. But this time we've won. So you'd better drop your toys, you little tarts! Drop them, and get those rags off — we're gonna screw all of you, one at a time."

Anka looked around at the thugs standing or concealing themselves, guns at the ready, and answered with a sigh:

"Maybe you don't need all of us — maybe just me's enough?"

"Ha, ha, bitch! See, now you're singing a different tune," the leader responded over the laughter of his buddies. "We shan't be satisfied just with you — we're gonna teach you all a lesson here. After this you're gonna be working for us, bitches!"

"An' jest where are you goin' to get the stud power to take on all of us?" Anka responded with a laugh. "You'll be lucky if you have enough for just one!"

"Shut your trap, bitch! We'll screw all of you, several times over!"

"I doubt that! I bet you won't be able to take on even one of us!"

"We'll keep screwing you all night long!"

"You know, sweetcheeks, you're startin' to get on my nerves — you an' your 'promises'. I don't believe 'em, I don't believe you're *man* enough!"

"You'll find out soon enough, bitch! I'm gonna smash that pretty face of yours in!" wheezed the leader, already seething with rage, putting on a pair of brass knuckles as he moved toward Anka.

Anka retreated a bit and called out to her group:

"Step aside, girls!"

The group of hookers took several steps back. Only the sullen plumpish 'cow' in the nightdress stood on the sidelines as though rooted to the spot, and when the tall and lanky leader took another step in Anka's direction, the 'cow', who before this had not spoken a word, suddenly said blandly:

"Hey, An — what're you waitin' for, An? Let's get started, eh?"

"Don't be in such a hurry, Mashka,"[7] replied Anka, taking another couple of steps back. "Well, go ahead, seein' you're itchin' to get on with it!"

---

[7] *Mashka* — like *Masha* and *Mashenka,* a colloquial variant of *Maria.*

The plumpish Masha, calmly and coquettishly tore open the flaps of her nightdress, scattering the buttons to the winds, exposing not only her bare breast and bikini briefs, but something else as well...

Under her nightgown the 'cow' was carrying a Kalashnikov assault rifle with a silencer and night-vision telescopic sight. She pulled the bolt, raised the butt stock to her shoulder, pressed her cheek to the stock and peered into the sight.

"Only remember, Masha, no automatic," Anka suggested. "This ain't no war zone. Just one bullet at a time. You know — every bullet costs money."

"Uh-huh," answered Masha, her eye still pressed to the sight, and fired off five shots, each about a second apart. But what shots they were! The first bullet tore off the heel from one of the leader's boots, apparently wounding his foot in the process. He jumped back in the direction of the water, limping. The other four shots landed right by each of the thugs in turn. Immediately they began looking for cover behind the rocks, and the ones who didn't have any cover handy lay face down on the ground.

"An, tell them to crawl into the water! Or they may get blasted by a ricochet!" Masha blurted out, her Kalashnikov still at the ready.

"You heard her, sweetcheeks! Into the water!" Anka ordered the big thugs already crawling toward the water's edge, gently reminding them: "Mashenka's not yet a good enough shot to be responsible for ricocheting bullets!"

A moment later, and all of them, including their leader, were standing waist-deep in the sea.

Ania went up to Anastasia, and for a while the two simply looked at each other, face to face, without saying a word. Then Ania said quietly, with just a hint of sadness:

"You, friend, wanted to go for a stroll with your companion there. So go ahead. It's a fine evening, quiet, warm..."

"Yes. There is indeed a pleasant air blowing over the city," Anastasia replied, adding: "You are tired, Ania, perhaps you would care to relax in a garden of your own?"

"Perhaps... but I feel sorry for me girls, an' I'm still so mad at those... blokes. Say, are you from the country?"

"Yes."

"Nice place, where you live?"

"Very nice. But I do not always feel at peace, especially when things are not going well for everyone in other places, as here right now."

"Don't mind them. Come whenever you like... Anyway, I'm off. Gotta work. Have a nice quiet stroll here."

Ania headed toward the cars, her entourage in tow. As they walked past the 'cow' still sitting on the rock, the Kalashnikov lying across her bare knees, Ania said:

"You stay and relax here a bit, Mashenka. We'll send a car for you later."

"I've got a client waitin' — I was with 'im when you called me. An' he's paid already!"

"We'll take care of your client. We'll say you had an upset stomach. Like, the quality of the champagne wasn't up to scratch."

"I had vodka. And only half a glass."

"Well, then, maybe you ate something..."

"I didn't have anything to eat — just a bit of candy and some pastries."

"So that's it, then — the pastries weren't too fresh. How many d'you eat?"

"Don't remember."

"C'mon — she never eats less than four at a time," said one of the girls. "Right, Masha?"

"Well, maybe you're right. At least leave me a cigarette. So's I don't get bored out of my skull."

Ania put a package of cigarettes along with a lighter on the rock beside Masha, and the girls walked on.

"Hey," came a voice from the water, "you gonna leave this gal of yours here on the rock?"

"She's stayin', sweetcheeks, she's stayin'!" replied Ania. "I told you right off, one of us is enough for the likes of you. You wanted all of us. And now it turns out it's goin' to be pretty boring for just one of us to stay here with you."

"Once this gets out, about how conniving you are..." one of the thugs called out. "Once it gets out... Well, no one will ever want to shag with you again. Even if *you* offer to pay *them*."

Five muffled shots rang out from the rock in quick succession. And five little splashes popped up in the water, one right beside each of the men standing there, making them retreat even further out from the shore. Ania turned to them and warned:

"Look, boys, just make sure you don't rile Mashenka here. When we like someone, we can be sweet and tender. An' loyal as dogs. When we like someone, understand? No matter who..." And then, as she clambered up the hill toward the cars, she struck up a song in a resonant, wistful voice:

The paths and roads are all overgrown there
Which my dear lover's feet have known there.

And the young prostitutes following her picked up on the tone of her voice, on the intonations of sadness and despair:

Overgrown there with mosses and grasses:
He's taken up with another of the lasses.
Where does he travel, my lover?
It makes my heart only sorrow and suffer.

And off they drove, still singing the song about the pathways and roads, as they headed back to work.

CHAPTER TWENTY-THREE

Your desires

It was almost midnight by the time Anastasia and I got back to my apartment. As I put the key into the lock, I felt a sense of exhaustion after all the intense experiences the day had brought. Upon seeing my bed, I told Anastasia that I was extremely tired, and went to take a shower. When I came out of the shower, Anastasia told me she'd already made up my bed, and that she herself would lie down on the balcony.

It's probably too stuffy for her in one of these mass-produced apartment blocks, I thought, and went out to the balcony to see what kind of bed she had made for herself there. It turned out she had put a little strip of rug down on the balcony floor and covered it with some white paper, which my landlord had got ready for wallpapering the flat. In place of a pillow she had folded her cardigan, and put a small tree-branch at the head of her makeshift bed.

"How can you get a good night's sleep here, Anastasia? It's hard, and you'll be cold. At least let me fetch you a blanket."

"Not to worry, Vladimir. I shall be fine here. The air is fresh, and I can see the stars. Look up and see how many stars there are! There is a soft, warm breeze blowing — I shall not be cold. You go lie down, Vladimir, and I shall sit on the edge of your bed for a while, and once you fall asleep, I shall lie down, too."

I lay down on the bed Anastasia had made up for me and thought I was so tired that I'd nod off right away, but it didn't work out quite like that. The thought, or realisation, that Man — i.e., every single individual — was nothing more than a plaything in the hands of some sort of coincidences, kept gnawing away at my mind, giving me no peace. This led to a growing feeling of irritation at those who had arranged these coincidences, and Anastasia too. Anastasia in particular, since I considered it a definite possibility that she had actually participated in the formation of these coincidences, at least as far as my life was concerned.

"Is something disturbing you, Vladimir?" Anastasia calmly enquired, and I even raised myself slightly on my elbows.

"As if you didn't know!... I believed you... I wanted to believe... I particularly wanted to believe that Man — every Man — is capable of making his own life happy. I especially believed in the eco-communities you talked about, where people can live a secure existence thanks to their own family plot of land, and raise their children to have a happy life. And that there would be good schools there for the children. I believed you when you said that every Man is the beloved child of God. 'Man is the summit of creation' — you did say that, didn't you?"

"Yes, Vladimir, I did tell you that."

"Of course you did! And how convincing you made it all sound! I not only believed you, I started acting on it, started organising a community. I've already submitted the necessary paperwork to the authorities. The Anastasia Foundation is collecting people's applications. A design's been commissioned, along with a layout for gardens and all sorts of plantings. It would have been all right just to believe you and all that, but I actually started carrying things out, and with pleasure! *You knew!* You knew I'd carry things out!"

"Yes, Vladimir, I knew. After all, you are an entrepreneur. You are always ready to carry out practical actions, to make things happen..."

"Always ready?" I echoed. "How simple it all is! Of course. No need to be a clairvoyant to see that. As long as an entreprenur believes in something, he will start to act. And I, fool that I was, started too."

I couldn't stay lying down any longer. I jumped out of bed, walked over to the window and opened the *fortochka*,[1] since I felt a sudden wave of heat — either in the room or within me.

"Why did you think your actions foolish, Vladimir?" Anastasia calmly asked.

And her equanimity, along with her feigned ignorance, as I then considered it — made me even more angry.

"And you just sit there talking all calm-and-collected-like? Calm and collected! As if you didn't know all along that Man is a puppet in somebody's hands. *They* control Man through various circumstances. Each Man is easily controllable by some kind of forces. If they feel like it, they can plunge half the human race into war. They plunge people into war and then take up a position somewhere up above or on the side-lines to watch us kill each other. If they feel like it, they'll slip some sort of religion into the proceedings and watch, once again, as people go to war over their faith. If they feel like it, they can play with just a single individual. I'm convinced of it. I've been convinced by people who are smart enough to analyse what's going on."

"And just how did these 'smart people' succeed in convincing you that Man is just a plaything in the hands of some kind of forces?"

"I listened to a report. They were talking about me. Some smart people became interested in public reaction to the books. They became interested in you, and in me too. They followed my every move during my time on Cyprus, while I was working on the fourth book. They recorded everything

---

[1]*fortochka* — a small openable window in the upper corner of a larger window-frame.

and then analysed it. And, if you can believe it, I'm not mad at them for following me. I'm even grateful to them — for finally opening my eyes. They showed how Man is being toyed with. Coincidences don't just happen, they're arranged, and I've become convinced of this through my own experience."

"What experience is this, Vladimir? Have you been conducting an experiment?"

"*I* haven't, but they've been conducting an experiment on me. When I was on Cyprus, I happened to mention freshwater fish, and *presto!* — freshwater fish appeared. I mentioned cedars, and cedars appeared. I wanted to pay a night-time visit to a church — and, lo and behold, there was a church, and the church doors were open at night. A whole lot of other things happened — all I had to do, no doubt, was write what they wanted me to.

"But the main thing — the granddaughter of the goddess Aphrodite appeared. I mentioned to several people on Cyprus that I wanted to meet with her granddaughter, since I had had it up to here with their Aphrodite. There were posters everywhere about her Baths, and people were forever carrying on about her. Anyway, I told them I was going to meet with the granddaughter of this goddess Aphrodite. I mentioned this, and a few days later along comes this girl with fire in her eyes — anyway, the way things turned out, everybody decided that Aphrodite had indeed sent her granddaughter, and was working miracles through this girl, and the girl herself underwent some kind of transformation.

"But who arranged all these circumstances one after another? Who? I certainly didn't arrange anything. If only one thing like this happened to take place, well, okay, but here was a whole chain of them together, and if you take them altogether, it's no longer a coincidence, it's a *pattern*. This is the conclusion the academics came to. And I'm convinced they're right. And you can't persuade me otherwise."

"But I was not about to deny that there is a pattern to what has been happening, Vladimir," Anastasia calmly observed.

I felt my whole insides turn cold, and I was suddenly overwhelmed with some kind of extraordinary sense of apathy following these last words of Anastasia's. I did have a hope — a faint one, but still a hope — that she would be able to dissolve the whole feeling that had been building up in me of Man's utter insignificance — not just my insignificance but all mankind's — but this she didn't do. In any case, how could she have? Who would dare deny what is so patently obvious? Indifferent to everyone and everything, I stood by the window in a room lit only by moonlight, and looked out at the stars.

Somewhere out there, perhaps on one of those very stars, lived those who were controlling us, toying with us. *They* were living, *they* were real! But could *our* existence really be called life? A toy in subjection to somebody's will cannot be said to live an independent life — which meant only one thing: *we were not living*. This is why we are indifferent to so many things.

Once again Anastasia began talking in that same quiet and calm voice. But this time her voice didn't arouse in me any emotions whatsoever — it was more like some kind of extraneous sound.

"Vladimir, you and the people who sent you that cassette with the report were right: there really are energies out there capable of changing time, joining together into a single chain various events or, as happened with you, arranging a chain of circumstances required to achieve a predetermined goal. Pure coincidences do not happen — that is already clear to many people. Coincidences, even those which seem to be the most far-fetched, are programmed. Everything that happens to each individual is programmed. And what happened to you on Cyprus, which served as a clear illustration for the researchers as well as, naturally, for you, was also programmed, and then turned into reality.

"Tell me, please, Vladimir, would you not like to know where the one directly responsible for programming your co-incidences is now?"

"What difference does it make where he is? Doesn't matter to me. On Mars, the Moon... Whether he feels good or bad."

"He is right here in this room, Vladimir."

"That means, it's you?... If so, that still doesn't change anything. I'm not even surprised. And I'm not angry. I simply don't care. We are manipulable, and that's the hopeless tragedy of the human race."

"I am not the one in charge of programming your coincidences, Vladimir. I am able to exercise but a tiny speck of influence."

"Then who *is* in charge? There's only two of us in the room. Or is there a third — a programmer who's invisible?"

"Vladimir, this programmer is right within you — it is *your desires*."

"How so?"

"Only Man's desires and aspirations can launch any kind of programme of action. This is the law of the Creator. Nobody, none of the energies of the Universe, can ever break that law. Because Man is the master of all the energies of the Universe! Man!"

"But I didn't launch anything on Cyprus, Anastasia. Everything happened all by itself, by coincidence, apart from me."

"There were indeed certain minor incidents that were not part of the more significant events — though they contributed to their realisation — and these incidents did happen apart from your will. But the basic events themselves were preceded by your desires. Was it not you who wanted to meet with the granddaughter of the goddess Aphrodite? You expressed your wish in the presence of witnesses and repeated it a number of times."

"Yes, I did..."

"And if you remember that, then how can you call servants carrying out the will of their lord masters, and how can you call the master a plaything in their hands?"

"Yes, that *would* be silly. Interesting, how all this is turning out! Wow! Desires... But why then aren't all our desires fulfilled? Many people wish for things, but their wishes aren't fulfilled."

"So much depends on how meaningful the goal is. On whether the desire corresponds to the light or the dark. On how strong the desire is. The more substantial and bright the goal, the more the forces of light are drawn to fulfil it. To bring it about."

"And if the goal is a dark one — let's say, for example, to get drunk, or get into a fight, or plan a war?..."

"Then the dark forces take over — Man through his desire has given them the opportunity to act. But, as you can see, it is still Man's desire that is first and foremost! Your desire, Vladimir."

I began to ponder what Anastasia had said, and my heart felt better and better. The very pleasant moonlight filled the whole room, and it seemed as though the stars in the sky were shining not with a cold light, but with a warm one. And Anastasia, sitting there on the edge of the bed, seemed to look even better than before. I said to her:

"You know, Anastasia, back there, when I first arrived on Cyprus, to be honest with you, I very nearly went on a binge. Because at first I couldn't find anything there I liked. Nobody spoke Russian. It was too noisy to work — people were whooping it up all around. *Why on earth did I end up here,* I thought, *maybe to get to know some hookers?* There are lots of women there, shall we say, of loose behaviour — from both Russia and Bulgaria."

"You see, Vladimir? You had the desire, and there they were. You got drunk on vodka, and set up a date with them.

With one woman from Bulgaria, and another from Russia. Only even before that you wanted to meet with Aphrodite's granddaughter — your first desire proved to be stronger, and *she* appeared, and saved you from all the wretched stuff. She helped you."

"Yes, she did. And just how might you know about the Bulgarian girl?"

"From my feelings, Vladimir."

"I don't understand that, but never mind. Tell me rather: this girl, Elena Fadeyeva, she's not the daughter of the goddess Aphrodite — she's Russian, she's simply an employee of a tourist agency on Cyprus. But I was talking about Aphrodite's granddaughter. Does that mean these forces of light were too puny to show me the real granddaughter of Aphrodite?"

"They are by no means 'puny'. And they did show you. The goddess Aphrodite today exists as energy. She is capable of connecting for a time with the energy of any Man — if she can see some meaningful reason to do so. That Elena Fadeyeva, whenever she was with you, had two energies inside her. There was a lot she could do during those days. There was a lot she succeeded in doing, and she managed to help you, too."

"Yes, I'm grateful to her. *And* to the goddess Aphrodite."

All my concerns and unpleasant sensations, connected with my assumption that all people were simply pawns in the hands of some kind of forces, literally flew out the window. Now, after my talk with Anastasia, a sense of confidence and peace set in.

For some time I just watched silently as Anastasia sat on the edge of my bed in the moonlight, her hands meekly folded atop her knees. And then... to this day I cannot figure out how this happened, but I suddenly came out with:

"I realise that you, Anastasia, are a great goddess." And as I said this I fell on my knees before her.

A cry of pain and despair burst from Anastasia's lips. She immediately rose and stepped back from me, leaning against the wall and clasping her hands to her breast as though in prayer.

"Vladimir, I beg of you, get up off your knees — you should not bow down to me. O God, O God, I have overdone it, I have been in too great a haste — forgive me for not making myself clear enough to Your sons. In God's sight, Vladimir, all people are equal. They should not bow down to one another. I am simply a woman — *I am Man!*

"You are so vastly different from all other people, Anastasia, so if you are simply Man, then who are we? *Who am I?*"

"You are Man, too, only as you are living out your life in vanity, you have not yet been able to think of what your purpose is."

"Moses, Jesus Christ, Mohammed, Rama,[2] Buddha — who are they? And how do you relate to them?"

"Those are my elder brothers you have named, Vladimir. I am not in a position to judge their works, but I shall say one thing: none of them had their fill of earthly love."

"That can't be — every single one of them has millions of worshipping followers, even today."

"But worship does not mean love. It only exhausts the worshipper's power of thought — a power exclusive to Man. Great is the *egregor*[3] of my brothers — for millions of years many people have fed it through their worship, and in so doing each worshipper lost some of his energy. Over the centuries there have been many willing to condemn the deeds of my brothers. And I could not understand why they made such

[2]*Rama* — a god-king and an earthly incarnation of Vishnu (in the Hindu tradition).

[3]*egregor* — a unifying collective psychic entity or field — see footnote 3 in Book 3, Chapter 14: "Who are you, Anastasia?".

great efforts to feed their own *egregor*, building up its energy over thousands of years. Nobody has been able to guess their secret until the dawn of the present age. And my brothers decided to gather the accumulated energy into a single whole, in order to distribute it to souls now living on the Earth. A new millennium will soon be given birth, in which the gods will settle the Earth — those people whose conscious awareness will allow them to accept this energy in all its worth.

"Vladimir, I beg of you, get up off your knees! It is painful for any father to see his son bowed down and enslaved. It is only the dark forces that have always tried to demean Man's significance. Vladimir, get up off your knees, refuse to betray yourself. Do not separate yourself from me."

Anastasia was extremely upset, and I did as she asked. I got up off my knees and said:

"I wasn't separating myself from you. On the contrary, it seems I've just begun to understand you. Only I don't agree that worship interferes with love. On the contrary, all believers say that they love God. And I am bowing before you as a goddess, but you are frightened for some reason, you've become upset."

"We have known each other for five years now, Vladimir. A lot of time has gone by since that night when our son was conceived, but ever since that time, not once have you had the desire to touch me, to give me the look you give to other women. Lack of understanding — and now, worship — do not allow love to reveal itself. Worship does not bring forth children."

"Well, that's because you're not exactly a woman, Anastasia. You've become a kind of information node. It's not just me — others too don't get your meaning right off. For example, what does 'don't betray yourself' mean? Why did you say that in reference to me?"

"You wrote a letter to the President of Russia, Vladimir, but at the same time you have come to doubt yourself — you almost perished. You have ceased creating on your own and handed your problems to others — basically to a single President."

"That's because he's the only person in Russia who can realistically do anything."

"One person cannot do it by himself — the will of the majority is required. Besides, why did you send your letter only to one president? There are presidents in Ukraine, Belarus, Kazakhstan..."

"But you've always talked about Russia. Besides, Russia is my Motherland."

"But your passport[4] says you are a Belarusian."

"That's right. My father was Belarusian."

"And you spent your whole childhood in Ukraine."

"Well yes, I did. And that was the best part I remember from my childhood. I remember the white cottage with its straw roof, and the weir where I fished for mud loaches along with the neighbourhood lads. And my grandma and grandpa never once quarrelled in my presence, and never punished me."

"Yes, yes, Vladimir, and remember how you and your grandfather planted tiny seedlings in the garden..."

"I do remember. Grandma would water them from a bucket."

"But you know that even today in the village of Kuzdnichi, in Ukraine, in the village where you were born, that garden has been preserved, its trees are all crusty now, but they are still bearing fruit — they are waiting for you."

"So then, where is my Motherland, Anastasia?"

"It is within you."

"In me?"

---

[4]*passport* — in this case, an internal identity document, which states one's ethnic origin.

"In you! You can materialise it forever on the Earth, wherever your soul indicates."

"You're right — I have to figure it all out somehow. At the moment I get the feeling I'm scattered all over the land."

"Vladimir, you are tired. This whole day has brought a lot of emotion upon us. Lie down and go to sleep. By morning your sleep will have built up fresh strength for you, and you will have a new conscious awareness..."

I lay down on the bed, and could feel Anastasia taking my hand in hers. Now a deep sleep would ensue, and I already knew that she could make it deep and peaceful, so that everything would be all right by morning. But just before I dropped off I managed to say:

"You know, Anastasia, could you please see to it that I shall be able once again to catch a glimpse of Russia's splendid future?"

"Fine, go to sleep, Vladimir. You will see it."

And Anastasia started singing very quietly — a wordless song, like a lullaby. *Anyway, it's great that people can program everything for themselves,* I managed to think before plunging into a peaceful and pleasant dream about the future of Russia.

CHAPTER TWENTY-FOUR

Eternity lies ahead for you and me

The rising Sun shone through the uncurtained windows straight onto the bed, waking me up. I had such a wonderful sleep! Some kind of extraordinary strength (fantastic!) was making its presence known inside me — I even felt like I wanted to do push-ups or some other kind of physical exercise. And I was in an excellent mood.

From the kitchen I could hear the clatter of dishes. *Wow!* I thought, *Don't tell me that's Anastasia trying to make breakfast?! She doesn't know how to cope with all the kitchen gadgets, or even how to turn on the gas. Maybe I'd better help her?* I put on a track suit and opened the door to the kitchen. No sooner had I caught sight of Anastasia than a hot flash seemed to run through my entire body.

This was the first time I had seen the Siberian recluse not in a taiga forest, not in her glade or by the seashore, but in a modern city woman's most typical surroundings — the kitchen. She was leaning over the gas stove, trying to regulate the burner. She kept turning the gas knob up and down, but the old cooker was not designed for any settings except 'high' and 'low'.

In the kitchen Anastasia appeared to be a completely normal woman. Now why did I go and scare her last night by bowing down on my knees? I'd probably had too much to drink and was beastly tired to boot.

Anastasia felt my gaze upon her, and turned to face me. One of her cheeks sported a dab of flour, and from underneath her bandana a braid of hair clung to her slightly perspiring forehead. Anastasia smiled. And her voice — that marvellous voice of hers!

"A splendid good morning for the coming day to you, Vladimir! You see, I have almost finished preparing breakfast. Just a wee bit more to do. You go and wash up, and by then everything will be ready. You go wash up, and do not worry — I shall not damage anything here — I have figured things out."

Instead of heading for the bathroom right off, I stood there dumbfounded, just looking at Anastasia. For the first time in the five years we'd known each other I caught a glimpse of just how extraordinarily beautiful this woman really was. There are no words to describe a beauty like this. Even with a flour-spotted cheek, even without a fancy hairdo (her hair was simply tied back in a bun) — not to mention her plain, unfashionable clothing — she was still extraordinarily beautiful.

I headed off to the bathroom, did a careful job of shaving and took a shower. During all this time I could not get my thought off this woman's beauty. When I came out of the bathroom, I sat down on the bed (which by this time had already been made). Instead of going into the kitchen, I just sat there, my mind still racing with thoughts about Anastasia.

It's been five years now that I've known this woman, this recluse from the Siberian taiga. *Five years...* And how my whole life has changed over these five years! Even though we rarely get together, it seems she's always around. And it's really her!

Of course, it was thanks to her that I was able to patch up my relationship with my daughter. We get along famously now. And as for my wife, well, even though I haven't been home in five years, I *have* talked with her on the telephone, and I can tell by her voice that my wife now speaks to me without any sense of coldness or resentment. She tells me that everything's fine with the family.

Anastasia... After all, she was the one who cured me. The doctors weren't able to, but she was. I knew myself that I was in danger of dying, and she cured me, and she made me famous, too. Now I'm getting big royalties for my books, but they're still her words, after all. And she always talks so tenderly, never gets angry. Even if I get mad at her without meaning to, she still won't get angry. Of course she's changed my life drastically, but she's changed it for the better. It was she who bore me my son! Sure, it's not your normal situation — my son lives in her glade in Siberia, but it's probably better for him there, with her.

She's so very kind. I need to say something nice to her, and do something nice for her. Only what? There's nothing she needs. Funny how it turns out — even if you owned half the world, she'd still have more than you. Still, I really felt like giving her some kind of gift. A long time ago I had bought her a pearl necklace. Not artificial, but large, natural pearls.

I decided this was a good moment to go and give it to her. I took the little jewellery box out of my suitcase, but instead of heading straight for the kitchen I decided, for some reason, to change my clothes. In place of the track suit I put on a pair of trousers, a white shirt and even a tie.

Then I put the necklace in my trouser pocket, but I was still too excited to go out to the kitchen. So I stood by the window, looking neat as a pin, until I managed to get a hold of myself. *What's going on here, anyway?* I thought to myself. *It's high time! Enough of this silly emotionalism!* And I walked out to the kitchen.

Anastasia was sitting at the table she had got all set for breakfast, waiting for me. She rose to greet me. By this time she had done her hair and put on a very neat appearance. She got up and silently gave me one of her tender looks with her greyish-blue eyes, while I just stood there, not knowing what to say. Then I said, unexpectedly using the formal form of address:

"Good day to you, Anastasia!" My formality completely took me aback. But she replied in all seriousness, as though she hadn't even noticed:

"Hello, Vladimir! Please, sit down. Breakfast is waiting."

"Okay, I'll take a seat. But first I wanted to say... I have something to tell you..." But I couldn't remember the words.

"So, tell me, Vladimir."

But I completely forgot what I was going to say. I went up close to Anastasia and gave her a kiss on the cheek. Whereupon my whole body flared up — I felt hot all over. And Anastasia's cheeks flushed a deep red, and her eyelids fluttered faster than usual. And when I spoke, it didn't sound like it was me at all, but some kind of constrained voice:

"That's from all my readers, Anastasia. So many people are grateful to you."

"From your readers? A big thank-you to all the readers. Thank you very much!" Anastasia quietly whispered.

And then I gave her a quick kiss on her other cheek and said:

"That one's from me. You are extremely good and kind, Anastasia. And you are extremely beautiful. Thank you for being you."

"You think I am beautiful, Vladimir? Thank you... Do you really think so?"

She was excited, too. I didn't know what to do next. But then I remembered the pearl necklace in my pocket. I hastily pulled it out and began trying to undo the clasp.

"This is a gift for you, Anastasia. Those are pearls... real ones... they're not fake. I know you don't like anything artificial, but those are real."

But the clasp wouldn't budge. I jerked at it, and the thread broke, and all the little pearls that had been threaded onto it clattered to the floor and scattered in different directions. I sat down on the floor to pick them up. Anastasia began picking them up too, only she managed to go faster. I watched as she deposited the pearls into the palm of her hand. She took a careful look at each one, and I just sat there entranced with her movements. I sat there on the floor, leaning against the wall, and watched her in astonishment.

I thought to myself how common the standard kitchen was, but how uncommon and marvellous I felt everything was in my heart. Why? Probably because *she* was here in this very kitchen — *Anastasia*. She was right beside me, but for some reason I couldn't muster up enough resolve to embrace her.

This woman, who back there five years ago in the taiga had seemed to be a somewhat abnormal recluse, now appeared as a star which had dropped in for a few moments from heaven. Here she was right beside me, yet as a star she was unreachable. And the years... Pity, the difference in years between us! I watched intently as Anastasia rose and put the pearls she had collected into a saucer on the table. Then she turned her head toward me. Entranced, I went on sitting there on the kitchen floor, leaning against the wall, and looking into her greyish-blue eyes. And she never averted her tender gaze even for a moment.

"Here you are right beside me, Anastasia, but now I can't touch you. I feel as though you're a distant star in the sky."

"*A star?* That's how you feel? Why? Look! Here she is at your feet — this little star, turned into an ordinary woman."

Anastasia quickly got down on her knees and sat next to me on the floor. She put her hands on my shoulder and rested her head on her hands. I could hear her heart beating, only *my* heart was beating a lot stronger. And her hair smelt of the taiga. Her breath was like a warm breeze infused with the intoxicating scent of flowers.

"Oh why, Anastasia, why couldn't I have met you when I was young? You're so young, and just look at how old I am! I've lived almost half a century already!"

"But it has taken me ages to break through to your wandering soul! Do not chase me away now."

"I'm getting old, Anastasia. And my life will soon be at an end."

"But while you are getting old, you will be able to plant your own family tree, and lay the foundation for a city with a splendid future, and a marvellous garden."

"I'll try. Pity I shall have such a short time to live in this garden myself. It'll take quite a few years to grow."

"If you set it up, you will always live there."

"Always?"

"Of course. Your body will grow old and die, but your soul will take flight!"

"The souls of the dead take flight — I know that. The soul takes flight, and that's the end of it."

"Oh, what a marvellous day we have today! Why are you creating a joyless future, Vladimir? You are creating it for yourself."

"It's not me creating it. That's objective reality, plain and simple. First comes old age, then death — for everyone. And even you, my dear, sweet dreamer, cannot come up with any other scenario."

Anastasia shuddered all over and moved slightly to one side. Her kind and cheerful eyes peered into mine and sparkled — radiating a joyful confidence that nothing could withstand.

"I have no reason to 'come up with' anything. There is only one truth. Death exists for the flesh — that is clear to everyone. For the flesh! In every other aspect death is a dream, Vladimir."

"A dream?"

"Yes, a dream."

Anastasia got up on her knees and began talking, looking me straight in the eye. But somehow the way she talked

silenced the kitchen radio, the sounds of voices and other
noise outside the window, as she spoke in a gentle voice:

"My dearest! Eternity lies ahead for you and me. Life will
always claim its own, you see. The littlest ray of sunlight glis-
tens in the spring, and the soul enrobes itself in its new things.
But the decaying body does not embrace the ground in vain.
Come spring, from our bodies will sprout new flowers and
grass again. You shall forever hear the birds sing, and drink in
the drops of rain. In the blue sky above, the clouds — again
and again — will entrance you with their dance.

"And if you, my dearest, should find yourself scattered
across the unfathomable Universe as little specks of dust, still
refusing to believe, then from these specks of dust wandering
through eternity I shall begin to gather you up. And the tree
you plant will help me do this: in the early spring, to the place
where your soul lies in unfeeling peace, it will stretch out its
branch above. And those you have been kind to upon the
Earth will remember you with love. And if the sum total of
earthly love is not enough to materialise you once again, then
there is one — one whom you know, and on every plane of being she will be flaming with a single breath of desire, namely:
materialise yourself, my love! — there is one who will give herself
over, for a moment, unto death."

"That will be you, Anastasia? Are you sure you will be able
to do such a thing — really?"

"Any woman possesses the ability to do it, if only she can
compress the Logos into her feelings."

"And what about you, Anastasia? Who will help *you* return
to the Earth once more?"

"That I can do for myself. I need not bother anyone about it."

"But how shall I recognise you? After all, our lives will be
quite different from before."

"Once you materialise upon the earthly plane, you will become a youngster once again. You will notice a snotty little

red-haired girl in the garden next door to yours. Say a kind
word to this slightly bow-legged youngster, pay attention to
that little maid. After you grow into your teens, you will start
to notice pretty girls. Do not be in a hurry to join your destiny to theirs. In the meantime, in the garden next to yours
your friend will be growing, too. Her face will be all freck-
led — she will not appear beautiful yet. At some point you
will notice her following you out of the corner of her eye. But
do not laugh at her, do not chase her off when she approaches
you to draw your attention away from a more mature beautiful woman. Three springs will pass, and the neighbour girl
will become a truly beautiful young lass. One day you will
look at her and feel yourself aflame with love. And you will be
happy with her. And she will be happy, too. And it is my soul
that will be living in that happy girl you choose."

"Thank you for that marvellous dream, Anastasia, my pre-
cious storyteller!"

I carefully embraced her by the shoulders and drew her
close to me. I wanted to listen to how excitedly her heart
was beating, to feel the fragrance of this marvellous woman's
hair — a woman who believes only in good, in eternity. And
possibly to grasp hold of, if only like a straw, her incredible
dreams. Her words about the future made everything around
me seem more and more joyful.

"Maybe what you say, Anastasia, is all just words, but still
they are marvellous words, and I feel more joy in my soul
when I hear them."

"The words of a dream can set a tremendous energy in motion. Man creates a future for himself through his dream,
through the thoughts he cherishes. Believe me, Vladimir,
everything will happen for the two of us exactly as I have described. But you are free in your dream, and you can change
anything you like just by speaking different words. You are free,
you have the liberty, and every Man is a creator for himself."

"I shall change none of the words, Anastasia, spoken by you. I shall try to believe in them."

"Thank you."

"For what?"

"For not spoiling eternity for the two of us."

On this splendid sunny day the two of us swam in the sea and sunned ourselves on the deserted seashore. That evening Anastasia took her departure. As usual, she asked me not to see her off. I stood on the balcony and watched as she made her way along the pavement by our building, her head covered with her kerchief, wearing the plainest of clothing and carrying her hand-made cloth bag. She walked along, trying not to stand out among the other pedestrians — this same woman who had created a splendid future for the whole country.

And it will definitely come. People will turn her dream into reality and start living in this splendid world themselves.

Before disappearing around the corner, Anastasia paused, turned in my direction and waved. And I waved back in farewell. I could no longer make out her facial features, but I was sure she was smiling. She is always smiling, because she believes in and creates only good. Perhaps it has to be that way. I waved back, whispering to myself: *Thank you, my dear, sweet Anastasia!*

Appendix

Desertification has affected the lands of the Rostov Region[1] (up to 50% of the Salesian Steppes), the Altai Territory[2] (a third of the Kulunda Plain) and thirteen other regions within the Russian Federation. Altogether 6.5 million hectares of Russian farmland have now been taken over by blowing sands, the largest single segment being in the Caspian Lowlands, covering as much as 10% of their total area.[3] The overall area of Russian farmland subject (either actually or potentially) to desertification approaches 50 million hectares.

According to agrochemical indicators, Russia's agricultural lands are, on average, not very productive, especially outside the Chernozem Belt.[4] The layer of topsoil does not contain a sufficient quantity of nutrients for proper cultivation:

---

[1] *Rostov Region* (Russian: *Rostovskaya oblast*) — a prairie region comprising just over 100,000 square kilometres around the city of Rostov-on-Don, bordering on the Sea of Azov (just north of the Black Sea) in Russia's south, including the fertile *Salesian Steppes* (Russian: *Sal'skie stepi*).

[2] *Altai Territory* (Russian: *Altaiski kray*) — a partially mountainous territory of 169,100 square kilometres in the south-western part of Siberia, south of Novosibirsk at the headwaters of the Ob River, centred around the capital Barnaul. Almost two-thirds of its area is covered by the *Kulunda Plain* (*Kulundinskaya ravnina*), which is suitable for farming.

[3] *Caspian Lowlands* (Russian: *Prikaspiiskaya nizmennost*) — a semi-arid lowland area (as low as 28 metres below sea level) covering approximately 200,000 square kilometres around the northern end of the Caspian Sea in both the Russian Federation and Kazakhstan.

[4] *Chernozem* (lit. 'Black Earth') *Belt* — a zone of forest and farmland containing a layer of dark-coloured soil (ranging from 1 to 6 metres in depth)

nitrogen, phosphorous, potassium, calcium, magnesium, micronutrients (especially cobalt, molybdenum and zinc). At least a third of the farmlands have acidic soil, and soil containing low concentrations of available phosphorous and potassium amount to 30% and 10%, respectively.

Over 43% of arable lands have a low humus content; in 15% of them (45% outside the Chernozem Belt) the proportion is critical. More than 75% of the farmlands of the Kaluga, Smolensk, Astrakhan and Volgograd Regions,[5] as well as the Republics of Kalmykia, Adygeya, Buryatia and Tuva[6] are low

---

in southern Russia and Ukraine. It is characterised by a high percentage (up to 15%) of humus, as well as large quantities of acids, phosphorous and ammonia. A similar belt (also known as Chernozem) is found in the prairielands of the province of Manitoba in Canada. (The original Russian term is pronounced *chernoz-YOM*.)

[5]These regions are all named after the cities at their respective centres: *Kaluga* — a city on the Oka River about 200 km southwest of Moscow, originally the domain of the princely Vorotynsky family. *Smolensk* — one of the oldest cities in Russia (dating back to AD 863), located about 360 km west-southwest of Moscow, and described in an ancient history text as one of the key stations on the trade route between Scandinavia and the Mediterranean. *Astrakhan* — at the mouth of the Volga, on the Caspian Sea, in the Caspian Lowlands; formerly the capital of a Tatar khanate, the city was conquered for Russia by Ivan the Terrible in 1556. *Volgograd* (originally *Tsaritsyn*, known as *Stalingrad* from 1925 to 1961) — a city founded in 1598 at the confluence of the Volga and Tsaritsa Rivers, about 400 km northwest of the Caspian Sea.

[6]These republics are all part of the Russian Federation: *Kalmykia* — just southwest of the Astrakhan Region in the northern Caucasus, covering an area of 76,000 square kilometres, bordering on the Caspian Lowlands. *Adygeya* (pron. *a-di-GAY-ya*) — a small republic (7,600 sq. km) surrounded by Russia's Krasnodar Territory (northwestern Caucasus), with prairie lands in the north and mountains in the south. *Buryatia* — a large, primarily mountainous republic of 351,000 sq. km in south central Siberia, situated on the eastern shore of Lake Baikal. *Tuva* (pron. *too-VAH*) — also in south central Siberia, covering an area of 170,500 sq. km, not far to the west of Lake Baikal; the western section of Tuva comprises a dry lowland.

in humus. Experts believe that, on average, with irregular and insufficient applications of organic fertiliser and improper cultivation practices, a significant depletion has taken place in Russia's soil content. Humus levels have been reduced to a minimum — 3.5–5.0% of topsoil in the central Chernozem regions and only 1.3–1.5% outside the Chernozem belt. Annual humus losses in farmland topsoil are pegged at 0.6–0.7 tonnes per hectare (as much as 1 tonne per hectare in Chernozem areas). This means an annual nationwide loss of approximately 80 million tonnes.

It has been proved that there is almost a perfect linear relationship between the humus reserves in basic soil types and the productivity of major agricultural crops. A one-tonne-per-hectare increase in humus levels means an increase in average long-term productivity of cereal crops of 10–15 kg/ha. For a number of crops cultivated under various soil/climatic conditions, this amount corresponds to 30 kg of cereal crop units. For every 1-centimetre decrease in humus depth in Chernozem topsoil under the influence of either natural or man-made factors (e.g., erosion), cereal crop productivity falls by 100 kg/ha.

Over the course of many years Russia's soil resources have been extensively exploited[7] by various means, and nutrients have often been eliminated through the harvesting process at a faster rate than they could be replenished.

Agricultural scientists warn that such extensive exploitation of the soil's fertility will lead to an irreversible degradation. Trends in overall cereal output are cited as evidence of this. The annual manure application required to maintain constant humus levels in the soil should amount to between

[7]*extensively exploited* — In Russian the term 'extensive' (*èkstensivnoe*) here refers specifically to using up more and more land resources, as opposed to increasing fertility on the lands already under cultivation.

7 and 15 tonnes per hectare. This means adding to the soil a minimum of 1 billion tonnes of organic fertiliser every year. Russia today employs only about 100–120 million tonnes, or approximately 10 times less than is required.

What is the current situation with regard to conservation of soil resources?

Centralised financing of soil-improvement projects has been completely cut off, and the scope of these projects has been drastically reduced. Financing now comes out of local budgets — since 1993 out of land taxes, with 30% of the conservation-programme expenses to be paid by land-users. As a result, from 1994 to the present all projects for applying peat-manure compost in non-Chernozem areas, as well as lime treatment of acidic soils, delivery of liming materials and bone-meal, and phosphate application have pretty well ceased on most Russian territory because local authorities do not have funds for carrying out agrochemical projects.

This has contributed to the failure of practically all comprehensive federal soil-improvement and agricultural development programmes initiated by the Russian government and the Ministry of Agriculture and Food.

In view of the above, we can now speak of the escalating degradation of Russia's topsoil, which threatens its ecological and food security, as well as its national security as a whole.

THE AUTHOR, Vladimir Megre, born in 1950, was a well-known entrepreneur from a Siberian city of Novosibirsk. According to his account, in 1995 — after hearing a fascinating story about the power of 'ringing cedars' from a Siberian elder — he organised a trade expedition into the Siberian taiga to rediscover the lost technique of pressing virgin cedar nut oil containing high curative powers, as well as to find the ringing cedar tree. However, his encounter on this trip with a Siberian woman named Anastasia transformed him so deeply that he abandoned his business and went to Moscow to write a book about the spiritual insights she had shared with him. Vladimir Megre now lives near the city of Vladimir, Russia, 190 km (120 miles) east of Moscow, devoting himself to writing. If you wish to contact the author, you may send a message to his personal e-mail **megre@online.sinor.ru**

THE TRANSLATOR, **John Woodsworth**, originally from Vancouver (British Columbia), has over forty years of experience in Russian-English translation, from classical poetry to modern short stories. Since 1982 he has been associated with the University of Ottawa in Canada as a Russian-language teacher, translator and editor, most recently as a Research Associate and Administrative Assistant with the University's Slavic Research Group. A Certified Russian-English Translator, John Woodsworth is in the process of translating the remaining volumes in Vladimir Megre's Ringing Cedars Series.

ORDERING INFORMATION

USA:
- *on-line* — www.RingingCedars.com
- *tel. / fax (toll-free)* — 1-888-DOLMENS (1-888-365-6367)
- *tel. / fax (from outside US & Canada)* — 1-646-429-1986
- *e-mail* — sales@RingingCedars.com
- *mail (US)* — send US$14.95 per copy plus $3.95 shipping and handling for the first copy and $0.99 s&h for each additional copy in your order to:

    Ringing Cedars Press
    c/o PSSC, Suite 3
    46 Development Rd.
    Fitchburg, MA 01420

Make a check or money order payable to "Ringing Cedars Press". Please indicate clearly the quantity and title of the book(s) you are ordering and be sure to include your US postal address with your payment. Allow 2-4 weeks for delivery.

AUSTRALIA:
- *order on-line* — www.RingingCedars.com.au
- *by phone* — 1300-65-27-65
- *e-mail* — books@RingingCedars.com.au

NEW ZEALAND:
- *order on-line* — www.RingingCedars.co.nz
- *by phone* — 64-9232-9792
- *e-mail* — sales@RingingCedars.co.nz